Barcode in Back

W9-DAX-091

DISCARD
HUMBER COLLEGE
LAKESHORE CAMPUS
LEARNING RESOURCE CENTRE
3199 LAKESHORE BLVD. WEST
TORONTO, ONTARIO M8V 1K8

INTERNATIONAL
COMMUNICATIONS
STRATEGY

INTERNATIONAL COMMUNICATIONS STRATEGY

Developments in cross-cultural communications, PR and social media

Silvia Cambié and Yang-May Ooi

HUMBER LIBRARIES LAKESHORE CAMPUS
3199 Lakeshore Blvd West
TORONTO, ON.   M8V 1K8

**KOGAN
PAGE**

London and Philadelphia

Publisher's note

Every possible effort has been made to ensure that the information contained in this book is accurate at the time of going to press, and the publishers and authors cannot accept responsibility for any errors or omissions, however caused. No responsibility for loss or damage occasioned to any person acting, or refraining from action, as a result of the material in this publication can be accepted by the editor, the publisher or any of the authors.

First published in Great Britain and the United States in 2009 by Kogan Page Limited

Apart from any fair dealing for the purposes of research or private study, or criticism or review, as permitted under the Copyright, Designs and Patents Act 1988, this publication may only be reproduced, stored or transmitted, in any form or by any means, with the prior permission in writing of the publishers, or in the case of reprographic reproduction in accordance with the terms and licences issued by the CLA. Enquiries concerning reproduction outside these terms should be sent to the publishers at the undermentioned addresses:

120 Pentonville Road
London N1 9JN
United Kingdom
www.koganpage.com

525 South 4th Street, #241
Philadelphia PA 19147
USA

© Silvia Cambié and Yang-May Ooi, 2009

The right of Silvia Cambié and Yang-May Ooi to be identified as the authors of this work has been asserted by 2009 in accordance with the Copyright, Designs and Patents Act 1988.

ISBN   978 0 7494 5329 9

British Library Cataloguing-in-Publication Data

A CIP record for this book is available from the British Library.

Library of Congress Cataloging-in-Publication Data

Cambié, Silvia.
  International communications strategy : developments in cross-cultural communication, PR, and social media / Silvia Cambié and Yang-May Ooi. – 1st ed.
        p. cm.
  Includes bibliographical references and index.
  ISBN 978-0-7494-5329-9
 1. Intercultural communication. 2. Social media. 3. Public relations.
4. Leadership. I. Ooi, Yang-May. II. Title.
  HM1211.C36 2009
  659.2–dc22
                                                2009008501

Typeset by JS Typesetting Ltd, Porthcawl, Mid Glamorgan
Printed and bound in India by Replika Press Pvt Ltd

To my mother, for her support.

Silvia Cambié

To my parents, who encouraged my love of writing.

Yang-May Ooi

Contents

About the authors

Silvia Cambié is a cross-cultural communicator and a journalist. She was raised in Southern Europe, educated in a German-speaking environment, speaks five languages and spent her entire career working in an international context.

Her background includes reporting from Eastern Europe and the former Soviet Union for major British and German print media as well as managing communications and public affairs for Brussels-based international trade associations.

She blogs about the cross-cultural communication challenges facing the business world at X-Culture and is read by an audience of 8,000 each month.

Silvia is based in London, where she advises clients on strategic communication, stakeholder relations and social media. She is a recognized public speaker on multicultural communication.

Silvia serves on the boards of two organizations with global outreach, the International Association of Business Communicators and The International Alliance for Women.

Yang-May Ooi is a writer specializing in cross-cultural issues and social media. She grew up in multi-racial and multi-faith Malaysia and now lives in London, where she runs her cross-cultural blog Fusion View, an East/West view on people, society and technology. Fusion View is read by over 8,000 unique visitors a month from all over the world, and has been featured on the BBC Radio programme Pods & Blogs. Yang-May has also published legal thrillers with Hodder & Stoughton.

Yang-May also has many years of senior executive experience working in local government and corporate environments as a lawyer. She currently works part-time in a management role in a financial institution in the City of London where she has developed and facilitates a blog for the housing finance sector.

About the authors

Preface

Understanding other cultures and building bridges between ways of thinking have always been important to us. In the course of the years we spent studying and working in environments different from the ones where we grew up, we had the opportunity to develop a number of ideas. Some of these have helped us manage the interactions we had every day with people from backgrounds we knew very little about. Others have become our inner compass, a system we instinctively refer to every time we have to communicate in an international setting.

With globalization gaining pace and the world becoming more interconnected, we felt that the time had come to put these ideas on paper. This book is the result of our passion for connections that defeat the cultural divide. We have focused and reflected on three major phenomena that, we believe, are about to change the global narrative beyond recognition.

Emerging economies are becoming more and more active on the global business scene and we will soon be working for their multinationals. Technology and social media are widening our horizon and creating new cultures that have nothing to do with shared nationality or demographics. Social business is challenging our collective thinking around resource allocation and the organization of human society. New ways of working and producing wealth are bound to come from this innovative approach.

We have researched a number of emerging patterns and observed their impact on current communication practices. We have tried to go beyond seeing what the mainstream sees.

We are thrilled to have had the opportunity to add our voices to the global debate on the transformation of communication in the era 3.0. We believe that this change will be very much driven by cultural sensibility.

Acknowledgements

Many people shared their experiences, knowledge and expertise with us in many different ways and we are grateful to everyone for their input, advice and support. We would like to thank expressly the following:

Haifa Fahoum Al Kaylani, Chairman, Arab International Women's Forum, London, UK; Kevin Anderson, Blog Editor, *The Guardian*, London, UK; Asohan Aryaduray, New Media Editor, *The Star*, Kuala Lumpur, Malaysia; Tudor Aw, Digital Convergence Partner, KPMG, London UK; Mai Badr, Editor in Chief, *Hia* Magazine, Dubai, UAE; Ariana Bradford, Director, Global Outreach, UK Office, Rotman School of Management, University of Toronto, UK; Sharon Bakar, creative writing teacher and literary impresario, Kuala Lumpur Malaysia; Lea Chambers, Associate, Marketing and Communications, Golder Associates Corporation, Calgary, Canada; Angela Corrias, Italian freelance journalist, writer and photographer, London UK; Richard Dennison, Head of Knowledge Management Strategy, British Telecommunications, London, UK; Gerry Ditchling, Director and Managing Partner, Filgifts.com; Jay Drayer, CEO of CareFlash, Houston, USA; Eric Forbes, Editor of MPH Books, Kuala Lumpur, Malaysia; Xinran Eady, Founder, Mother's Bridge of Love, UK and China; Rauf Hameed, Communication Manager, Tetra Pak Arabia, Jeddah, Saudi Arabia; Tim Gingrich, Marketing Services Executive, Asia Pacific, Weber Shandwick, Beijing, China; Rodolfo Guttilla, Director of Corporate Affairs, Natura Cosméticos, São Paulo, Brazil; Anthony Hazell, Head of Relationship Management, Democratic Alliance Party, Johannesburg, South Africa; Victoria Hale, Founder, Institute for One World Health, San Francisco, USA; Neville Hobson, communicator, blogger, podcaster, forimmediaterelease.biz, UK; Patrick Hofman, User Interface Designer, Google, Australia;

Francis Ho, Director of Kuching Kayak, Kuching, Malaysia; Virak Hor, blogger and web developer, Cambodia; Emma Huang, former Editor, International News Section, *Hangzhou Daily*, Toronto, Canada; Jennifer James, Urban Cultural Anthropologist, USA; Kati Kerenge, Corporate Communications Manager, Tanga Cement, Dar es Salaam, Tanzania; Stanislav Krans, Chief Representative in PRC, RIA Novosti, China; Rajeev Kumar, Senior Practice Consultant, Tata Management Training Centre, Pune, India; Alan Lane, Reputation Management Expert, VASGAMA, London UK; Juny Lee, Account Manager, Edelman Korea, South Korea; Valery Levchenko, Deputy General Manager, RIA Novosti, Moscow, Russia; Paul Littlefair, Campaigns Officer, International Department, RSPCA, London UK; Mean Lux, blogger advocate, Cambodia; Gina McAdam, Director, Stratemarco Ltd, London UK; Di Macpherson, News Editor, East Coast Radio, Durban, South Africa; Warren G. Makgowe, Public Relations Officer, University of South Africa, South Africa; David Marash, US Anchor, Al Jazeera, Washington, USA; Roger Martin, Dean and Professor of Strategic Management, Rotman School of Management, University of Toronto, Toronto, Canada; Dirk Matten, Hewlett-Packard Chair in Corporate Social Responsibility, Schulich School of Business, York University, Toronto, Canada; Diane Morris, President, The International Alliance for Women, London, UK; Bish Mukherjee, President, Misha Network PR, Chennai, India; 'Patroklus Murakami', Second Life resident; BL Ochman, social media strategist, New York, USA; Ramon Ollé Jr., Account Planning Director, Grey Iberia, Barcelona, Spain; David Robertson, partner in web design firm Out of the Trees, London UK; Zoe Robinson, co-founder of T-Vox, UK; Adam Rugel, CEO, 71miles, California, USA; Erika Ruiz Ramos, Communications Manager, Boerhinger Ingelheim Promeco, Mexico; John Russell, Executive Vice President Asia Pacific, Powell Tate, Beijing, China; Anna Sayburn, Editor, BMJ Publishing Group, London, UK; Mark Schumann, Managing Principal, Towers Perrin, Houston, USA; Nada Serajnik Sraka, Senior Communication Advisor, Government Communication Office, Ljubljana, Slovenia; Felicia Shiu, Director, International Executive Board, International Association of Business Communicators, Toronto, Canada; Kenny Sia, blogger, Kuala Lumpur, Malaysia; Paulo Henrique Soares, General Manager, Communications Department, Vale, Rio de Janeiro, Brazil; Ramata Sore, Journalist and Blogger, Burkina Faso; Lucy Soutter, Art Photographer and Lecturer, London, UK; Michael Spencer, Managing Director, Sound Strategies, London, UK; Alan Stevens, media coach and crisis communications specialist, MediaCoach.

co.uk, London, UK; Marc Wright, Publisher, simply-communicate. com, London, UK; Nan Yang, freelance writer, translator and teacher, China; Kai Xing, Manager, Client Services International, Schulich Executive Education Centre (SEEC), Schulich School of Business, York University, Toronto, Canada; Betty Yao, Programme Director, Asia House, London, UK.

Where we have referred in the book to information derived from websites, blogs, magazines, journals and wikis which are freely available online, we have aimed to acknowledge the source in the text or as a footnote. We have also occasionally quoted short extracts from such sources to illustrate a point, with an acknowledgement.

Part 1

International communications

1 The world we live in

It was well after midnight. Co-author Cambié had landed in the middle of Kazakhstan, only three years after the fall of the Soviet Union.

She had read a number of spy novels and was feeling rather nervous at the prospect of having to go through immigration as the only European on the plane.

Little did she know that the exchange she would have with a smiling Kazakh officer would change her way of looking at the world.

Still under the influence of cold-war mythology, the last question she had expected to be asked in the middle of post-communist Central Asia was whether the football team of her home town in Italy would continue to move from victory to victory. The immigration officer's passion for football was so strong that it lit up his entire face and created an instant bond between him and Cambié.

Communication is not only about producing messages you want other people to hear. It is about understanding what moves the listener. And in order to be able to do that, you need to know the listener's points of reference, their culture, their values, their ways of relating to the world.

What Cambié experienced that night in the heart of Central Asia was a simple lesson in cross-cultural communication. It came at a time when the world had begun to change dramatically after the fall of the Soviet Union.

Change is still happening. It is drawing everybody closer to other parts of the world. And it is making us realize that we need to look at them in a different way. We can no longer expect people in other cultures to adopt the way we think and communicate. We are experiencing the end of one era and the beginning of a new one.

The media are already writing about the termination of the one-way globalization of Western culture that reached its peak in the 1970s and 1980s.[1] *New York Times* columnist Thomas Friedman believes that 'Globalization 3.0 is going to be more and more driven not only by individuals but also by a much more diverse – non-Western, non-white group of individuals'.[2]

We are indeed experiencing the end of the era of complacency. A combination of new phenomena has been creating a new awareness. And this awareness is making audiences around the world more sophisticated.

It is good news for the communication profession, which for years has been fighting for recognition. Business executives are waking up to the idea that they need communicators to produce much more than colourful brochures. They need experts able to get the message across to new audiences and new markets by using new technologies. The time has come for corporations to have a much more strategic view of communication.

Friedman writes that in order to thrive in the 'Globalization 3.0' era, individuals have to have 'a certain mental flexibility, self-motivation, and psychological mobility'.[3] In other words they need to be highly creative. Communication is about creativity. This is why we believe that our time offers unprecedented opportunities for communicators.

Let's have a look at the phenomena of the new era and the impact they are having on the way we talk to each other.

China's global role

The world is about to undergo a major political and economic power shift.

The investment bank Goldman Sachs expects the list of the world's ten leading economies in 2050 to be very different from the one we have today. Over the next 50 years, Brazil, Russia, India and China – what the bank calls BRICs – are likely to play a much more prominent role in the global economy. By 2025, they will most probably account for more than half the size of the G6, even if today they are worth less than 15 per cent.[4]

And the impact of the rise of China is already being felt outside Asia. The country is playing an important role in Africa, where it has bought stakes in oil companies and has been strongly contributing to the local infrastructure. Sudan's economy is already heavily dependent on China, which owns 40 per cent of its largest oil firm.[5] Angola was the largest exporter of oil to China in 2006 and the beneficiary of a major influx of Chinese construction companies.[6]

Africa will be able to profit from the growth model that China is exporting to this continent. It is building a hub for copper and other metals in Zambia by linking the country by rail, road and shipping lanes to the rest of the world. China is also creating a trading hub in Mauritius that will provide its businesses with access to the common market of East and Southern Africa. Africa is being transformed by the competition to attract Chinese investment.[7]

China used to be nothing more than the factory to the world and is now moving to leave a strong mark.

We can also expect China to make an impact on international communication practices. The country is used to dealing with ambiguity, with problems like political corruption, environmental degradation, violation of human rights and rural poverty. It is used to thinking in terms different from the black-and-white scenario typical of the Euro-and-North-America-centric view of the world. Since Globalization 3.0 is bound to bring us in contact with other countries facing ambiguity, China might be better equipped to communicate with them.

We used to think of China as the mass producer of fake designer goods, but those days are over. China is embracing creativity and its universities are graduating thousands of design students every year. They offer programmes in design strategy, innovative thinking and sustainability.[8] The country seems to be finding a new way of expressing itself. And we can expect China to want to play a leadership role in the global community and to influence the way it communicates.

Courting the fledgling consumer

The global market has been courting other BRIC countries besides China. The reason for this attraction lies largely in their growing middle class.

India's middle class totals 200 million people and accounts for 20 per cent of its population.[9] The country's economy has already more than doubled since economic reforms began in 1991. And the swelling middle class is leading its expansion through a new consumer boom. The number of India's mobile-phone subscribers rose from 2 million in 2004 to 55 million in 2007 and is expected to reach 250 million in 2012.

These are highly promising figures if we consider that mobile phones are tipped to become the next major source of advertising income, much bigger than television, radio, print media or internet advertising. According to forecasts, annual expenditure will reach US$11.4 billion by 2011.[10]

International consumer brands are now chasing the huge Indian consumer market. When you operate in a complex reality like that of India, you need to develop a new kind of creativity. You need to stretch your imagination and put yourself in the shoes of a public that might be very remote from every experience you have ever had in your life. This is what Nokia did with the Indian version of its 1100 mobile phone. To respond to the needs of local consumers living in areas troubled by power shortages, Nokia developed a shock-resistant phone with a battery that lasts for two days and a built-in flashlight that can be used as a torch in case of emergency.

This is the kind of imagination required by Globalization 3.0. And India is becoming an inspiration to the rest of the world in terms of innovative business.

According to Naina Lal Kidwai, HSBC India's Chief Executive, 'India is a market for experimentation for many companies; new technologies and trial runs of products are often undertaken in India, and this grants the poorer classes access to goods that were previously unavailable – laptops, mobile phones, cars.'[11] This attitude combines entrepreneurship with social business and creates products for a low-wage earning market, which are likely to benefit other parts of the world.

Tata Nano, the world's cheapest car, was launched in India in 2008 and is expected to be made available also in Latin America, South-East Asia and Africa. Ratan Tata, the chairman of the company that makes the Nano, came up with the idea while watching Indian families of three or four travelling on a motor scooter. He wanted to make it possible for India's emerging middle class to buy their first car ever. Nano, also referred to as the 'People's Car', costs only 100,000 rupees (US$2,500). It is the result of five years of research conducted by a team of 500 engineers. Tata minimized costs by limiting the use of steel and providing the car with a no-frills interior.

Nano is expected to have an impact on India that goes beyond opening up the car market to low-income consumers. So far, the growth dynamic of the country's economy has been based on technology services rather than manufacturing expertise. The success of Tata Motors's latest invention could shift this focus.[12]

Communicators will need to keep India on their radar screen not only because of its huge consuming classes. India's media and entertainment business is also experiencing strong growth, thanks to the higher income younger generations are earning. The sector is expected to develop from US$11 billion to US$25 billion by 2011.[13] Bollywood, the Mumbai-based film industry, is teaming up with other media groups around the world and is becoming a household name among international audiences. How long until the style and values associated with Bollywood movies enter the international entertainment business? How long until they have an impact on other forms of communication? Probably not very long. Bollywood dance steps seem to have been as effective as Japanese anime, or animation, in penetrating global youth culture.[14]

India is not the only place where the consumer goods industry and its communicators will be hunting for new audiences. In Brazil and Mexico, sales of cars, computers and consumer electronics have been booming. In the whole of Latin America, 15 million households moved out of poverty between 2002 and 2006. Following this trend, a small majority is expected to have joined the middle class by 2010.[15] This is good news for the most unexpected products. Thirty years ago, deodorants were almost unheard of in Brazil. Unilever, the world's largest producer of deodorants with brands like Dove and Axe, now has yearly sales worth 400 million euros in this country. In Argentina, its share of the deodorants market increased from 50 per cent in the late 1990s to 70 per cent in 2006.[16] And with only half of the world's population using deodorants, Unilever's hopes in emerging markets are still high.

A new type of multinational

The Boston Consulting Group (BCG) published a report in 2008 on the 100 best performing companies from emerging economies. BCG's '100 New Global Challengers: How Top Companies from Rapidly Developing Economies are Changing the World' lists local enterprises from countries like China, Brazil, Mexico, India and Turkey that have begun operations in other parts of the world and are making their mark on the international brand landscape.[17]

One of these is Hisense, a Chinese manufacturer of consumer electronics, with factories in North Africa, Eastern Europe, Iran, Pakistan and South Africa. It leads the market for TV sets in China and is pursuing an active foreign expansion strategy. In Europe, it has already conquered 2.5 per cent of the French market for flat panel display TV sets.

Another Chinese multinational on BCG's watchlist is Chery, the car manufacturer. It started off by selling cars to Syria in 2001 and is now the country's major exporter of cars and automotive parts, with sales to over 60 countries. Chery is also engaging in international philanthropy. Its Russian subsidiary donated US$100,000 to three universities in Moscow that will serve to finance the studies of 150 Russian students.[18]

In Latin America, BCG singled out the Brazilian aerospace conglomerate Embraer, which has become the world's third-largest manufacturer of commercial jets after Boeing and Airbus. Embraer has signed a joint venture with China Aviation Industry Corporation II and has been delivering planes to China Southern Airlines, the country's largest airline. Cemex, the supplier of building material, is Mexico's raising star. Its acquisition of the British RMC Group turned it into the worldwide leader in ready-mix concrete.

A number of Indian companies have been buying businesses in Europe, North America and Asia as part of an effort to build global empires. Undoubtedly the most famous case is that of Mittal Steel, which bought Arcelor of Luxembourg in 2006 to build the world's largest steel company. Another is Bharat Forge, the manufacturer of auto components, which emerged as the world's second-largest manufacturer in 2007, after buying companies in Germany, Sweden, the United Kingdom, North America and China.

The rise of the emerging-markets multinationals and the pace of their foreign acquisitions have been opening up unprecedented opportunities for communicators. Every time one of these multi-nationals enters a new market, it has to educate the local public about its brand and has to learn to relate to local audiences. This effort requires solid advice that communication practitioners are ideally positioned to provide.

At the same time, working for these new players can be rather daunting for communicators used to the old standardized Western practices. They have to become accustomed to new work cultures. In India, it is a long-established practice for managers to ask their staff to carry out tasks that are not strictly part of their job description. A director of public relations (PR) might be asked, for example, to review facts and figures from a financial statement and to comment on it. This approach is based on trust in the ability of an employee rather than on rigorous corporate organigrams. However, it can be rather confusing for someone not familiar with the culture.

Another cultural challenge is presented by the fact that multinationals from emerging economies are often owned or controlled by families. This factor has an impact not only on the way in which the company makes decisions but also on the brand image it wants to project. The brand in these cases is likely to be an extension of the owners' personal brand or that of their family. Or it could be rooted in the family's history. The role of the communicator then becomes that of a storyteller. He or she will have to take the public on an emotional journey and have them arrive at their destination with a new awareness of the heritage and the values behind the brand.

Another example is corporate social responsibility. The causes supported by the company are likely to be closely connected with the image of the family behind it and their set of beliefs.

Not what it used to be

The radical transformation that journalism is experiencing is a clear example of how the world of communication is changing. Audiences around the world are growing tired of the dominance of big media, and want to hear more than one story. They want to read about the local angle.

And that is what channels like Al Jazeera English and France 24 are offering. The new era we are entering requires a new type of reporting. Al Jazeera tends to use local journalists embedded in the culture of the country/region they write about.[19] 'It is their home territory and they therefore have a wider set of contacts', said Al Jazeera's US Anchor David Marash. 'Much more is at stake for them. There is a tendency to believe that sources in the developing world are behind the sophistication curve. It is the task of these journalists to prove the opposite to the rest of the world.' And the sources they use are much more likely to be loyal to these kind of reporters than to fly-in–fly-out journalists unable to relate to their lives and experiences.

This approach to journalism is bound to make audiences around the world more aware of the existence of different realities and different ways of looking at them. It is also starting to influence the world of communication by forcing practitioners to include local angles in their messages. We will no longer be able to produce one story and cascade it down into the different markets where we want to generate media coverage. We will have to study the history and culture of the audiences we want to reach and use local points of reference.

Delivering the views of ordinary citizens has always been an important part of journalism, but in our era of new web technologies this aspect is gaining a whole new meaning. Citizen journalism is still considered a fringe phenomenon, but it is bound to have an impact on the way in which people consume information. To public relations practitioners, the idea of having ordinary citizens rather than journalists writing stories and posting them on the internet might sound like the ultimate nightmare. How do we reach these people? How do we influence them? What can we expect them to write? Where do their loyalties lie? As unsettling as it might seem to a seasoned communicator, we believe that participatory journalism is here to stay. It is what people want.

One of the most popular citizen journalism sites is OhMyNews, founded by Korean journalist Oh Yeon Ho and launched under the motto 'Every citizen is a reporter'. The site has more than 60,000 citizen journalists in more than 100 countries worldwide and 65 full-time staff reporters. Many stories written by citizen journalists have a personal angle. Someone in a particular country might read about an issue in their local paper that does not get covered internationally. They might want to write about it for an international citizen journalism site and add their personal angle to it. The story could be about a power shortage in a particular region and how people in the writer's village reacted to it. It is written by one of the people affected by the situation. It is a real-life story. Readers will be able to imagine what it is like to live in that particular part of the world, having to cope, for example, with power shortages. This kind of content is much more powerful than the sterile reporting offered by the major international networks.

Citizen journalism is bringing back personalization to content creation. It is also adding pressure to the environment ordinary journalists are operating in. It is forcing them to stay ahead of the curve. PR practitioners are dealing with a whole new media ecosystem. It feels like a moving target. But we believe audiences' increased need for local perspectives to be good news for the communication profession. Business executives will need communicators to decipher other cultures and convey local messages.

The 'most unappreciated growth story'

The slick shape of the Burj Al Arab hotel in Dubai has become the symbol of the growth the Arab world has experienced. Global energy prices have brought hundreds of billions of dollars to the region. Its governments have been focusing on capital formation and capacity building. Now, its major challenge is job creation, given the young age of its population.

Saudi Arabia produces 200,000 new graduates every year. In the next 20 years alone, the Arab world will have to come up with 100 million new jobs, more than during the entire 20th century.[20] And it is already exploring new sectors where those jobs could come from.

PricewaterhouseCoopers expects the region's entertainment and media market to grow by about 60 per cent to US$10 billion annually, outpacing Brazil and Russia.[21] Sumner M. Redstone, the chairman of media group Viacom, calls the Arab world 'the world's most underappreciated growth story'.[22] Viacom launched MTV Arabia in 2007 and calls it 'Arabic MTV made by Arabs for Arabs'.[23]

Sixty per cent of the people of the Arab world are under the age of 25. Social media and other web technologies are likely to play a major role in the way they perceive the world and share information. We believe the Arab world to be one of the communication stories of the future. Its growth is likely to be realized through an interesting mixture of local values and imported techniques.

The upside of global warming

Few would say that global warming has produced positive side-effects. However, there is one. Pictures of melting glaciers and stranded polar bears have made people understand how closely interconnected world economies are. Audiences in one country have become aware of the impact that those who emit greenhouse gases are having on the quality of life of people in other parts of the world. The prospect of disruptive climate change has made them think beyond the geographical borders of their countries. And this factor is contributing to the new global awareness that is currently surfacing. People want to know what is really happening in other parts of the world and how it is going to change the way they live.

Al Gore's Oscar-winning documentary, *An Inconvenient Truth*, has played a major role in making climate change part of popular culture. So has celebrity endorsement of global warming concerns. The website Ecorazzi[24] covers celebrity gossip from an environmental angle. As its tag line 'The latest in green gossip' suggests, you can read about Hollywood stars endorsing green technology or about the sins of celebrity journalists who forgot to pay sufficient attention to climate change during important TV debates.

There are those who believe that public figures and celebrities will soon tire of supporting green activism and move to the next corporate social responsibility issue trendy enough to stir popular imagination.[25] However, the phenomenon has already reached critical mass. Global warming and its challenges have become part of the communication equation. They are likely to remain a constant feature of communication strategies.

The clean-energy business is bound to develop into one of the leading economic sectors of the future. Experts believe that nothing less than a total makeover of the US $6 trillion global energy business will be needed in order to stop global warming.[26] The preoccupation with global warming has moved to the next stage, with a significant number of venture capital firms investing in green technology. This phenomenon has communication implications. Communication practitioners will play a major role in explaining the advantages of these clean technologies to public audiences. They will be instrumental in turning their interest into passion.

Public awareness of the global consequences of climate change is high and businesses can expect their sustainability practices to be scrutinized by people living on the opposite side of the world. It used to be that all a business needed to do was to comply with national environmental regulations and engage with local stakeholders. Not any longer. We live in a global economy in which multiple voices are heard. A company trying to buy a business in another part of the world can expect its commitment to the environment to be scrutinized by the communities that business is serving. And that is where cross-cultural communication comes in. In order to convince local audiences of its solid environmental track record, the potential buyer will have to do communication work that goes beyond glossy sustainability reports. The company will need highly skilled communicators able to penetrate the local culture and to engage with consumers, non-governmental organizations (NGOs), regulators and other interest groups.

Environmental protection has always required transparent information. Environmental protection in the twenty-first century will require culturally sensitive information.

Gearing up for the new era

All these phenomena are contributing to creating a new awareness. Even disturbing ones like terrorism and other societal risks have contributed to pushing our boundaries and increasing our perception of external forces.

A presentation on post-conflict civil society organized by the Ismaili Centre in London in 2008 reported about the results of a study conducted in the United Kingdom with school children. These children were asked to associate the word 'conflict' with an image. While in the past this word used to make them think of fights on the playground, the answer they came up with this time was terrorism and violence in other parts of the world.

The awareness of terrorism and its impact on many aspects of our lives, from global travel to exports, has produced a new attitude of borderlessness. In this new global environment, you will be asked to suspend your identity as a citizen of a country or an employee of a corporation and stretch your horizon to process new realities from a different point of view. It might feel unsettling at first but this new way of perceiving our audiences and their environment will need to come naturally to us. It is not only globalization and the interactive internet that are forcing us out of the comfort zone. It is also people's conscious choice as to whom they want to trust. Public perceptions are shifting. This means that we will be communicating in a completely different business context. Where does this leave the professional communicator? Which core skills will the communicator of the Globalization 3.0 era need?

We are looking at a radically different profile. Our feeling is that some of the skills that have been so important in the past, like producing annual reports or organizing press conferences, will fade into the background. While others, like the ability to decipher environments or build relationships with selected audiences, will come to the forefront. Sensibility will be key, and in particular cultural sensibility. Although communicators were often required in the past to understand the background of target audiences, this skill tended to be considered secondary. The emphasis has often been on the message and the ability to package and broadcast it.

The level of sophistication of today's audiences and their ability to select information calls for a paradigm shift. Corporations will need communicators who can educate them about the cultural background of a certain audience and the best way to address its needs.

Therefore, in order to succeed in the Globalization 3.0 era, a communicator will need to gain exposure to other cultures, learn other languages and develop a curiosity for other ways of thinking. We are basically talking about a set of skills that will enable us to interpret complexity. In the coming years this is where much of the value added by the communication function will come from.

We will also be required to help staff find meaning in a rapidly changing world. We might be working for a German company that has just been bought by a Chinese corporation with headquarters in Dubai. Our task in this case will be to guide employees through the different cultural changes while remaining a constant point of reference. Situations like this call for the ability to mediate between cultures, a skill that will become an integral part of the communicator's profile.

In the words of Josep Maria Esquirol, professor of philosophy at Universitat de Barcelona in Spain, we need to develop a new mindset.[27] We need to move closer to other cultures in order to be able to appreciate and respect them. And this might prove a balancing act. 'One of the key points about respect is the need to keep the right distance.' Professor Esquirol believes that there are no standard measures to guide us in this process. 'Success depends on our capacity to perceive and focus our attention.' According to him, to communicate is 'to establish a relationship, to create a connection that enables sharing'. Communicators operating in a new multicultural context will be asked to harness the knowledge of the different nationalities working for a company. And sharing will be at the core of this process. This kind of information sharing will require a shift in thinking, a new openness and acceptance of ideas alien to the mainstream culture we have been used to.

The communication function will become a meeting point for all the cultures represented in an organization. It might be helpful to think of communicators as 'fruit salads'. It will be up to us to study these cultures, find the most effective elements and merge them into a new narrative representative of the company, one that most employees will be able to identify with.

These are exciting times for communicators. We can all sense that we are at the beginning of a new era. We have to be prepared. Here is how we can get up to speed:

● Monitor trends: Trends influence corporate strategies and the sustainability of a company's business model. They affect our target audiences. At the same time, if properly interpreted they provide communicators with new opportunities to add value. Think of trends like alternative energy, virtual education or online publishing. It is important to study and understand their impact on communication before they become mainstream.

- Develop cultural proficiency: Geneviève Hilton, senior vice president at the PR agency Ketchum in Hong Kong, wrote in an article that what we need to develop is cultural proficiency. This means 'knowing when to listen, when to ask for help and when – finally – to speak'.[28] These simple instructions summarize well what we have to do in order to develop a sensibility that allows us to tune into other cultures. One can start by developing an interest in how other people live and think, how they grew up, what their values are. If you are designing a communication campaign for a country you do not know, learn about the history. Read a book by its most famous writer.

- Study communication styles: people in different cultures have different communication patterns. Develop an ability to appreciate historical backgrounds and honour experiences that might contradict your way of looking at life. Know that they are all an integral part of the personality of the people you will have to interact with. Co-author Cambié was once chairing a meeting at a Brussels-based international trade association. A representative of a Slovak organization asked to see her before the start to discuss an issue on the agenda. The meeting began and Cambié was moderating the discussion. She noticed that the Slovak colleague was being rather quiet and was not mentioning the interesting point he had raised just a few minutes earlier in her office. She therefore asked him to take the floor and share his point of view. The colleague looked embarrassed and declined the invitation. Cambié quickly realized that what she had done was a major cultural faux pas. During the Cold War era, her Slovak colleague had had to survive in a climate of general secrecy and mistrust. He had to learn to be careful with sharing information. His superiors and colleagues could have abused his openness and used it to spot his weaknesses. This is why he felt comfortable expressing his views in a private one-to-one conversation but not in an open forum like the meeting Cambié was chairing.

- Widen your horizon: To gain real insight we have to go beyond what we have been trained to see. Only then we will be able to reach a better understanding of people, their perceptions and their expectations. The communication environment of Globalization 3.0 will be much more nuanced than anything we have experienced before. We will need to leave the cookie cutter behind and develop strong antennas able to recognize emerging patters and to interpret information intuitively.

Notes

1. S Hamm, Children of the Web, *BusinessWeek*, 2 July 2007, p. 53.
2. T Friedman, While I Was Sleeping, in *The World is Flat*, p. 11, Picador/ Farrar, Straus and Giroux, New York, 2007.
3. T Friedman, The Untouchables, in *The World is Flat*, p. 278, Picador/ Farrar, Straus and Giroux, New York, 2007.
4. Goldman Sachs, Dreaming with BRICs: The Path to 2050, 1 October 2003.
5. Vivienne Walt, Khartoum Boom, *Fortune*, 27 August 2007, p. 34.
6. Alec Russell, The New Colonialists, *Financial Times Magazine*, 17/18 November 2007, p. 26.
7. Mark Leonard, China's New Intelligentsia, *Prospect*, March 2008, p. 29.
8. Elizabeth Woyke, Rise of the Asian D-School, *BusinessWeek*, 15 October 2007, p. 66.
9. Chakravarthi Ram-Prased, India's Middle Class Failure, *Prospect*, September 2007, p. 28.
10. The Next Big Thing, *The Economist*, 6 October 2007, p. 85.
11. Naina Lal Kidwai, India's Emerging Role in the Global Economy, The XXIst World Traders, Tacitus Lecture delivered at the Guildhall in the City of London, www.world-traders.com, 3 March 2008, http://www.world-traders.com/.
12. The World's Cheapest Wheels, *Newsweek*, 14 January 2008, p. 40.
13. Jason Overdorf, Bigger than Bollywood, *Newsweek*, 10 September 2007, p. 43.
14. Steve Hamm, Children of the Web, *BusinessWeek*, 2 July 2007, p. 53.
15. Adios to Poverty, Hola to Consumption, *The Economist*, 18 August 2007, pp. 23–24.
16. The Legacy That Got Left On The Shelf, *The Economist*, 2 February 2008, p. 76.
17. 17 Companies Join the Boston Consulting Group's List of 100 Emerging Giants in this New Edition for 2008, consultingpulse.worldpress.com, 11 March 2008, http://consultingpulse.worldpress.com/2007/12/10/new-global-challengers-pose-growing-threat-to-established-industry-leaders-according-to-a-new-report-by-the-boston-consulting-group/.
18. Chery Shines at Moscow Auto Show 2007, cheryglobal.com, 11 March 2008, http://www.cheryglobal.com/mtzx/text_detail.jsp?artId=1188 8731830001&columnId=11700520360001.

19. David Marash, US Anchor, Al Jazeera, in discussion with co-author Cambié, March 2008.
20. Hamid Jafar, Chairman Crescent Petroleum and Chairman Dana Gas, speech at Mansion House for Arab International Women Forum, aiwfonline.com, 3 January 2008, http://www.aiwfonline.com/.
21. Emily Flynn Vencat and Zvika Krieger, Media Meccas, *Newsweek*, 5 November 2007, p. 50.
22. Kerry Capell, The Arab World Wants Its MTV, *BusinessWeek*, 22 October 2007, p. 80.
23. Kerry Capell, The Arab World Wants Its MTV, *BusinessWeek*, 22 October 2007, p. 81.
24. March 2008, http://www.ecorazzi.com/.
25. The Final Cut, *The Economist*, 2–8 June 2007, p. 34.
26. Marc Gunther and Adam Lashinsky, Cleanup Crew, *Fortune*, 26 November 2007, p. 58.
27. Josep M Esquirol, PhD, Professor at Universitat de Barcelona and Director of the Institute of Technoethics, Values and Communication: In Search of Valuable Communication, IABC 2008 EuroComm Conference, Barcelona, Spain, 5 February 2008.
28. Geneviève Hilton, Becoming Culturally Fluent, *Communication World*, November–December 2007, p. 35.

2 Rethinking public relations

No aspect of the communication profession is more misunderstood than public relations (PR). If you move from journalism to PR, this is something that will dawn on you very quickly. Many corporate executives believe that it is all about packaging messages, sending them out and trying to get journalists to write your story.

If you began your career in journalism, you know that this cannot possibly happen. Everything you have been taught as a reporter runs contrary to this model. So you try to convince senior management that the emphasis should be placed on the word 'relations'. Time should be spent studying the culture of a particular medium as well as the background and eventual agendas of its publisher. And more time should be dedicated to establishing a relationship with its journalists. This work is of even greater importance if you are operating in a market you know little about.

There is no end to the misunderstanding. PR practitioners are known the world over as 'those who put people in the papers'. Their work is often limited to a reactive role as companies try to avoid the media and resort to PR only when they have to respond to negative reporting. However, this scenario is about to change. The role of the PR practitioner is defined by the way in which members of the public consume information. In the new era, it is becoming increasingly difficult to control the message. We can no longer rely on our audience to get its information from the media.

According to the 2008 Edelman Trust Barometer, the agency's annual trust and credibility survey, the man/woman in the street still trusts a 'person like yourself', and trusts experts more than senior executives. Generation Y, who Edelman calls 'Young Influentials', uses multiple sources of information, and trusts it only if it is confirmed by several spokespeople. In emerging markets like China and Russia which have a history of government control over the media, young people tend to use mainly online sources, such as social networks and video-sharing sites, when they are looking for information about companies.[1]

If you want to practise public relations in the social media era, your focus should be on the word 'public'. The new phenomenon of citizen journalism has brought home to us the fact that amateurs and professionals have access to the same resources and compete for the same audiences. It is the ability of Journalism 2.0 to add the local component and personalize a story that makes it so attractive to different people. People want to know which impact a particular piece of news is bound to have on their lives.

Becoming part of the story

Open-source reporting done by ordinary citizens with the help of camera phones and blogs is bound to bring people in different parts of the world closer to each other. Imagine a housewife in Denmark reading the article of a citizen journalist reporting on the impact of a mud slide on his home town in Peru. She will be able to relate to the troubles of the working mother who has to travel twice as far to take her children to school. This story is likely to resonate with her much more than any piece of journalism about the impact of a natural catastrophe on the economy of a country and the stock market.

Open-source journalism is a way for readers around the world to learn about other cultures' unique perspectives. We learn to see life in other countries through the eyes of local citizen journalists, and we begin to relate to their experiences. Pakistan is a powerful example. During the judicial crisis of 2007, a number of ordinary citizens used their mobile phones and laptops to report on what was happening after the declaration of the emergency order in their country. Muhammad Aslam Khan is a citizen journalist who writes regularly for OhMyNews. He is the winner of the first award granted by the South-Asian Citizen Reporters Network (SACRN), an initiative aimed at promoting open-source reporting in the region.

Aslam Khan believes that 'as an ordinary citizen, [it is] my duty to report from danger zones during this critical juncture in the history of our country… For me, it's no longer just a case of filing stories but rather documenting history for future generations of South Asians.'[2] His account of the Red Mosque siege in the summer of the 2007 in

Islamabad and the storming of the building by government troops is particularly captivating because of the conversational tone he uses and the real-life feel he is able to convey in the story:

> Having just returned from the OhmyNews Forum, I was very tired after my long Thai Airlines flight from Seoul to Islamabad. I landed here on Monday at 2 p.m. So Tuesday morning, I preferred to rest up after breakfast. I was reading the local Urdu newspapers after many days abroad and was enjoying some of my favorite columns.
>
> Suddenly I heard huge blasts that were followed by the uninterrupted firing of automatic weapons.
>
> I immediately left my bedroom, which was located on the first floor. I could see black smoke in the sky and clearly heard the heavy firing. It was time to act, not rest. My cell phone was continuously ringing. Calls from around Pakistan were pouring in because my close friends knew that my residence is very near the Red Mosque. All were curious to know what was going on there.
>
> ... I immediately put on my favorite jogging shoes and got ready to report.
>
> ... The area was buzzing with loud ambulance sirens, heavy gunfire and bomb blasts. Teargas shelling was also irritating our eyes as we proceeded up the street.
>
> ... Within minutes we were at the crossroad of Lal Masjid [the Red Mosque] and the Islamist girls' school, where Rangers were deployed and heavily concentrated.
>
> They had constructed bunkers and concrete posts in front of Lal Masjid. In any case, we were keenly aware that we could become caught in the crossfire.
>
> Then there was a calm before the storm. After severe teargas shelling it was the interval. Ambulances were at the main gate of Islamist girls' school. Actually the female students were badly affected by the severe teargas shelling.
>
> Rangers and police targeted the inside of the school compound. Sirens were blaring and it was hard to hear. Students were chanting slogans against the government and President Musharraf.
>
> ... Inside the building a youth was standing, armed with automatic assault rifle. He was wearing a modern gas mask. When I was taking pictures of that youth, an intelligence officer in modern khakis tried to stop me.[3]

We can picture the writer having breakfast in his home, immersing himself in his favourite reading and being rudely brought back to reality by the firing of weapons in the streets. This kind of reporting makes us feel part of the story. We become engaged at an emotional level. And emotions together with passion are the motivators communicators have to use if they want their message to leave a mark in this new era.

The Red Mosque story on OhMyNews also comes with a picture of Aslam Khan wearing a flak jacket and holding the mobile phone he had been using to take pictures and videos for the article. This real-life touch makes the report even more tangible. The reader might be an office worker, surfing the internet in his spare time from the safety of his bedroom in Canada. He will want to know what the reporter looks like, how he managed to keep safe in such a risky situation and what he used to take pictures. All of a sudden, he can sense the danger described in the story. Thanks to the reporting style used by this citizen journalist and to his camera phone, the crisis in Pakistan has become extremely tangible.

Participatory journalism can also take the form of blogs, as in the case of Inside Iraq. The Iraqi staff of the Bagdad office of the news agency Knight Ridder/McClatchy use this blog to write about their daily experiences. Their posts are left unedited and the English is that of the writers. This style adds a powerful emotional component to the stories. Here is an extract from an intense post written by Laith in the winter of 2008 about sectarian violence in the country:

> The 55 years old taxi driver start his talking with a strange sentence. He said 'the only winner in this country is the bachelor'. After a while, we started talking about the old days and I asked him like twenty questions about the life during the sixties and the seventies. After tens minutes of the heated discussion, I could reach the main point.
> The man lost his son who was kidnapped in one of the western neighborhoods of Baghdad more than a year ago.[4]

The best way of defining this new type of open-source reporting is with the comment a fan of Inside Iraq left on Cambié's blog XCulture: 'A good example of grass roots reporting which tells more about the ground situation than a 1000 word article in good English.'[5]

It's all about lemons

Another powerful example of citizen journalism is Yoani Sánchez. Her blog, Generatión Y, describes the tribulations experienced every day by the average Cuban. All over the world, observers of the Castro regime have been stunned by the freedom this blogger enjoys. Correspondents of foreign newspapers would have been thrown out of Cuba if they had tried to address some of the privations so faithfully described in her posts. Sanchez rarely writes about politics. She doesn't need to. The picture she paints of Cubans' everyday lives is highly effective at shedding light on the failures of the island's regime. She might talk about the Cuban currency disturbingly morphing into 'money from a Monopoly game' or the Kafkaesque conformity of the newly established Cuban parliament.

Sanchez is not a journalist. She was trained as a philologist and, after being denied a career in academia, she had to make a living working in Havana's tourism sector. Her reporting is so powerful because she talks the language of social media. She writes about the average citizen of Cuba for the average citizen of the world. Her readers don't want political analysts writing about the future of Raul Castro. They want to know how it feels to live day-in–day-out in one of the remaining bastions of communism. And they can certainly get the feeling from the following post written by Sanchez in the winter of 2008:

Search and seizure

Today I got up with a sore throat. The guilty party was the impertinent cold wind in the Malecón, to which I exposed myself last night while talking with a friend. During an hour we talked – thinking that we were fixing the world and the Island – without realizing that the temperature was falling. That's why this morning I woke up with a cold and my whole body was asking for a hot lemon tea.

With that imperative I went to the closest agricultural market and asked for the green citrus of my cravings. One of the vendors told me: 'Lemons are lost. You better buy a guava'. I didn't let him convince me and continued with my whim of a warm lemon with a hint of black tea. I walked then towards Old Havana and in passing through several markets I realized that they didn't have what I was looking for either. My throat was hurting even more and at that point I had to rethink if would be better to take a C Vitamin pill; but since my stubbornness is genetic, I insisted in searching for the missing fruit.

Close to two in the afternoon I gave up. I could barely swallow because of the burning in the throat, nothing compared with the disgust that provoked in my the 'disappearance' of the lemons. The useless 'search and capture' has generated in me an ill feeling more long lasting than the cold. I has left me with some hard questions: How is it that with so much fertile land and so many people with desire of producing, commercialize and sell, they don't combine themselves and materialize an abundant offering of lemons in the market? Why is still Marabú the 'king of the Cuban countryside' (go in a road trip by the highway to Pinar del Rio and you'll see), while oranges, tangerines and – not to mention – grapefruits, go to the inventory of the exotic? When will the land belong to those who will make it produce and not of a State that sub-utilzes it in its abandoned parcels? Do I keep the hope or forget about the flavor of lemons?[6]

In 2008, *Time Magazine* included Sanchez in its list of the 100 most influential people in the world. The same year, the Spanish newspaper *El Pais* awarded her the prestigious l'Ortega y Gasset prize. Although she was forbidden by the regime to travel to Madrid to collect the prize, Sanchez enjoys a freedom of expression paper-bound reporters on the island can only dream of. Cuba experts believe it is the power of the online community that has kept Sanchez out of jail and in the international headlines. Any action against her would send instant ripples across cyberspace and result in a massive attack against the regime by the thousands of 'netizens' who are faithfully reading her blog.

A two-way communication

Citizen-powered reporting is just one aspect of the 'localization' phenomenon that has been sweeping the world of journalism. 'Refrigerator journalism' is another. This term was invented by Don Ranly, a professor of journalism at the University of Missouri.[7] According to him, a story has to be written in a way that will make people want to cut it out and put it on their refrigerator or bulletin board. Often these stories are about people they know or admire. They are about real people living normal lives.

In our era of globalized content, readers are looking for a local angle they can relate to. And by 'local' we do not necessarily mean a geographical community. According the 2008 Edelman Trust Barometer, a 'person like yourself [is] defined by common interests rather than shared demographic features and attributes. Communities are not geographically contained'.[8]

Historically, PR practitioners have been trying to influence the media. Now we rely on the broader public, organized in communities of bloggers and social networkers, to tell our story.

But what does this mean for us in practice? How is the PR profession going to change?

According to David Marash, US Anchor of Al Jazeera, 'when you formulate a position or design a campaign, you have to know that everyone in the world will be able to access that information. [These days] you can no longer get away with segmented messages. You are talking to the whole spectrum including consumers, competitors and adversaries. And it's a two-way communication. Their response is played back to you.'

Instead of trying to control the message, we have to communicate our passion and inspire the public so that they will spread the message for us. This is no easy task. It calls for a mind shift. But it also means a big step up the food chain for PR practitioners. Communication with the new general public requires intensive research into their cultural differences, beliefs, expectations and affiliations. We are talking about intelligence gathering here, not to be compared with old-style PR, which tended to be very much about writing news releases and compiling lists of press contacts. PR practitioners are no longer needed in their capacity as crafters of messages. They are finally assuming the role of strategic consultants, able to sense the environment in a particular country or market and to advise senior management on which course to take.

Studying the spirit of the time will become a large part of the brief of the PR practitioner in the Globalization 3.0 era. To many of us, this is nothing new. The PR sector has always been one of the first to have to react to political and social changes.

Warren G Makgowe, public relations officer at the University of South Africa, writes in an article about PR in the post-Apartheid era:

> Democracy in South Africa has ushered opportunities for organizations, at the same time, customers now demand more from them. Organizations are now obliged to do market research in order to respond appropriately to customers' needs. The task of engaging with stakeholders in order to understand them better has become an integral part of the PR practice and in so doing they are able to advise and provide management with the necessary information for business decision making. This has resulted in management appreciating and recognizing the PR practice as important for the success of organizations.[9]

Coming of age

In emerging economies, PR is coming of age and shaping up as an integrated discipline. The pressure is coming in part from the media sector. In China, three media outlets are being funded by the government, People's Daily, China Central Television (CCTV) and Xinhua News Agency. Journalists working for the rest of the sector have had to learn to attract audiences and to care about advertising revenue. Ten years ago PR practitioners could count on journalists to attend a simple product launch and report on it. These days they will only attend if they can get a newsworthy story out of it.[10]

The Chinese are also beginning to listen to new voices. One of these comes from another BRIC country, neighbouring Russia. RIA Novosti, Russia's largest public news agency, has been producing news in Chinese since 2006 for subscribers in mainland China as well as Hong Kong, Taiwan, the USA, Australia, Japan and Europe. 'Every Chinese correspondent in Moscow begins their working day by surfing RusNews.cn [RIA Novosti's Chinese site] to get an idea of what is currently happening in Russia', says Stanislav Krans, chief representative of the agency in China.[11] In 2008, RIA Novosti was the first Russian news agency to be authorized by the Chinese authorities to sell its services directly to Chinese subscribers.[12] The agency has been viewing this development as an important step for the RIA Novosti brand in China and its further expansion. RIA Novosti has cooperation agreements with news agencies in other emerging economies, including India, Mexico and Argentina.

These developments call for a higher level of sophistication in the PR industry. 'Thirty years ago PR people [in India] would be sent to the airport to pick up foreign visitors', pointed out Bish Mukherjee, a communications expert based in Chennai. 'These days we have a very vibrant PR sector.'[13]

With multinationals from emerging economies becoming increasingly active in the global mergers and acquisitions arena, communicators from these markets are experiencing the need to educate their senior management on more strategic forms of PR. The acquisition of Daewoo's truck division by the Indian company Tata Motors, for example, was supported by an intense PR strategy aimed at shifting the perception in Korea that a European candidate would have been more appropriate to take over the ailing company. 'Tata executives were enrolled in Korean language classes, company brochures were translated into Korean, and Tata began making presentations to employees, the local auto association chief, the mayor of Gusan [the city were the plant is based], officials in Seoul, even Korea's Prime Minister.'[14]

New tools

In China, the focus of major PR campaigns is shifting from events and media relations to other dimensions, including corporate reputation and social media. The interactive web is providing communication practitioners with new creative tools, as demonstrated by Pampers' 'Absolute Baby' campaign developed by the Shanghai office of the communication agency Weber Shandwick.[15]

The year 2007 marked a baby boom in China, with millions of parents seeking advice on how to care for their children. The Absolute Baby campaign was aimed at informing young mothers of the changing needs of babies as they grow, a concept defined as the Baby Stages of Development (BSOD) by Pampers.

Most Chinese have limited experience with parenting due to the country's one-child policy. According to research by the Shanghai Municipal Population and Family Planning Commission, 98.4 per cent of families with a newborn baby require parenting guidance. Mothers across six provinces admitted in a survey that they were lacking in information or that the information they had received was 'out-of-date' or 'old-fashioned'.

Weber Shandwick identified the pervasive need for information on baby care and health in China as an opportunity to position Pampers as a trustworthy source of information and to support sales of its leading-edge products. Based on research from consumer and healthcare professionals, the Absolute Baby campaign identified its target audience as two specific kinds of mothers in major urban centres with babies aged between 0 and 24 months: 'Achievement Moms' and 'Relationship Moms'. The former are well-educated, have a relatively high income, can afford good products and expect access to knowledge that allows them to be perceived as leaders among their peers. 'Relationship Moms', on the other hand, look to peers and friends as sources of information. They are frequent internet users and look for online baby care information and tips from other mothers. Fathers and other family members were also target audiences, especially for offline events such as Pampers Baby Carnivals organized in major cities.

At the core of the Absolute Baby project was research showing that the interactive web with its bulletin boards plays an important role for mothers seeking information in different parts of China. The campaign also used blogs to capitalize on the strong emotional investment parents have in their babies as a result of the country's one-child policy. Parents were given the opportunity to upload baby photos and submit essays on their parenting experiences. All babies registered on the Pampers site could be voted on by visitors as part of the Talent Baby competition.

It was this competition that made Weber Shandwick discover the unpredictability of participatory sites and the flexibility needed to deal with them. When the site users were invited to vote in Talent Baby, some parents submitted multiple votes for their babies, resulting in a flurry of angry posts on the Pampers site bulletin board. An IT company had to be brought in to find out which votes were invalid. The response was quick and helped to boost Pampers' reputation. Another lesson learned is that unpredictability has its advantages. Visitors to the Pampers site pasted the company's baby care knowledge onto other sites, creating a wave of third-party endorsements that continued to echo the campaign's key message across the cyber sphere. Weber Shandwick tracked these articles and found that 400,000 mothers had read them and had posted 70,000 responses. Despite a sharply reduced PR budget, the use of social media produced stronger results than the previous year's campaign. Weber Shandwick's Absolute Baby campaign won a certificate of excellence at the 2007 Asia Pacific PR Awards.

Interactive media are transforming PR into a two-way conversation between a company and its audiences. As demonstrated by the Absolute Baby campaign, PR practitioners need to understand the cultural context – in this case the emotional consequences of China's one-child policy – before engaging in a dialogue with them.

The middle way

As the communications spectrum in emerging economies becomes broader and more diverse, we are beginning to experience a shift in the perception of PR professionals from service providers to business partners.

In a market like China, whose companies are eagerly courting public listings on international stock exchanges, communicators have the opportunity to reinvent themselves as the key to Western markets. It is all about building corporate reputations to support strong brands.

Chinese corporations might be running a successful business but their brands still have some way to go, at home as well as abroad. The Chinese subsidiary of the communications agency Hill & Knowlton conducted a survey in 2004 together with the Chinese media *Seventeen Magazine* and Sinomonitor International to discover the aspirations of Chinese students and their definition of 'cool'. Half of the young people surveyed in Beijing and Shanghai used terms like 'individuality and innovation' to describe a 'cool' company. The Nike brand came top of the list, with 30 per cent of the students' votes. Adidas was second. Also on the list were Microsoft, Samsung, Nokia, IBM and Christian Dior. Only two Asia brands were mentioned, Samsung and Sony.[16]

More than half of the respondents do not believe that China has cool brands. But when asked specifically to mention cool Chinese brands, they came up with household appliances manufacturer Haier, followed by computer-maker Lenovo and sports good manufacturer Li Ning.

Li Ning is an interesting example. It is named after its founder and executive director, a famous athlete who won the highest number of medals at the 1984 Olympic Games in Los Angeles. The company dominated the market in the 1990s. That was before the entry of Nike and Adidas into China. Now it has a mere 18 per cent of the market, while its Western competitors have 20 per cent each.[17] In spite of having an inspirational leader, Li Ning is still struggling to carve out a distinctive identity. In an attempt to add a strong Chinese flavour to its products, it has developed a shoe named after Lei Feng, a youth hero from the 1960s who still features in movies that are part of the mandatory primary school curriculum.

The pace of development of the communication profession in an emerging economy like China is being dictated by the fight for the consumer. Local companies need to catch up with their Western competitors in terms of marketing skills and, at the same time, harbour aspirations of penetrating foreign markets and attracting foreign investors. It is all happening very quickly. It is this speed that is bringing sophistication into our profession. Media relations are no longer sufficient to shape the profile of a company. Corporate reputation management is needed to create the character and identity behind a brand. And a brand is kept alive thanks to a solid strategy and active issue management.

Operating in emerging markets means dealing with a certain amount of complexity. One has to consider a number of factors simultaneously. And these might be factors you have never encountered in your work in Europe or North America. Take the surge of Chinese nationalism that followed both the Tibetan crisis in the spring of 2008 and the protests triggered by the Olympic torch relay. An intriguing expression of this phenomenon was the digital red heart followed by the word 'China' which the users of the Microsoft networking platform MSN China were invited to put in front of their name as a sign of support for the Olympic games. More than three million people joined the 'Love China' campaign. The reactions on the China Daily online community were mixed.[18] This message was posted by one of the users:

> Do you have (L) China on your MSN?
> I do!
> What does this mean to you?
> To me, it means that I love my adopted country, and I am very thankful for all China has given and done for me!
> It also means, that there is ONE CHINA, and will never be torn apart! No matter what the HATERS say or do!

A more subdued comment read: 'have it... because someone told me to have it'.

Creative cross-cultural communication is all about observing phenomena of this kind and distilling the cultural elements that produce specific behaviours. The next step then implies mixing communication practices already applied in other contexts with strong local components.

Experts believe that a country like China with a 3,000-year tradition of oriental philosophy will develop its own way of doing PR rather than simply emulating the Western model. According to David Weiner, senior partner with *National Public Relations Communications Monthly*, 'China will take the middle way, striking a balance between traditional Chinese values and international business practices.'[19]

The same holds true for other emerging markets. The middle way is what communication practitioners the world over will have to familiarize themselves with in the years to come. The frontiers between the developed economies and emerging markets are dissolving. What the concrete result will be in terms of communication models is anybody's guess. But there are already a number of promising signs.

Instigating change

Among the promising signs is the development of the media sector in the Arab world. Economic growth coupled with a more open political environment and new technologies has led to the launch of a series of new publications and TV channels.[20] With literacy levels rising, the region is discovering a new appetite for foreign, specialized publications. For example, the Saudi Specialised Publishing Company acquired the rights to publish the Arabic editions of *Domus*, an Italian magazine covering interior design, and *Quattroruote*, an automotive magazine also from Italy.

With foreign publications streaming into the market and more Arabs travelling abroad, demand for quality and international content has increased and is putting pressure on local publications. *Hia*, the leading magazine for 'affluent Arab ladies', reacted to this trend by focusing more on experts' advice for its readers and offering a mobile phone service, a so-called Jawal service, that provides subscribers with news and tips. Shortly after its launch on the Saudi market, this service attracted more than 800 users. *Hia* runs four 'Jawal channels', covering news about the Saudi royal family as well as tips on beauty, health, fitness and fashion. The magazine has a total circulation of 45,000. It is distributed throughout the Middle East and North Africa as well as Europe. *Hia* has been profiting from a new trend. An increasing number of young women in the Arab world are pursuing higher education and want to start new businesses.[21] According to the Arab International Women's Forum, a network advocating women's involvement in the economic and political life of the region, 70 per cent of university graduates in the Arab States in 2007 were female. Women in the Gulf control an estimated US$40 billion of personal wealth that they are channelling into specialist investment funds managed for and by women.

'The Arab Society is becoming more open towards empowering women to join various fields including media', says Mai Badr, *Hia*'s editor in chief. 'Media can act as an instigator of change.' The region is, however, still experiencing a shortage of qualified female journalists. In 2008, Princess Hassa Bint Salman Bin Abdulaziz of the Saudi royal family set up a scholarship in cooperation with the Prince Ahmad Bin Salman Institute for Applied Media to encourage Saudi women to study journalism.

The other side of the coin

In our interconnected world, countries have a character just like people and companies. They are constantly being rated according to 'how they do what they do, how they keep promises, how they make decisions, how things really happen inside, how they connect and collaborate, how they engender trust, how they relate to their customers, to the environment, and to the communities in which they operate etc.[22] Few issues are more delicate for a country than the introduction of a new currency. Money is part of its national identity. It is one of the most important points of reference for its citizens. The right kind of PR is crucial at this time in history. Modern PR calls for an integrated approach aimed at targeting different groups of people with different communication tools. The right kind of communication is what makes the difference between a smooth transition to a new monetary system and a highly unsettling experience bound to turn into general insecurity.

Slovenia, once part of Yugoslavia, joined the European Union in 2004, and the following year it began preparations to join the twelve countries that had already adopted the euro, the European single currency. This small republic was the first country from Eastern Europe to replace its old currency with the euro.

Slovenia viewed its entry into the Eurozone as a milestone. A broad consensus had to be reached among the population. Public surveys were conducted and 57 per cent of the respondents revealed a positive attitude towards the euro, while 66 per cent expressed interest in the changeover to the new currency.[23] Polls showed that 78 per cent of the Slovenes did not expect to experience problems as a consequence of the introduction of the euro. The majority of the population was not concerned about potential abuses, nor did it fear a loss of national identity.

Nevertheless, the government needed to develop a communication campaign that would increase public knowledge of the new currency and explain the advantages as well as the obligations connected with its introduction. Effective communication was also deemed essential in order to guarantee a smooth and swift changeover to the new currency and avoid problems with its use. A third goal was the retention of high levels of confidence in the euro after its introduction. At international level, it was important to achieve a positive assessment of the overall changeover process by the EU institutions and to impress the broader public.

The communication campaign of the Slovenian government was aimed at the average citizen, with the objective of answering any question they might have about the practical aspects of the change-over to the new currency. An inter-institutional working group led by the Government Communication Office and the Central Bank of Slovenia was set up to guarantee that all the parties involved would speak with one voice. The group included key organizations like the Banking Association of Slovenia, the Ministry of Finance, the Ministry of Economy, the Chamber of Commerce and Industry, the Chamber of Handicraft and the Association of Consumers. A tagline 'Evro za vse nas' (Euro for us all) was developed to convey this message.

The government of Slovenia focused in particular on direct communication, rather than relying only on media relations and advertising. This strategy enabled its communicators to devote more attention to the members of the public who required specific assistance, like people who were blind and partially sighted, disabled people and the inhabitants of rural areas.

The campaign included a website (www.evro.si), a toll-free number, publications and calculators distributed to every household, conferences held by experts, and presentations given in schools, shopping centres and retirement communities. Printed material had to be produced not only in Slovene and English but also in the languages of the country's ethnic minorities (Hungarian, Italian, Albanian, Bosniak, Croat, Macedonian, Serbian and two Roma dialects).

The Slovenian government was aware of the necessity to address the emotional components of the changeover. The risk was that the replacement of its money could be perceived as a loss of national identity. However, the country knew it could capitalize on previous experiences of the Slovenian public. The euro is the fourth currency to have been introduced in Slovenia in the past 15 years. After the fall of Yugoslavia, the dinar was replaced by vouchers, which gave way to the predecessor of the euro, the tolar. The familiarity of the public with the process for the introduction of new currencies made the communication effort easier. A certain anxiety remained, however, around the fact that the euro was now an international currency and was therefore more vulnerable to abuse and criminal activities.

The public also had to realize that the euro coins had a higher value than the ones they were used to. The 'Small change is no longer small change, you can buy a lot for it' message was meant to sensitize Slovenians to their right to a fair conversion and fair prices.

Another cultural aspect that had to be dealt with was the tendency of elderly people to keep their savings 'under the mattress' as a result of different waves of inflation experienced in the past. The campaign had to convince them to put their money into a bank, where it would be changed into euros free of charge.

Deloitte Consulting praised the Slovenian campaign for being 'comprehensive, effective' and for having 'clearly added value, particularly in targeting those relatively few target groups in Slovenia which were not already familiar with the Euro'.[24]

According to a report compiled by the European Commission, the executive arm of the European Union, 92 per cent of the Slovenian population felt well informed about the introduction of the single currency and 91 per cent were satisfied with the information provided by the public authorities.[25]

Fine-tuning the message

Here are some factors to bear in mind when doing PR work in a new cultural environment:

- Respect should be high on your agenda. Be respectful of the practices used in a particular country and the way in which relationships are built. Listen to the locals. Don't try to take something out of the context of your country of origin and apply it to another. Don't impose your models.
- Understand the role of the media in a particular country and how it functions, especially the limitations under which it operates. In China, for instance, given the government control on traditional channels, the role of online and social media is more important than in other markets. In many cases it drives consumer and stakeholder attitudes.
- Be respectful in your relations with the press. Show that you are making an effort to understand their way of working. A simple way to do this could be to organize media training sessions for senior management focused on media relations in the new markets your company is trying to penetrate. This approach will help them to understand the context. The next time they will have to face the press in this new environment, they will be sensitive to their priorities and agendas and will be able to fine-tune their messages accordingly.

- Be mindful of cultural nuances. Your tone needs to be adjusted to the style of the environment you are operating in. Take Tanzania, for example, where people tend to be soft-spoken and do not take well to aggressive behaviour.[26] In this case, you would need to ensure you do not come across as too forceful.

- Before choosing your audiences, consider social dynamics. In some countries, like the USA, people are more individualistic, while in others groups play an important role. This element has a strong influence on the way an audience takes in information. You need to study your audience before drafting your message. When introducing a technology product in an Anglo Saxon environment, for example, you might want to use an image of a business man/woman happily experimenting with it in the privacy of their office. In Spain, however, you might want to show the user of the new technology surrounded by his peers or friends.[27]

- Analysing audiences in emerging economies implies working through different layers of complexity. You need to add other factors to the ones you are used to analysing, such as social hierarchy, gender issues, the level of literacy or the number of languages in which you will need to translate your message. India, for example, has 800 languages and 2,000 dialects. Its Constitution lists 22 official languages including Hindi and English.[28]

- Make good use of local experience and expertise. You might need local experts to endorse your message if you want public opinion to take you seriously. Adding a renowned local specialist to the line-up of a press conference will not only increase your credibility in a foreign environment but will also help to 'translate' your message into terms and concepts familiar to local people.

- Make an effort to understand and appreciate local traditions, politics and heritage. Take the time to cultivate local contacts, not only in the media but also among other influential stakeholders.

Notes

1. Edelman Trust Barometer 2008, edelman.co.uk, 28 February 2008, http://www.edelman.co.uk/trustbarometer/.
2. SACRN Best Reporting Award 2007, sacrn.com, 5 March 2008, http://sacrn.com/SACRNAward2007.htm.

3. On the Front Lines of the Red Mosque Battleground, ohmynews.com, 5 March 2008, http://english.ohmynews.com/articleview/article_view.asp?menu=c10400&no=370300&rel_no=1.

4. Silence is Important, washingtonbureau.typepad.com, 5 March 2008, http://washingtonbureau.typepad.com/iraq/2008/02/silence-is-impo.html.

5. A Blog I Like, chandacom-xculture.com, 5 March 2008, http://www.chandacom-xculture.com/?p=87#comments.

6. Search and Seizure, desdecuba.com, 20 June 2008, http://desdecuba.com/generationy/?p=51.

7. The Basics of Ranly's Refrigerator Journalism, thefreelibrary.com, 17 November 2008, http://www.thefreelibrary.com/The+basics+of+Ranly's+refrigerator+journalism-a059328478.

8. Edelman Trust Barometer 2008, edelman.co.uk, 28 February 2008, http://www.edelman.co.uk/trustbarometer/.

9. Warren G Makgowe, Public Relations Officer, University of South Africa (UNISA), *Public Relations in the New South Africa*, October 2007.

10. Emma Huang, Insight into Public Relations in China, unpublished paper, Continuing Education Division, Ryerson University, Toronto, Canada, 12 April 2008.

11. Stanislav Krans, Chief Representative in the People's Republic of China, RIA Novosti, in discussion with co-author Cambié via e-mail, November 2008.

12. RIA Novosti Becomes First Russian Media Outlet to Sell News to China, en.rian.ru, 25 November 2008, http://en.rian.ru/russia/20080411/104800925.html.

13. Bish Mukherjee, President, Misha Network PR, in discussion with co-author Cambié, March 2008.

14. Manjeet Kripalani, Tata: Master of The Gentle Approach, *BusinessWeek*, 25 February 2008, p. 64.

15. John Russell, Executive Vice President Asia Pacific, Powell Tate, in discussion with co-author Cambié via e-mail, March 2008.

16. China's Youth Define 'Cool', chinabusinessreview.com, 17 October 2008, http://www.chinabusinessreview.com/public/0407/smith.html.

17. Joe Nocera, Chinese Have Dreams of Global Brands, *International Herald Tribune*, 12–13 April 2008, p. 10.

18. LOVE CHINA!!! HEART CHINA!!! (L) CHINA!!!, bbs.chinadaily.com.cn, 16 April 2008, http://bbs.chinadaily.com.cn/viewthread.php?gid=2&tid=600896.

19. Public Relations in China Pursue the Middle Way, national.ca, 22 April 2008, http://64.233.183.104/search?q=cache:LUIPl9TGkvsJ:www.national.ca/china/Interview.pdf+David+Weiner+%2B+national+Public+Relations+Communications+Monthly&hl=en&ct=clnk&cd=1&gl=uk.

20. Mai Badr, Editor in Chief, *Hia* magazine, in discussion with co-author Cambié in Dubai, UAE, May 2008.

21. Lina Saigol and Roula Khalaf, More Women on Boards in Kuwait and Oman than Italy and Japan, *Financial Times*, 19 May 2008.

22. Friedman to Wall Street: Get Your HOWs Right, howsmatter.com, 18 November 2008, http://www.howsmatter.com/thomas-friedman-to-wall-street-get-your-hows-right/.

23. Attitudes of Slovenian Citizens to the Introduction of the Euro, evro.si, 22 April 2008, http://www.evro.si/en/slo-and-euro/opinion-surveys.

24. Review of the Slovenian Changeover by Deloitte, evro.si, 22 April 2008, http://www.evro.si/za-novinarje/dokumenti/final-report-deloitte.pdf.

25. The Introduction of the Euro in Slovenia, ec.europa.eu, 22 April 2008, http://ec.europa.eu/economy_finance/the_euro/your_country_euro9155_en.htm.

26. Kati Kerenge, Corporate Communications Manager, Tanga Cement, in discussion with co-author Cambié in San Antonio, USA, February 2008.

27. Ramon Ollé Jr, Account Planning Director, Grey Iberia, in discussion with co-author Cambié, March 2008.

28. List of the National Languages of India, axistranslations.com, 17 October 2008, http://www.axistranslations.com/translation-article/national-lanuages-of-india-list.html.

3 The global language of corporate social responsibility

Corporate social responsibility (CSR) is a product of globalization. In order to be able to operate successfully in foreign markets, these days a company needs a broader understanding of the world, which includes the ability to recognize the needs of local communities and the art of establishing sustainable relationships with them.

Many definitions exist for CSR. We like the one from Wikipedia because this online encyclopaedia tends to reflect the view of the man/woman on the street:

> Corporate Social Responsibility is a concept whereby *organizations* consider the interests of *society* by taking responsibility for the impact of their activities on *customers*, suppliers, *employees*, shareholders, *communities* and the environment in all aspects of their operations. This *obligation* is seen to extend beyond the *statutory* obligation to comply with *legislation* and sees organizations voluntarily taking further steps to improve the quality of life for employees and their families as well as for the local community and society at large.

Wikipedia also goes on to say that:

> The practice of CSR is subject to much debate and criticism. Proponents argue that there is a strong business case for CSR, in that corporations benefit in multiple ways by operating with a perspective broader and

longer than their own immediate, short-term profits. Critics argue that CSR distracts from the fundamental economic role of businesses, others argue that it is nothing more than superficial window-dressing

And communication is perceived as being part of that 'window-dressing' exercise. In its special report on CSR published in 2008, *The Economist* magazine wrote: 'True, much of what is done in the name of CSR is nothing of the sort. It often amounts to little more than the PR department sending its own messages to the outside world.'[1]

Where does it come from, this confusion about the role of the communication function? What is puzzling is the inability of business strategists to see the obvious connection between solid corporate citizenship work and effective reputation management.

Communicators play a crucial role, not only in bridging the gap between a company's sustainability efforts and the public, but also in shaping its CSR policies. In order to be able to draft a viable corporate citizenship strategy, a company has first to understand the interests and agendas of its stakeholders. The mapping of stakeholders and analysis of audiences is what communicators do every day to target a company's outreach. Communicators are also the guardians of corporate reputation and brand values, two key components of the soul of a company with a major impact on its CSR profile.

The importance of this contribution is still widely misunderstood. However, corporations are becoming more aware of the power of perception. They are beginning to grasp the value of intangible assets like reputation and access to networks. According to *BusinessWeek*, 'a company's reputation for being able to deliver growth, attract top talent, and avoid ethical mishaps can account for much of the 30-to-70 per cent gap between the book value of most companies and their market capitalization'.[2]

Corporate reputation requires CSR to go beyond merely publicizing philanthropy. Communicators will find themselves engaging with senior management inside and outside the organization as an integral part of the delivery of business objectives.[3]

It is the relentless pace of globalization that makes the perfect case for the involvement of communication practitioners in the early stages of CSR processes. If companies want to manage risks in a globalized business setting, they need a broader understanding and insight into a complicated patchwork of rules. What is expected from them in terms of CSR initiatives changes from country to country.

Until recently, multinationals headquartered in the global North had a tendency to cascade down into the developing markets CSR practices that were developed for their countries of origin. They used to develop codes of conduct and impose them on suppliers. In the words of Dirk Matten, Hewlett-Packard Chair in Corporate Social Responsibility at the Schulich School of Business in Toronto, 'After having forced suppliers to deliver at the lowest prices possible, corporations would pull out codes of conduct and tell them to stick to them.'[4] Factories in China and India resented this practice and began to view it as a new form of neo-colonialism.

The limits of this approach have become evident. Multinationals are now opting for a different kind of relationship with their suppliers. They prefer to sign contracts for the long term and to work together on issues like factories' sanitary conditions or the minimum age of female workers. Instead of dictating conditions, Western companies are beginning to treat their suppliers like subsidiaries and to use a more inclusive style.

India: The soda controversy

The profile of non-governmental organizations (NGOs) is also changing. They are becoming more globalized, with operations less bound by national borders. The internet provides for the lack of geographical perimeters. Therefore, CSR approaches that can reach across borders are needed.

PepsiCo learnt this lesson in India in 2003 when the Centre for Science & Environment (CSE), an NGO based in New Delhi, claimed that its soft drinks, along with those of Coca-Cola, contained residues of harmful pesticides. Sales of Pepsi's soda drinks fell dramatically. Activists used blogs and e-mail to attack the multinationals. Protesters took to the streets of Indian cities, burning images of soda bottles. Soda sales were banned or restricted in a number of states.

PepsiCo's reaction was slow. It denied CSE's claim and used scientific analysis to prove its point. Chief executives now wish they had acted differently. PepsiCo's CEO, Chennai-born Indra Nooyi, who at the time had a different top job in the company, admitted in an interview with *Fortune* magazine 'I was the face of India. I should have hopped on a plane right away and said, "Guys, I assure you, these products are the safest"... Now if it happened – man, I would be there in an instant.'[5]

CSE continues its battle under the leadership of its passionate director Sunita Narain. In the summer of 2006, it issued a press release entitled 'CSE dares cola companies to come clean – No more spins, no more half truths. Clean up your bottles, says CSE in an open challenge to the soft drink majors.'[6] According to studies by the NGO, PepsiCo and Coca-Cola products in India are unsafe because they contain pesticide residues above safe standards. It also holds the soda companies responsible for not using the technology available to them to clean up the groundwater.

In the same press release CSE accuses them of being 'masters of spin' intent at misleading the Indian public. It quotes Indian actor, Shahrukh Khan, saying 'We are a filthy country,' and is quick to ask the question 'Is he therefore implying that we deserve filthy products?' Khan is the face of Pepsi in India. He smiles and sings away in a series of endless commercials rebroadcast on YouTube. But is Bollywood glamour what PepsiCo needs to convince Indians that safe products are one of its core values?

Nooyi recognizes that the company's marketing strategy and its glitzy ads peppered with celebrities 'had made matters worse'.[7] It would have been better to highlight the work done by PepsiCo to promote water and crops.

The soda controversy has been going on for a number of years in India. It has contributed to turning CSE director Narain into an NGO celebrity, quoted regularly in the international media. In 2005, Narain received the Padma Shri from the Government of India, an award given to citizens in recognition of their contribution in areas such as arts, education, social service and science. The same year, the King of Sweden presented her with the Stockholm Water Prize for 'a successful recovery of new knowledge on water management, a community-based sustainable integrated resource management under gender equity, a courageous stand against undemocratic, top-down bureaucratic resource control, an efficient use of a free press, and an independent judiciary to meet these goals'.[8]

Narain was called a hero on Mominnows,[9] a blog that monitors the media in India:

> Heroes come in different shapes, with different roles, and all real heroes are important because heroism cannot be quantified by the size [of the achievement]. Heroism is the courage, the faith, the stamina and doing something to the best of oneself in given circumstances and place that separates heroes from mere mortals. With that said we tip our hats to Sunita Narain.

India's PepsiCo and Coca-Cola saga is very indicative of the increasing importance of NGOs in the international arena. Their strength is that they are using the emotional card to communicate with the public. Their tone and rhetoric are in line with the Zeitgeist.

In the past, we used to talk about influencers when referring to important target groups that were key to the success of our communication campaign. In the era of social media and globalized messages, it is the 'passionists' we want to convince. These are average citizens who use blogs and social networks to talk about issues that really move them. It might be the quality of the air in Chinese cities or the right of women to participate in public life in the Middle East. What these issues have in common are the heated debates they engender. And those who participate in them are looking for authenticity and strong messages. NGOs know how to speak this language while multinationals are often still trapped in the vicious circle of corporate speak. What they lack is the ability to tune into the spirit of a new era in which emotions are becoming the driving factor. If you want to be heard in this new environment, you have to appreciate cultural sensitivities and beliefs.

This is what PepsiCo failed to do in India. Water occupies a particular place in the Indian psyche. Purification with water is an important ritual procedure in Hinduism. Water becomes an Indian's last home once their ashes are scattered in the River Ganges. On top of this, the country has been experiencing problems with water supply and water shortages for years. No wonder the issue of pesticides in soda drinks is so emotionally charged.

China: Mounting pressure

In China, problems with toys and pharmaceutical products have led to safety issues abroad. Consumer concerns in the United States and Europe have had an impact on Chinese manufacturers where the supply chains of Western brands are based. According to John Russell, Executive Vice President for Asia Pacific at the strategic communication firm Powell Tate, Chinese companies with international aspirations are beginning to learn that industrial issues, previously managed and contained by traditional methods and controlled media, cannot be contained once products and services leave their shores.

Pressure is mounting also on China's domestic front with an increasingly investigative media, a rise in the influence of NGOs and the proliferation of social media and consumerism. These developments create a great demand for a systematic approach to reputation, issues and crises. Conventional relationship models of PR continue to be important, but are no longer sufficient for success.

Enter the Chinese Federation for Corporate Social Responsibility, launched by Chinese enterprises and foreign multinationals including China Merchants Bank, IBM and Nokia. Its aim is 'to promote the construction of corporate social responsibility in China by the promotion of government agencies, supervision of non-government organisations and the self-discipline of corporate entities'.[10]

The CSR news coming out of China ranges from campaigns with touches of local folklore, to the announcements of crackdowns on the various offenders of international import regulations. Here are two examples:

Beijing Considers Spit-Free Day

A mobilization meeting of Healthy Olympics, Healthy Beijing has issued news that Beijing will set a No Spit Day within the year.

A representative from Beijing Municipal Health Department says that spring is the peak time for the occurrence of various respiratory diseases, so to call for a sanitary lifestyle and remove bad habits of spitting from its citizens, the city will set a No Spit Day sometime in the new year. The detailed date for the No Spit Day is still under discussion.[11]

Jiangsu Suspends Toy Manufacturers' Production

News from Jiangsu Provincial Administration of Quality Supervision, Inspection and Quarantine is that Jiangsu has suspended the operations of 85 toy manufacturers since the province initiated a special campaign last year...

Hu Guangjun, a director of JPAQSIQ, has told local media that the main problems of these 80 companies include not paying attention to the international toy import regulations, having bad management or production conditions, and incomplete product tracking system. Hu says that these 85 companies can not resume their production until they pass the relevant reviews of JPAQSIQ.[12]

CSR is being recommended to foreign companies operating in China as an acceptable way of engaging with the local community. It also enables multinationals to make donations to local schools, sports teams or orchestras without running the risk of being accused of bribery. China has a tradition of gift giving, but it is unusual to give gifts in a business context.[13]

The day the world changed

At 2.28 pm on 12 May 2008, an earthquake recording 8.0 on the Richter scale hit China's Sichuan province, north-west of Chengdu. The Xinhua News Agency reported the news 18 minutes later. An hour and a half after the quake, Party Secretary Hu Jintao had already made public his plans for emergency relief efforts and Premier Wen Jiabao had announced that he had left for the scene of the disaster. This reaction speaks volumes about the way in which China has changed and has become aware of the way it is perceived abroad. Thirty years earlier, when the Tangshan quake shook the country in 1976, with 240,000 victims, it took the government three years to release the total number of deaths, making it possibly the largest earthquake of the 20th century, by death toll. Those were different times. It was the year Mao Zedong died and the country was nearing the end of the catastrophic 10-year-long Cultural Revolution. The government refused all international aid and used the quake as an opportunity to boast about superiority and self-reliance.

China is now in a different era. Some experts say that the Severe Acute Respiratory Syndrome (SARS) outbreak of 2003 has taught government officials the virtues of transparent news sharing. It has convinced them that open news reporting doesn't necessarily lead to chaos and loss of control but, on the contrary, can be used to increase public confidence in the government. Other China observers believe that it was the wave of negative press the country experienced for its handing of the pro-Tibet demonstrations in the spring of 2008 that led to this change of strategy. China had not expected to be the subject of negative publicity during the Olympic torch relays. In spite of the progress achieved by its economy in recent years, there were still people around the world who disliked what China stood for. This came as a shock for its government and led to an unprecedented awakening.

When the Sichuan quake struck, Chinese leaders knew that the eyes of the international community would be on them. They therefore decided to allow foreign journalists free access to the region. The natural disaster marked the beginning of what many believe to be a new attitude towards the outside world as well as the birth of civil society in China.

On the afternoon of 19 May 2008, a week after the earthquake, the whole of China stood in silence for three minutes to remember the dead, in the first ever nationwide public display of respect for the victims of a natural disaster since the founding of the People's

Republic of China in 1949. Decades of reform have shifted the focus to the individual and the importance of human life. Because of the top-down nature of China's political system, volunteerism used to be a limited and widely misunderstood phenomenon. The disaster claimed more than 69,0000 victims and motivated many citizens to organize themselves at grass-roots level and head for the quake-hit areas. Citizen groups mobilized on the internet and offline. The day after the earthquake, 57 civic society organizations issued a joint statement asking all NGOs to join forces and deliver disaster relief. Fifty-one other NGOs jointly established an office in Chengdu to coordinate relief activities.[14]

The new awareness has jump-started citizen activism in China that for 10 years had existed only on a small scale, with organizations keeping a low profile. One of the 51 NGOs, 1kg.org, for example, has been in existence since 2004. It is web-based and organizes college students to carry 'one more kilogram' of books and small supplies when they tour rural areas and poor regions.[15]

According to Xinran Eady, founder of the UK-based charity Mother's Bridge of Love (MBL), the Chinese government has little experience with organizing volunteers. In 2004, she tried to register MBL, which helps Chinese children living in destitute conditions, and was surprised to find that in China there was no office that would register NGOs. 'There is no tradition of charities in China. People often confuse them with religious missions. To this, you have to add the fact that the military has been doing most of the work traditionally done by NGOs in the West.'[16] Eady believes that reality often precedes policy in China and what the country now needs is a new legal structure to enable NGOs to operate. 'We need to train the local government on how to deal with NGOs from both a legal and a fiscal point of view. We also need to train the volunteers to run NGOs in a professional way.' The Chinese public has become more aware, not only of what citizens can do, but also of the kind of contribution companies should make to society.

'Don't be too Wang Shi'

It all started with Vanke, China's largest publicly traded property developer. Its high-profile CEO Wang Shi announced shortly after the quake that the company would donate 2 million yuan (US$293,000)[17] to the Sichuan area and his employees should not donate more than 10 yuan (US$1.5).[18] He was also reported to have said that donations for relief support should be a sustainable practice and not a burden for companies. These comments were torn apart by Chinese bloggers who began to criticize Wang Shi, a popular blogger himself, for being stingy. The phrase 'Don't be too Wang Shi' began to circulate on the internet.[19] This is a pun on another expression that has entered the Chinese internet vernacular: 'Don't be too CNN.' Chinese netizens came up with it during the Tibet crisis of 2008 and accused CNN of using cropped photographs for its coverage of the clashes with Tibetan monks.

Vanke's share price, which had nearly tripled in 2007, took a plunge and dropped by 29 per cent. The company's shareholders had to come to the rescue. In a statement to the Shenzhen Stock Exchange released in early June 2008, they announced their decision to donate 100 million yuan to rebuild homes in Sichuan over the following three to five years. The company also decided to use a spokesperson in the future and pledged to desist from actions that would hit its share prices.

Wang Shi should have read his audience better. He should have known that the limelight was shining embarrassingly bright on the Chinese construction industry. In the immediate aftermath of the tragedy, reports kept streaming in about schools that had collapsed as a result of builders using poor materials and not following anti-earthquake standards. With a public so emotionally charged the last thing you want to do is use the words 'donation' and 'burden' in the same sentence. Other Chinese companies learned the lesson quickly. China Life Insurance, the largest life insurer in China, pledged to adopt all the orphan victims from the earthquake and to pay their living expenses until they are 18 years old.

Multinationals operating in China were not spared by this wave of criticism. Demonstrators gathered in front of the local McDonald's branch in Nanchong, Sichuan, and posted a sign on the front door denouncing foreign companies for delivering too little to the relief effort compared to the large profits they were making in the country. Walmart was shamed on the online community China Daily for donating less than Formosa Plastics, the US supplier of resins and petrochemicals. Formosa was called an 'Earthquake Corporate Hero' in one of the posts on China Daily's online community.[20] Zglobal wrote five days after the quake:

Formosa Plastics Corp.

Formosa Plastics Corp. donated 100 million yuan (14.3 million dollars) while Foxconn Technology Group contributed 60 million yuan (8.6 million dollars). What a fantastic effort by Formosa Plastics.

100 million yuan. Consider this against Walmart at 3.5 million YUAN. Formosa Plastics is not even a household brand name. We can see how much walmart cares for the community...

These developments are bound to put pressure on Chinese companies and multinationals to continue contributing to society in a sustainable manner. The web site CSR Asia, which promotes corporate social responsibility in the Asia-Pacific region, published a set of recommendations in June 2008 encouraging companies to use a strategic approach for their contributions to the relief effort:

1. Companies should set up a local special team (ie CSR department) or utilize knowledgeable local staff to set up a more detailed plan for working on CSR issues. Having local specialists enables companies to track local concerns and respond quickly.
2. The internet plays a powerful role in criticising corporate actions especially when there is such important events such as the earthquake. Companies should make good use of online communication channels in the future. These online channels allow companies to collect the most updated information on special issues and know how corporate giving or CSR programs are being portrayed on BBS forums and blogs in China.
3. As the reconstruction of Sichuan needs to take a few years, companies should consider co-operating with local NGOs, which have expertise, technology and facilities to provide useful advice in helping the reconstruction. Apart from corporate giving to NGOs, companies should keep check on where the money is being spent and monitor the effectiveness of the reconstruction program. This can help to build a safe home for Sichuan sufferers in the future. [21]

Brazil: The future of biodiversity

Instituto Ethos is the voice of the CSR movement in Brazil. The members of this NGO are 900 private companies from different sectors of the economy with a total of 1.2 million employees. Their annual revenues amount to 30 per cent of the country's GDP. They have joined this initiative because they wanted to share knowledge about CSR practices and needed tools that could help them assess their commitment to corporate citizenship.[22]

Under the leadership of founder Oded Graje, a member of the UN Global Compact's Advisory Council, Instituto Ethos developed a set of indicators that companies can use to assess how well their managers perform in terms of incorporating CSR practices into their work. Managers are asked to fill out a self-assessment form that is sent to Ethos for evaluation. The institute then compiles a confidential report, which compares the company's score against the average and against a benchmark group of the ten highest-scoring companies. To serve the needs of different sectors better, Instituto Ethos has developed indicators for small and micro enterprises as well as for the bakery, mining, financial, energy and paper and cellulose industries.

The Brazilian NGO is also reaching out to the media. More than 300 journalists are members of its Ethos Journalist Network, which spreads information and organizes training sessions on CSR topics.

Instituto Ethos works closely with the public sector to strengthen the Brazilian government's awareness of CSR and to promote partnerships with private enterprises. Its programme includes a number of activities:

1. The Decent Work Agenda, which focuses on combating child labour, the eradication of slave labour and on an equity and diversity programme.
2. The I Want To Read Program, the objective of which is to reduce to zero the number of towns in the country that still do not have public libraries. This programme is run in conjunction with the Ministry of Culture, state and municipal culture secretaries and private initiatives.
3. Pro-Councils that envisage the creation of forums for debate with all of the public policy councils in the country.
4. National Citizenship and Solidarity Week, an initiative on behalf of a network of social and corporate organizations initially structured by the Ethos Institute, and brought together to encourage social conscience and promote citizenship and solidarity nationally in a convergent and integrated manner.
5. Local initiatives in which governmental and private sector initiatives unite in order to raise the HDI (Human Development Index) rating of the neediest towns in Brazil, particularly in the north and north-east.[23]

One of Brazil's top CSR performers is Aracruz Celulose, the world's largest producer of bleached eucalyptus pulp. It was the only forestry company to be included in the Dow Jones Sustainability Index 2007/2008 of the New York Stock Exchange. The index screens corporations worldwide according to their economic, environmental and social performance.

Aracruz has a broad CSR program with goals that span from the conservation of biodiversity to the commitment to viable solutions in land disputes with indigenous communities, to the support given to low income communities, for example through the training of local teachers.

Brazil also boasts a world leader in the sustainable use of raw materials from biodiversity. Cosmetics company Natura is praised in international CSR reports for its cooperation with bodies like the Forest Stewardship Council and the Sustainable Agriculture Network to guarantee the proper sourcing of the resources used for its products. It has launched the Plant-Based Raw Material Certification Program to guarantee that its raw materials are extracted in an environmentally friendly and socially just way. In 2007, the company invested some US $48,000 in the project, which promotes sustainable cultivation and forest management through the certification of native forest and plantations. It also helps to build corporate citizenship by including family farms and traditional communities into the Natura supply chain. The company currently works with 19 communities of suppliers including 1,684 families in biomes such as the Amazon and the Atlantic Rainforest. These groups are often poor and heavily dependent on the cosmetics industry and its fashions.[24] Their products are bought by processing companies that, in turn, sell the industrialized raw materials to Natura. 'Even though they are not direct suppliers, they are important for our business', says Rodolfo Guttilla, director of corporate affairs at Natura. The company has put together a multidisciplinary team responsible for managing the relations with the communities. 'When we need new raw materials, we first try to purchase them from our current partners instead of building new relationships. We seek to provide the best conditions for these producers and help to reduce the impact of discontinued products on them'.[25]

South Africa: Helping a country to surface

No environment is more promising for CSR than that of a country in political and economic transition. This setting provides a foreign company with a number of opportunities to do interesting work that can make a difference. Creativity is what is needed. A society in transition is a society in the process of reinventing itself, of discovering its new identity and that of its various stakeholders. There is therefore a lot of room for helping these stakeholders shape their mission and for becoming a true partner of the new fledgling local institutions.

Take the case of Unilever South Africa. The consumer products giant helped post-Apartheid South Africa develop a brand for the country. The initiative resulted in the stylised South African flag, which we see featuring on many advertisements, and the tagline 'Alive with Possibility'. The South African government had identified tourism, trade and investment as major drivers of GDP growth and was looking for a partnership that would help it realize its vision. Unilever offered its branding expertise and marketing background and worked with South Africa's International Marketing Council to develop a message and a brand that could be used for tourism and business purposes. The initiative was also instrumental in putting South Africa on the map as the host of the 2010 World Cup. According to data from South Africa's tourist board, tourism in the country grew at twice the global rate during 2004 and 2005.[26]

Unilever also worked with South Africa's government to set up the Unilever Mandela Rhodes Academy of Communication and Marketing for the Public Sector. Students come from various provinces and different levels of government to learn how to develop communication programmes around matters of public policy.

Offering the government of a country the support it needs to create a policy environment conducive to attracting foreign investment is a unique way to create brand awareness. It also enables the foreign company involved in this process to establish a strong credibility, which can be used as a basis for future communication campaigns.

Granted, major political shifts like the end of apartheid in South Africa don't happen every day. But with more and more emerging economies surfacing and looking for their place in the global arena, opportunities like the one seized by Unilever might be coming around soon.

CSR starts at home

So far, a number of companies might have been paying little more than lip service to CSR, but there is no doubt that this discipline is becoming one of the pillars of successful reputation management and sustainable employee engagement. Environmental and social issues occupy an important place in the psyche of young generations. Globalization, the interactive web and the green awakening have changed the background against which young graduates develop a vision of their career and future life. To them, the opportunity to contribute to global causes is as important as climbing the corporate ladder.

Recent studies demonstrate that employee volunteering is becoming an increasingly important component of social responsibility programmes. It is a way for employees to share knowledge, acquire new skills, learn about community issues and gain new insight into their own business. 'The volunteers also build internal networks which become supports in the workplace and contribute to further volunteer recruitment. Community actors claim that employee volunteering enables leverage of resources, institutional capacity building, and enhanced staff skills and knowledge.'[27]

Corporations are applying a more structured approach to volunteering and have started to consider it one of the core responsibilities of the community relations function that often reports to the head of corporate communications. More and more employees are allowed a certain number of working hours in a year to do work for organizations like community schools or youth empowerment centres. These activities build social networks and allow a company to gain a better understanding of community issues. This knowledge can then be used to design more powerful outreach programmes. It can also benefit the company's bottom line and strengthen its role in the community. Years of engagement in community initiatives can help a corporation gain public support for controversial initiatives like the development of a production facility. Or it can lead to the development of new products tailored to the needs of underprivileged customers.[28]

CSR experts agree that employee volunteering is a powerful tool for discovering stakeholders' expectations. However, it can only be successful if rooted in trusted relationships and shared values. This is why successful CSR initiatives start at home. A CSR programme has to be the expression of the company's soul. It has to be closely linked to its core values. And it has to have the support of the employees, who have to feel connected to the cause the company is trying to support. If you focus on the design of the programme without first getting your staff on board, you will miss a crucial phase and will most likely have to retrace your steps.

Communicating commitment

In 2003, the global ground engineering and environmental company Golder Associates Corporation set up a global corporate charity to improve the living conditions of children who had been orphaned or displaced by the AIDS pandemic in Africa.[29] The Golder Trust for Orphans enjoyed the support of senior management. It also reflected 'sustainability', one of the company's core values, meaning that Golder is committed to improving the lives of the members of the communities in which it works. There was, however, a problem. Donations to the Trust were slow to trickle in. A survey conducted in 2005 revealed that less than 10 per cent of Golder's staff had heard of the initiative, while fewer than two per cent were making monthly payroll donations.

Communication had begun in 2003 after the launch of the fund by means of occasional e-mail messages from the president. Several small fund-raisers had been held and the Trust had been mentioned in the company's annual corporate calendar and annual report. However, this had not been enough to raise the level of employee awareness and participation.

Golder had first to win the hearts and minds of a staff that was growing rapidly and becoming younger every year. The number of employees increased from 2,000, when the Fund was launched, to 5,000 in 2004. More than half of the new employees were under the age of 40 and the average age of senior leaders was 45.

The company had a goal: to have at least 800 employees by 2010 donating US$10 or more per month via payroll deduction. They also wanted to develop a global network of office champions to encourage awareness and fund-raising at office level and in the local communities. Golder operates in 30 countries worldwide. Another goal was to increase awareness of the Trust among Golder clients and the local communities.

An internal campaign was launched. It included a global intranet site, GoldNet, and a Trust intranet site with information from sponsored projects, marketing materials, presentations and links to HIV/

AIDS-related sites. An internal quarterly newsletter was designed, e-mailed to all Golder staff and posted on the intranet. Its purpose is not only to inform about progress made by the different projects but also to give the readers at Golder a sense of what it must feel like to operate in troubled parts of Africa under difficult circumstances. Here is an article published in the first quarter of 2008, about the impact of political unrest in Kenya on the local children's homes:

What's Behind the Violence?

Political veteran Mwai Kibaki claimed victory in controversial presidential elections in December 2007. His swearing-in for a second term in office prompted a wave of unrest across the country with accusations of 'rigged' polling. International and domestic observers have also raised their concerns.

An estimated 1,000 people have been killed to date and more than 25,000 people have fled their homes since the disputed presidential poll. Kenya, in the past, proudly boasted of its diversity. But today, it seems every conversation is dominated by ethnicity. People are becoming stranded prisoners in their own communities because their roads are so unsafe.

The Rift Valley is a geographical fault line that runs through Kenya. But it is also the centre of a political and ethnic divide. The Kikuyu are the largest and most economically-dominant ethnic group in Kenya. They have been at the heart of the violence in Rift Valley towns like Naivasha and Nakuru – as both perpetrators and victims.

The incumbent government in Kenya is perceived by the opposition as being Kikuyu-dominated, so the current political dispute is fuel for the smouldering embers of a land dispute which existed for decades.

How is the Violence Affecting Lewa Children's Home and Baraka Farm?

Lewa Children's Home and Baraka Farm are situated in Eldoret in the Rift Valley. In Eldoret, food prices have multiplied considerably, with a small bundle of green vegetables rising to 25Ksh from a 2007 value of 5Ksh (Ksh is Kenya shilling equivalent to 100 cents). The price of milk, which was already high due to the dry season, has risen dramatically with the problem exaggerated by people mixing the milk with water prior to sale. The price of fuel has doubled, if available at all!

Milk and produce sold by the farm in town goes rapidly as people are desperate and hungry. Sadly, the farm shop is currently blocked from continuing business and it is too dangerous to transport the milk.

> Further devastating news from the region includes the burning of another children's home close by. The destroyed children's home was managed by people from the same tribe as the president. The children from the home have been evacuated to the Eldoret Rescue Centre.[30]

An external campaign was developed to promote the Trust to local communities and the global philanthropic arena through external events, published articles and networking. As a result of these communication efforts, the number of employees donating increased from 50 in 2005 to more than 400 in 2007. The company has now 30 office champions in the USA, Europe, Canada, Australia and Chile with access to an internal blog where they can share ideas about fundraising activities. In the words of Lea Chambers, one of the Fund's trustees, 'having the Golder Trust for Orphans as a key part of our internal communications and external PR strategy has benefited the company – our employees appreciate it, our clients are proud of us for doing it, and our public applauds it'.

Going local

The task of a cross-cultural communicator is to educate senior management about the nuances of CSR. Social responsibility programmes are becoming more sophisticated. They are no longer about only one aspect of corporate citizenship or one project. And above all, the needs differ from country to country. Companies have to be aware of this reality. Sometimes the best approach is to learn from the locals.

In Africa, more and more small and medium-sized businesses are getting involved in projects that can change the lives of their employees and their communities. It might be setting up a microcredit bank or giving people in remote villages access to mobile phones so that they can call a doctor or check the current prices of their produce.

The first microcredit bank in Sudan, Family Bank, was founded by a local female entrepreneur, Widad Ibrahim. Ibrahim is a highly inspirational figure. She grew up on her grandmother's farm and used to sell eggs by the side of the street. In 1985, she got the idea to start selling apartments in Khartoum. Real estate was just the beginning. She now runs the Bee Group, an industrial conglomerate that employs 800 people and includes more than 40 petrol stations, 12 oil deposits, an aviation business, a transport company and a cement and lime factory.

Ibrahim visited Grameen Bank, the microfinance organization and community development bank established by the father of the microcredit movement, Nobel prize winner Muhammad Yunus, and decided to set up a similar bank in Sudan together with other women entrepreneurs. Family Bank now has more than US$35 million in its accounts. In 1992, she helped to establish the Sudanese Business Women Union. As a result, in 2006 for the first time in the history of Sudan, a woman was elected to join the executive committee of the Business Men Union. Ibrahim believes that in recent years, the Business Women Union has been playing an important role in providing the social support desperately needed by Sudan after 50 years of civil war and the crisis in Darfur.[31] Ibrahim and the Business Women Union have been promoting child education in refugee camps in Darfur. They help women to fight illiteracy and gain basic skills. They run first-aid workshops for female refugees in camps in South Darfur.

It is partners like Ibrahim, Family Bank and the Business Women Union that international companies operating in developing countries need to look for. If they want to make a real impact with their CSR programmes, they need to partner with local players who enjoy the trust of the community and are open to new solutions.

Microcredit projects have enormous communication potential. The fact that they touch so many aspects of the lives of the borrowers and their communities makes them a formidable source of stories. And stories are the most powerful tool in CSR communications. They give a voice to the soul of a project. They create an emotional appeal. They are much more effective than data and figures. Just think of all the stories that could be told around Grameen Bank's Sixteen Decisions, a set of social and personal commitments every new member of the bank is expected to learn and pledge to. Here are the most impressive ones:

2. We shall bring prosperity to our families.
3. We shall not live in dilapidated houses. We shall repair our houses and work towards constructing new houses as soon as possible.
7. We shall educate our children and ensure that they can earn to pay for their education.
11. We shall not take any dowry at our sons'weddings; neither shall we give any dowry in our daughters'weddings. We shall keep the center free from the curse of dowry. We shall not practice child marriage.[32]

We believe it is Muhammad Yunus's ability to tell the Grameen story in such an authentic and moving way that sold microcredit to the world. Co-author Cambié participated in an interview Yunus gave to a journalist at a congress in Berlin in 2000. To explain the essence of Grameen's mission, Yunus told the story of a woman he visited in Bangladesh during the bank's early days. She was sitting on the dirt floor of her hut in a small village, uncomfortable in the presence of a man. Yunus wanted to tell her about Grameen and explain to her how to borrow money. The old woman had probably never handled money in her entire life, a strict prerogative of men in her village. 'Go and leave me alone', she said. Yunus didn't give up. He asked whether there was anything else he could do for her. He could at least teach her to write. The woman could not believe her ears: 'I am a woman. I cannot write.' Yunus took a stick and began to write her name in the dust of her dirt floor. He then left the hut for a short while. When he came back, he saw that the woman had taken the stick and was copying his writing. 'Your name is Soma', he said. 'How do you know?' asked the woman with great surprise. 'Because you just wrote it.' At that moment, Yunus saw a light going on in her eyes. For the first time in her life, someone had given her a sense of dignity. There are no microfinance statistics that can match the power of this story.

'Entering a danger zone'

Communication as a discipline is becoming more and more integrated. As a result, CSR is beginning to include other aspects of the profession. Issue management is one of them. Companies are being asked to move beyond corporate giving. They are expected to take a position on global issues and to work together with government and other corporations to find sustainable solutions. One of these issues is the global food crisis that began in 2007. Food and energy prices reached new peaks in 2008, triggering political and economic turmoil and social instability in many developing countries. The Food and Agriculture Organization of the United Nations (FAO) expects food prices to ease from their record high in the course of the next 10 years. However, they are likely to remain at an average well above the levels of the past decade. More than 800 million people are affected by hunger in the world. The crisis threatens to worsen their situation and to push millions of other vulnerable people back into extreme poverty. In the words of World Bank president Robert Zoellick, the world is 'entering a danger zone'.[33]

The culprits are changes in diets in booming emerging economies, urbanization, agricultural subsidies, trade policies, higher fertiliser prices and expanding populations. Biofuels, which have been replacing food crops with ethanol and biodiesel, are another cause. Brazil is accused of cutting down carbon-absorbing rainforest and exploiting land used for food to provide land for fuel crops such as soya and palm. According to the FAO, fuel ethanol production tripled between 2000 and 2007 and is expected to double again between 2008 and 2017. Biodiesel production is predicted to grow from 11 billion litres a year in 2007 to 24 billion litres by 2017.[34]

Climate change, with its erratic weather patterns, has also been affecting crop production and is likely to continue to do so in the future.

Multilaterals like the World Bank and the United Nations have been joining efforts to put agriculture back on the development agenda. Eighty per cent of the world's rural poor earn their living in farming. Agriculture is the driving force in the economies of many developing countries. Two-thirds of the countries most severely affected by the crisis are in Africa. But other parts of the world have also been shaken by the 2008 food riots, including Uzbekistan, Yemen, Mexico, Haiti, Indonesia, and the Philippines.

Multinationals operating in regions vulnerable to the crisis will be expected to get involved at two levels. The first implies taking a position on the issue and helping to draw the attention of the international community to the needs of a particular region. A company might volunteer to use its international media contacts as well as its worldwide audience to put a region's specific issues on the map. The second level calls for a longer term commitment, one that goes beyond awareness building. Similar to the work done by multinationals in parts of Africa to fight HIV/AIDS, these companies will be expected to offer technical assistance to local organizations and farmers. They could advise the local government on the development of infrastructure and provide assistance for the improvement of irrigation systems, markets and rural roads. Or they could help to train farmers on how to use fertilizers, better seeds and more profitable methods of cultivation. They could also work with agricultural cooperatives and other organizations to develop weather-based insurance schemes to help farmers cope with floods, draughts and other calamities.

Such work will help to make the investment climate of a country more attractive. Agricultural growth relies on investment in infrastructure, including water supply, roads and railways, energy, communication and information systems. In order to attract foreign investment in these areas, a country needs to send signals indicating that it enjoys political stability and a safe investment climate. One of these signals could come from the fact that a multinational is helping the government re-launch agriculture in its rural communities.

Global interconnectedness is stretching the boundaries of CSR. Local community work is no longer sufficient. A corporation operating at international level will be expected to influence global debates on issues such as world food security. This will require an integrated approach to communication and the ability to position the company as a centre of intelligence on development issues.

Repositioning CSR

Here are some ideas to keep in mind when asked to design a CSR strategy in the new environment 3.0:

- Educate senior management about the complexity of modern CSR programmes and the need to involve the communication function at strategic level.
- Use your CSR programme to increase employees' well-being and sense of belonging. Powerful CSR begins with employees' support.
- Build an emotional link with your stakeholders. Learn the language of social media.
- When looking for NGOs to partner with in emerging economies and the developing world, don't limit your search to international household names. Contact local players with deep roots in their communities and the ability to relate to their needs. Africa has some powerful examples.
- Communication is becoming more and more integrated. Your PR strategy should reflect your approach to CSR. Treat the media like one of your stakeholders.
- Combine CSR with issue management. Integrate global issues like water management or climate change in your strategy and use them to position your organization as a partner for multilaterals and international institutions.

Notes

1. Do It Right, *The Economist*, 19 January 2008, p. 22.
2. Peter Engardio and Michael Arndt, What Price Reputation? *BusinessWeek*, 9 and 16 July, 2007.
3. John Russell, Executive Vice President Asia Pacific, Powell Tate, in discussion with co-author Cambié via e-mail, March 2008
4. Dirk Matten, Hewlett-Packard Chair in Corporate Social Responsibility, Schulich School of Business, York University, in discussion with co-author Cambié, June 2008.
5. Betsy Morris, The Pepsi Challenge: Can This Snack and Soda Giant Go Healthy? *Fortune*, 3 March 2008.
6. CSE Dares Cola Companies to Come Clean, cseindia.org, 3 April 2008, http://www.cseindia.org/misc/cola-indepth/cola2006/cola_press 20060807.htm.
7. Diane Brady (2007), Pepsi: Repairing a Poisoned Reputation in India, *BusinessWeek*, 11 June 2007.
8. Stockholm Water Prize, Wikipedia.org, 2 April 2008, http://en.wikipedia.org/wiki/Stockholm_Water_Prize.
9. India's Heroes, nominnow.blogspot.com, 3 April 2008, http://nominnow.blogspot.com/2007/10/indias-heroes.html.
10. CFCSR Established in Beijing, chinacsr.com, 3 April 2008, http://www.chinacsr.com/2006/10/20/799-cfcsr-established-in-beijing/.
11. Beijing Considers Spit-free Day, chinacsr.org, 2 April 2008, http://www.chinacsr.com/2008/03/13/2174-beijing-considers-spit-free-day/.
12. Jiangsu Suspends Toy Manufacturers' Production, chinacsr.org, 2 April 2008, http://www.chinacsr.com/2008/03/10/2160-jiangsu-suspends-toy-manufacturers-production/.
13. Emma Huang, Insight into Public Relations in China, Continuing Education Division, Ryerson University, Toronto, Canada, 12 April 2008.
14. A Civil Society Emerges From the Earthquake Rubble, globalpolitician. com, 10 June 2008, http://globalpolitician.com/24883-china-earth quake.
15. A Civil Society Emerges From the Earthquake Rubble, globalpolitician. com, 10 June 2008, http://globalpolitician.com/24883-china-earthquake.
16. Xinran Eady, Founder, Mother's Bridge of Love, in discussion with co-author Cambié, June 2008.
17. Universal Currency Converter, xe.com, 17 October 2008, http://www. xe.com/ucc/convert.cgi.
18. Universal Currency Converter, xe.com, 17 November 2008, http://www.xe.com/ucc/convert.cgi.

19. 'Don't be too Wang Shi': Business Attacked over Sichuan Quake Donations, csr-asia.com, 11 June 2008, http://csr-asia.com/index.php?id=11843.
20. Earthquake Corporate Heroes, chinadaily.com.cn, 10 June 2008, http://bbs.chinadaily.com.cn/viewthread.php?gid=2&tid=603793.
21. http://csr-asia.com/weekly_detail.php?id=11396
22. About Ethos, ethos.org.br, 1 April 2008, www.ethos.org.br.
23. Activities, ethos.org.br, 1 April 2008, http://www.ethos.org.br/DesktopDefault.aspx?TabID=3892&Alias=ethosEnglish&Lang=pt-BR.
24. Using Raw Materials Sustainability: Natura, wbcsd.org, 7 April 2008, http://www.wbcsd.org/Plugins/DocSearch/details.asp?DocTypeId=24&ObjectId=MjIxMTg&URLBack=%2Ftemplates%2FTemplateWBCSD2%2Flayout.asp%3Ftype%3Dp%26MenuId%3DMjU4%26doOpen%3D1%26ClickMenu%3DleftMenu.
25. Rodolfo Guttilla, Director of Corporate Affairs, Natura Cosméticos, in discussion with co-author Cambié via e-mail, November 2008.
26. Measuring Unilever's Economic Footprint: The Case of South Africa, businessfightspoverty.ning.com, 17 October 2008, http://66.102.9.104/search?q=cache:TPwwe4QQYEsJ:www.odi.org.uk/events/business_impact/Kapstein.pdf+Ethan+Kapstein+%2B+Unilever+%2B+South+Africa&hl=en&ct=clnk&cd=5&gl=uk.
27. Judy N Muthuri, Dirk Matten and Jeremy Moon, Employee Volunteering and Social Capital: Contributions to Corporate Social Responsibility, *British Journal of Management*, 2007, p. 10.
28. Judy N Muthuri, Dirk Matten and Jeremy Moon, Employee Volunteering and Social Capital: Contributions to Corporate Social Responsibility, *British Journal of Management*, 2007, p. 11.
29. Lea Chambers, Associate, Marketing and Communications, Golder Associates Corporation, in discussion with co-author Cambié via e-mail, April 2008.
30. Golder Trust for Orphans, Newsletter, Q1 2008.
31. Widad Ibrahim, Founder and General Manager, Bee Group Partners for Change, Realizing the Potential of Arab Women in the Private and Public Sectors, paper presented at Arab International Women's Forums Conference, Washington DC, USA, 24 June 2008.
32. Muhammad Yunus, The Microcredit Revolution, in *Creating a World Without Poverty*, PublicAffairs, New York, 2008, pp. 58–59.
33. G8 Must Act Now as 'World Entering a Danger Zone', Zoellick Says, worldbank.org, 4 July 2008, http://web.worldbank.org/WBSITE/EXTERNAL/NEWS/0,,contentMDK:21827981~menuPK:34463~pagePK:34370~piPK:34424~theSitePK:4607,00.html.
34. Agricultural Commodity Prices Expected to Remain High, fao.org, http://www.fao.org/newsroom/en/news/2008/1000849/index.html.

4 The dawn of leadership communication

Undoubtedly one of the most exciting aspects of the Globalization 3.0 challenge is leadership. When we sit down and think about the leader of the future, an image begins to form in our minds – that of an avatar, a three-dimensional being with highly developed sensibility able to tune into different cultural models and to connect with employees at a deeper level. This vision might sound a bit too futuristic. But the challenges and the skill set required to face them are for real.

We are at a fascinating crossroads. Developments around the world are signalling the need to leave behind old leadership models based on hierarchy and secrecy and begin to adopt new ones. Are corporations listening? Will they be able to read the writing on the wall? It is a major shift we are talking about. Communication as an integral part of effective leadership is at the centre of it. In this chapter, we use the term 'leadership communication' instead of 'internal communication'. It is because we believe that the time has come for this function to graduate to a higher level.

Generation Y

It was a sentence that brought it all home to us. The urban cultural anthropologist Jennifer James was speaking at the 2007 International Conference of the International Association of Business Communicators (IABC) in New Orleans about new technologies and the ability of younger generations to master them. 'When in history did we ever encounter a time when children were better at using elaborate technology?' she asked the audience. This is music to the ears of any communicator who spent years trying to convince senior management of the virtues of listening to employees.

Now the time has come. Will corporate leaders have to change their behaviour? Take job descriptions. They don't mean much to Generation Y, the 76 million Millennials born between 1982 and 2000. They are graduating from high school and college and entering the workplace. Employers are struggling to understand them and competing to attract them. 'This generation has had their pick of jobs most of their lives, and they will be picky now, opting for work that allows them to give back or make a difference over jobs that simply pay well.'[1]

What they are looking for is meaningful work. They want to be in a job that lets them express their potential. And a way to express this potential is by working for a company whose commitment to society and the planet reflects their personal values. This is why we believe that corporate social responsibility will be at the core of any successful recruitment strategy of the Globalization 3.0 era.

The question representatives of Generation Y ask themselves before going into a job interview is no longer 'What can I bring to the company?' but rather 'What can the company do for me?' On their minds is not only their professional, but also their personal, development. They are looking for an employer ready to give them an opportunity to pursue their interests and remain true to their beliefs.

Only a leader able to tell a compelling story will be in a position to attract this kind of talent. According to James, leadership used to be about control and mastery of the work but now, with the multiplication of data and the development of diverse, empowered teams, a leader has to have a higher level of sophistication and the ability to influence.[2] And corporate communication will have to help the leader of the future to tell an authentic story, one that resonates with deep-seated values.

The loyalty factor used to play a big role in the past. Not any more. We have all heard of the death of the job for life. Corporations become faster and faster at forgetting employees' years of seniority with every merger or restructuring they go through. However, this isn't something Generation Y is worried about. They have their own definition of loyalty and don't need a company to tell them who they can rely on. Their loyalty is to themselves and their networks. This generation grew up on Facebook and YouTube. They are used to functioning in groups of like-minded peers and expect to be able to operate in similar structures inside a company. They are only going to respect a leader who is able to create a culture based on knowledge sharing and collaboration.

For this reason, corporations are beginning to take internal networks seriously. Networks were a typical expression of corporate diversity policies. They were set up to reflect the ethnic representation and gender composition of a particular company. We can expect Generation Y to take this idea one step further and set up topic-oriented internal networks dealing with issues like global warming and human rights. The world this new demographic inhabits is both highly promising and at the same time endangered. The internationalized job market offers them unprecedented opportunities in terms of gathering professional experiences and visiting other countries. Their perception of this freedom, however, is limited by concerns for the planet and the changing physical environment.

Generation Y will make highly informed employees with an unprecedented awareness of the impact of global business. They are the product of the shift in global knowledge brought about by the interactive web. The voice they respect most is that of authenticity and competence, the voice of social media. A leader who wants to engage them has to be willing to tell the truth. We are experiencing the death of corporate mythology.

Cultural intelligence

The generational dimension is only one aspect of the kind of diversity that 3.0 leaders will have to manage. Another is cultural intelligence. The world is in need of a new approach to corporate leadership, one that combines the typical attributes of Western management schemes with qualities appreciated in other parts of the world like Southern Europe, the Middle East and Asia.

According to the Finnish management consultancy Pertec, pragmatism is what defines the Anglo-Saxon approach to business. Attributes that come to mind are effectiveness, assertiveness, fairness, independence, risk-taking and task-focus. The model pursued in Northern Europe and Scandinavia is similar. Its flavour is rationalism and its most cherished values are reliability, caution, order, scientific truth and process.

The shift we are currently experiencing is about merging these values, which in the past 60 years have been synonyms of business, with elements that other parts of the world consider important, when it comes to building relationships and making decisions. Humanism is the label used by Pertec for Southern Europe and the Arab world. The contribution of these regions to the global mindset is an approach that values relationships, closeness, belonging, communities and the expression of emotions. The lesson coming from the East is about Holism. It encompasses harmony, ambiguity, patience, acceptance and balance.[3]

The new leadership model will have to integrate many cultural elements in one common approach. Corporate values are a good example. There are still companies that like to come up with values at headquarters level and cascade them down to the countries in which they operate. These values are supposed to work even when they don't take into consideration the culture of a particular country or the local circumstances. This approach often results in a disconnectedness. Employees feel that they are being patronized. They end up ignoring the very same values that were originally conceived to help them identify with the company. The values don't mean anything to them because they are based on a different mindset. What the leader of the future will have to do is study local cultures and translate a particular value into their terms.

For example, if a company operates in a society where relationships and informal networks play an important role in the office life of its individuals, less emphasis should be placed on values stressing self-reliance and assertiveness. What employees want, in this case, is a value that highlights the social dimension of their work experience and gives them a sense of belonging. Being part of a community means more to them than the emphasis on tasks. Culturally aware leaders will be able to identify this need and turn it into a major motivational factor for their employees. If process-orientation and facts work well in the company's country of origin, it doesn't mean that employees in other parts of the world function in the same way.

Corporations need to develop a culture that gives their leaders the freedom to adjust global values to the mindset and circumstances of a particular country. Is this happening? Do we already have this freedom?

Integrative thinking

According to Roger Martin, dean of the Rotman School of Management at the University of Toronto and author of *The Opposable Mind*,[4] we still have a long way to go.[5] However, there is hope, as demonstrated by the experiences of the people he interviewed for his book. Martin talked to a number of leaders who had impressed him during the 15 years he spent working as a management consultant and as dean of Rotman. These include Isadore Sharp, founder of the Four Seasons Hotels and AG Lafley, CEO of Procter & Gamble.

What makes these leaders stand out, apart from their business talent and their dedication to innovation, is a skill Martin calls 'integrative thinking'. They all have 'the predisposition and the capacity to hold two diametrically opposing ideas in their heads'.[6] Martin believes that we are all born with an 'opposable mind', which can harbour two opposing ideas at the same time. The result is a productive tension able to produce a new and more advanced idea.

> Were we able to hold only one thought or idea in our heads at a time, we wouldn't have access to the insights that the opposable mind can produce… In business, we often look at decisions as a series of either-or-propositions, of trade-offs… But what if there was a way to satisfy both customers and shareholders without sacrificing the needs and interest of either party?
>
> Integrative thinking shows us a way past the binary limits of either–or. It shows us that there's a way to integrate the advantages of one solution without cancelling out the advantages of an alternative solution.[7]

And this insight is what the leader of the future will need to use if he or she wants to communicate successfully with their multicultural workforce. Integrative thinking applied to communication translates into the ability to consider two different cultural models without choosing sides. It also implies a new communication style, one based on Martin's 'assertive inquiry', a tool leaders can use to explore opposing models. Assertive inquiry is the opposite of advocacy. It involves a proactive search for another's point of view. When we communicate in this mode, we assert a point of view in an auditable way. We don't give conclusions. We couple our message with inquiry. We use questions like 'Could you help me understand what led you to believe that?', 'Could you give me an example to help me understand your point?'

According to Martin, assertive inquiry helps us to study someone else's mental model:

> you find saliencies that wouldn't have occurred to you and casual relationships you didn't perceive... Assertive enquiry isn't a form of challenge, but it is pointed. It explicitly seeks to explore the underpinnings of your own model and that of the other person. Its aim is to learn about the salient data and casual maps baked into another person's model, then use the insight gained to fashion a creative resolution of the conflict between that person's model and your own.[8]

You may have something to say, but someone else may have an idea that contributes to a better answer. A concrete example of this is what W G Lafley did when he became CEO of the consumer goods giant Procter & Gamble in 2000. Strategy meetings at this company used to be more about advocacy than dialogue. Product managers would be invited to present and go through what was usually a large number of slides. Lafley wanted to change this process and introduce a new model. He began to ask for presentations to be sent in advance. He would read them and identify three questions. His conversations with product managers would then be based on these questions and would be more interactive than the previous meetings.[9]

The leader of the future will have to become less fearful of dealing with opposing models. As long as we fear opposing ideas, we send out the message to employees that we don't want to hear disagreement. The view in large corporations is still that the only way to be successful is to be assertive. But something is changing.

Usually, the first reaction is denial. Many European companies, when they see their market share shrink because of Chinese competition, first enter a state of shock. Their reaction is to go through the existing processes, in a desperate search for confirmation that their leadership model is a good one and can be used indefinitely. Then, slowly, reality seeps in. They begin to realize that they are dealing with unprecedented market forces. A slight change, of course, won't be enough. We are talking about a whole new way of leading corporations into the future.

Martin believes that we have come to the end of the era of simplification. The whole 20th century was about simplification, about the decomposition of reality into simple models. The problem is that 'simplification makes us favour linear, unidirectional casual relationships, even if reality is more complex and multi-directional'.[10]

The leader of the post-modern era needs to be retrained to become an integrator, able to aggregate information and understand complex situations. In the Western world, the cradle of simplification, corporate leaders are standing at an epochal watershed. Will they insist on imposing simplification, in order to beat the new emerging economies into submission or will they realize that we have come to the end of the road?

The 'dance' between cultures

We believe it was simplification that produced models like those of the influential Dutch writers Geerdt Hofstede and Frans Trompenaar, focused on the differences rather than the similarities between cultures. So what is the best way to bridge cultural differences and merge them into a new leadership style? As we have seen, 'integrative thinking' helps. Another way is by creating a 'dance' between both sides of the cultural divide. Michael Spencer of Sound Strategies has been advising the Association of Japanese Symphony Orchestras for the past 14 years. He runs workshops and other creative learning exchanges in an environment where people are reluctant to express their views and to engage in an open dialogue. The 'dance', in this case, is about accepting both sides of the Confucian–Socratic coin and knowing when to challenge and when to accept.

Japan is a country where cultural issues run wide and deep. One of the aspects Spencer noticed first is the contrast between the personalised learning structures of Europe and the USA which emphasize individuality, and the collectivist nature of the Japanese education system, which concentrates on the integrity of the group and mutual support. 'Look in any Japanese school around lunch-time and you will see the pupils cleaning the premises, an unlikely occurrence in Western schools.'[11] According to Spencer, this is not just a matter of discipline, but rather of the contrast between Confucian and Socratic thinking: the 'shame–guilt', 'acceptance–challenge' dichotomy.

Nemawashi is a word unique to Japanese culture. It is used for a process that enables decisions to be taken not as a result of open discussion, but rather by a balance of influences and subtle exchanges 'behind the scenes'. In Japan, the act of volunteering an opinion can imply an assumption of responsibility and consequential risk of loss of face. 'No' is usually taken as a direct challenge and 'yes' should be taken as an acknowledgement rather than an affirmation of action.

The term 'dance' is a powerful metaphor for the exercise that enables exchanges between cultures. Understanding and respecting the other culture is only a part of it; you then have to know when to introduce elements of your own culture. These are core skills corporations will need their future leaders to master.

Welcoming ambiguity

The 3.0 leader will have to deal with paradoxes and ambiguity on a daily basis. Working for a multinational from an emerging economy presents new situations that Western leaders might not have encountered before. Take, for example, what happened to the Taj hotel chain owned by the Indian Tata Group. In 2007, it approached the American hotel chain Orient Express with the intention of building an alliance. Orient Express refused by saying that any association with a predominantly domestic Indian brand would affect the value of its luxury brand. The Indian group fought back, demanding an apology and declaring that Taj is one of the world's most trusted brands in hospitality.[12]

If you are used to managing the reputation of a Western brand whose credibility is taken for granted in most parts of the world, a situation like this will stretch your creativity beyond the limits of any work you have done before. How do you defend a valid business proposition from the biases of the very same culture you have been raised in? How do you protect a brand against cultural discrimination?

Working for the public sector of an emerging economy might pose a further dilemma for Western leaders. Chinese state-owned companies are among the international players with the most ambitious global acquisition strategies. They are called 'hybrids' because they combine the strong financial resources of the state with the freedom to operate like private companies.[13] These include, to name a few, the car manufacturer Chevy, energy group PetroChina and the petroleum company Sinopec.

China's investments in sensitive parts of the world like Sudan have received negative coverage in the international press and its multinationals are faced with the challenge of having to explain their decisions to the international community. China has been using a new model of business engagement in Africa. Its companies are offering much-needed infrastructure in return for resource extraction. Europe and the USA resent this practice, perhaps because they are afraid of its success and have not yet found a way to emulate it.[14] China and India have also replaced Japan and South Korea as the most important Asian markets for African goods. China has begun to import much more than fuels and minerals from Africa. Its imports now include commodities such as cotton and locally processed food.[15]

The foreign investment policies of a state-owned company are often considered an extension of those of its government. Managing the international reputation of this kind of company is a delicate balancing act. That's where the ability of a leader to deal with ambiguity will come in handy.

'Keep repeating'

There is no doubt that the 3.0 leader will have to be an avid communicator. And with Generation Y caring so much about authentic communication, the art of reaching out to employees in a genuine and engaging way will have to become second nature to corporations. To use the words of J J Irani, former CEO of Tata Steel, part of the Indian Tata Group, they will have 'to speak from the heart rather than the head'.[16]

During his time at Tata Steel, the flagship company of the Indian multinational, Irani had the daunting task of downsizing its workforce, which in 1994 amounted to more than 78,000 and was reduced to 45,000 by 2002. When economic reforms and liberalization began in India in 1991, Tata Steel felt the need to make the transition from a production-driven to a more modern, customer-driven enterprise. Its goal was to introduce a culture of change and innovation. It rearranged its structure from 13 to five layers at executive officer level in an effort to became a flat organization. Tata Steel also wanted to be able to compete on the international markets through costs and quality. And this is the message that Irani decided to communicate to his workforce. 'Compare figures with what is happening in the rest of the world and in India and show that we are behind in terms of productivity and that is why we have to improve. The main thing is to show the population, which is going to be affected, that whatever we are doing is for their own good and it is not for the good of management'.

The secret, Irani believes, is to avoid sending out messages that can be contradicted. 'If you say three and somebody shows it is four, then you have lost credibility.' A message should give correct facts without exaggerating or underestimating the problem and should be repeated as often as possible. Because yesterday's news is no longer news, 'if you want an impact, keep repeating, keep repeating'. Tata Steel kept working on its message, bringing it up-to-date, adding clarity and focus until everyone knew it by heart.

Irani is convinced of the role played by communication in a major change initiative like downsizing. The bigger the organization, the more crucial it is. 'If the organization consists of five people and they meet every day over a cup of tea, there is no problem with communication. Everybody knows each other's mind inside out. If there are 50,000 people or more, like in Tata Steel, the fellow who is ten levels down and 500 km away, how is he going to be drawn into making your plan successful unless there is proper communication?'

During the restructuring, Irani did his own message development. Being the chief planner, he believed that 'a good leader has to communicate'. As a matter of sincerity, he wrote his own scripts and did not use a speech-writer. He communicated to his direct reports, who in turn would communicate to theirs. This process created a need for consistency. 'Nothing is more harmful than sending a confused message.' Irani compares what sometimes happens in internal communication with a game he used to play when he was a child. Thirty children would stand in a row and pass on a message by whispering into the ear of the next child. Once the message reached the last child, it would have lost its identity and would be totally distorted. Irani's conclusion is that if you communicate directly to all thirty at once, you would achieve a better understanding. 'Communication has to be direct and as simple as possible.'

The first step Irani took when he was developing the strategy for the restructuring was to write a vision and a mission statement. It helped him to crystallize his thinking and to spell out what the company was trying to achieve through downsizing. 'What is the advantage? How much is it going to cost? Who are the people who are going to be impacted?' He then used communication to underpin this strategy. He likes to compare the communication process to the ritual of serving food. 'Strategy is planning the cooking, putting in masala, lemon, heating it or cooling it. Once the dish is ready, you bring it to the table and ask people to eat it... You can spoil it both ways. You can spoil the preparation or you can prepare it well and then, while serving, splash it all over, drop it on the table. Both have to be proper, the cooking and the serving.'

Send me an angel

Simplicity is an important lesson that we can draw from Irani's experience. The Globalization 3.0 era is one of sensational complexity and speed. Simplicity is a way to remain grounded and attentive to reality. We should not forget common sense, just because the environment around us is speeding up and heading for unprecedented transformation. A number of successful leaders are keen to remind us that communication begins with understanding others. They realize the importance of finding the balance between the global dimension and the need to appeal to employees through their local points of reference. Ramon Ollé, former Chairman of Epson Europe, is one of them. He firmly believes that the culture of the country where a multinational is headquartered should not be promoted as the culture of the entire organization. Corporate culture should integrate the history of the company with that of all the nationalities and demographics that contribute to the stability and growth of its business. Cultures of this kind attract leaders with a curiosity for different lifestyles, religions, age groups and traditions. This curiosity leads to understanding and to innovative ways of connecting with employees.

When Ollé was asked to explain Epson's values to his employees, he came up with a new idea. He decided to use angels, a figure common to several religions and spiritual traditions. Different angels would embody different values. After discussing the project with his internal communications department, he began to write a series of short chapters, one for each angel.

Ollé saw his 'angels' as a way to make abstract corporate values more tangible and to enable employees to identify with them. He believes that aligning the mindsets of employees with a particular goal is especially challenging in a multicultural organization. 'Organizations have to translate all these cultures, interpretations and mindsets into one set of policies, which means that management has to move from their mindset to outside action. In a complex multicultural organization this is a challenging process since integrating all these differences requires respect for all these cultural traits.'[17]

In his angel series, he uses metaphors and examples from his own professional life. In a chapter dealing with the importance of 'finding the right words', he recalls an exchange from his career:

> In 1988 we made a mistake in our organisation. I had to write a long letter to the president explaining the causes of the problem and the steps that had been taken to solve it. The following month, I met with the president in Japan and expected to be rebuked. Instead, he looked at me with a wise smile and asked me with a soft tone of voice: 'Have you learned from your mistake?' 'Yes', I answered. He then said that he considered himself lucky to have a manager with more experience. These words changed me. These words and the way in which he spoke left a strong mark on me. And that mistake never happened again.[18]

To explain another value, tolerance, he uses a text written by a monk in an old Spanish monastery: 'Our mistakes are like the quills of a porcupine. Others can see them and get hurt. We, however, are not aware and live quite comfortably with them'.[19]

The 'angel of team-spirit' begins by asking employees a series of questions:

- What kind of team would we like to be?
- How can we combine forces in this team?
- How can I use my abilities to make a positive contribution to the team?
- How can I motivate the other members of the team?
- How do I behave with the other team members?
- How can we guarantee maximum use of the team's resources and a well-functioning team?[20]

His advice to multicultural teams is to view the cultural differences between their members as advantages. It's the characteristics of all these people that make the team's performance possible, and as such they need to be respected. Ollé created further 'angels' to embody values like trust, the ability to spot and promote talent, creativity and motivation. They all contribute to create what he calls a sense of community.

Ollé's 'angels' are intriguing because they exist outside the realm of traditional corporate speak. Ollé was willing to volunteer examples from his own life and was ready to adopt a more down-to-earth language, which would create a stronger link between the values of the corporation and the personal values of its employees. This is the kind of language likely to resonate with Generation Y. The International Association of Business Communicators (IABC) conducted a survey among Generation Y, represented by its membership of 16,0000 professionals worldwide, and found that authentic communication holds a particular meaning for them. It goes beyond telling the truth. It implies sharing information in a way that takes into consideration the needs and communication styles of its different audiences.[21]

Mentoring across cultures

Every time we run a workshop on leadership or change, we hear the participants talk about self-confidence and positive thinking. These are frequently identified as key factors for a successful career and effective professional development. The challenge of the leader of the future will be to adopt a communication style conducive to positive thinking. With an audience as demanding as Generation Y, he or she will have to focus on creative ways for growing their staff at a professional and personal level.

Mentoring is often tipped as the leadership style of the future. Wikipedia defines mentoring as a 'developmental relationship between a more experienced mentor and a less experienced partner referred to as a protégé – a person guided and protected by a more prominent person'.[22] This is a rather old-fashioned way of looking at mentoring. The new demographics entering the workforce call for a more enlightened approach. In our own definition, mentoring is a structured interaction aimed at sharing knowledge and expertise. However, it can also be used as a communication style, one that requires openness and transparency as well as highly developed listening skills.

The traditional mentoring relationship described by Wikipedia is, however, still fairly common in the corporate world. Mentoring programmes of this kind are often designed for succession planning and talent retention. But more and more companies are opening up to reverse mentoring as an answer to the current demographic challenge. Younger employees possess the technical skills and experience necessary to understand new market trends and gain competitive advantages. And this applies not only to technology and Web 2.0. Generation Y is also much more aware of the role a company is expected to play in the community. This knowledge is very useful to help decipher the interests and agendas of different stakeholders.

Peer mentoring implies pairing up an employee with a peer in another department or division of a company. It helps to establish links that can be turned into resources for new projects and can be capitalized upon in case of change programmes. It can also be used as a tool to counteract a silo mentality.

We are great advocates of cross-cultural mentoring. This can take the form of an employee mentoring another about issues connected with working in a market or country he or she is knowledgeable about. Picture a new country manager arriving in an emerging market. A local employee could mentor him or her about how to deal with the government, which personalities from a certain institution are important to the company, what behaviours clash with the country's mentality and are most likely to upset local employees, etc. The country manager gains precious insight into important issues and challenges, and the employee feels that his or her knowledge is recognized and appreciated.

Another cross-cultural mentoring situation could imply employees from different ethnic backgrounds sharing knowledge and insight into their culture with senior management. This would not only help to promote diversity but would also provide the company with intelligence that could be used for entering new markets.

Mentoring, in general, works only if a company has a culture of giving and the success of its people is part of its key values. Cross-cultural mentoring adds an extra dimension. It contributes to creating a climate of respect and cultural sensitivity. It establishes a personal connection to a culture and helps to fight misconceptions and stereotypes. Cross-cultural mentoring also makes it possible for senior management to experience first hand in a direct exchange the problems employees from a particular ethnic or religious background might encounter at work or in their community. It gives them a broader understanding of the world out there.

More than anything else, mentoring is a state of mind that leads to an open and transparent leadership style. When it is used as a communication style, it becomes part of the information flow of a company. All interaction and exchanges of information are then based on the assumption that all parties have something to offer and are willing to learn from each other.

Maijo Bos, a Madrid-based leadership development consultant working with international organizations, wrote in a book on mentoring programmes for professional women:

> We often hear about executives rushing from one meeting to the next. In a business world focused on doing, mentoring requires participants to slow down and reflect on the knowledge they have developed over the course of their professional life in order to share it in a meaningful way.

This requires looking deep inside at what has shaped their values and character as a leader, and identifying which skills and abilities were needed in the process. Only then can they share the insights gained in a meaningful way.[23]

She interviewed a number of mentors about their motivations for entering a mentoring relationship:

- building a new and diverse network of relationships;
- strengthening succession planning;
- improving the spirit and environment of a company;
- increasing personal growth as a leader and teacher;
- leveraging a mentee as a sounding board;
- helping others find their voice as a leader;
- retaining executives through dedicated mentoring programmes that demonstrate the organization's commitment to its people;
- preserving stories and lessons learned for the next generation;
- leaving a legacy.

It will be the task of the leader of the future to recognize the mentoring potential of formal and informal relationships within a corporation. And what better way to promote active listening and the willingness to develop cultural intelligence.

The spirit of international networks

The secret of the 3.0 leader's success is based on the ability to develop a sophisticated understanding of new realities and to learn lessons from unorthodox environments. International associations and networks are one of these environments.

In the past, these voluntary groups of people, who come together to accomplish a common purpose, often had a tendency to pursue specific national interests and forget the global picture. However, in our knowledge-based society, this way of thinking is rapidly fading. The true spirit of international networks is experiencing a rebirth.

Members need their help to be able to deal with Globalization 3.0. The geopolitical axis is shifting. The Western world is experiencing a certain fatigue. While still entrenched in the old ways of conducting business, it is beginning to realize that something needs to change. When we go to work every day, we have the feeling that globalization is happening to us, while we would much rather prefer to be in control and understand what is going on.

What we need is a structure that can help us put our local issues in perspective – one that can make us understand how to translate global trends into tangible benefits for the part of the world, constituency or sector we are working in. In other words, international networks are the perfect platform where we can learn how to interact professionally with people from other cultures and develop ideas that will help us add an international component to our cause or business.

In the past, the work of international associations and networks was often limited to the representation of interests and the coordination of joint programmes. More and more networks are recognizing the importance of the new leadership role they are increasingly called to play. The confluence of today's global challenges is making them realize that they are being called to educate members about different cultural backgrounds. This applies to all kinds of international networks regardless of their area of activity. They don't necessarily need to have multiculturalism or conflict prevention as part of their mission. Their purpose might be to promote trade in a certain part of the world or to represent the interests of the manufacturers of a certain product. Today's global security concerns are adding an element of urgency to the agenda of any organization that operates internationally. We need each one of them to contribute to the creation of a new leadership style. We need them to help bring about a better understanding of the expectations and perceptions of different cultures.

In order to be able to play this role, international networks need to add new leadership skills and competencies to their structures. We can expect communication to be an important part of this change.

Change managers

The reasons why members join international networks have changed. They mirror their fears and hopes in a world that is undergoing major transformation. Members understand that globalization is upon us and would like a powerful ally to help them decipher the different trends looming on the horizon.

Take, for example, a group of manufacturers of building materials who are watching their market shrink due to fierce competition from Brazil or China. This kind of member is looking for orientation. They are trying to make sense out of a situation that is threatening everything they have ever worked for. They might not know exactly what to ask from their association. Their first reaction will probably be fear and confusion. What they need is an organization able to help them deal with this change by putting their situation in an international perspective and stretching their imagination. They might have never considered looking for manufacturing partners in a foreign country as remote as India. Doing business abroad would probably mean stretching their comfort zone. This is why the support of an international network is so essential. Its function, in this case, is no longer limited to identifying a foreign partner. It includes solid preparatory work aimed at familiarizing members with the idea of venturing into another culture and opening up their world to behaviours and practices never encountered before. It equals changing their mind-frame. This is no small task. It is one that requires visionary leadership skills and turns international networks into change managers.

The world's geopolitical axis is shifting. China and India as well as other emerging markets are becoming increasingly influential and are offering new prospects. While in the 1990s the challenge had been to make sense of the end of the Cold War and to engage with a part of the world everybody had feared for decades, changes in era 3.0 require us to understand the dynamics of the BRIC countries and other economies and to work out how to tie our fortunes to their growth.

The other major shift we are experiencing concerns the way in which we produce and exchange information. The interactive web has replaced hoarding knowledge with sharing resources. We are entering a new environment characterized by a climate of openness, which might seem rather daunting to established businesses that would rather stick to the status quo. The task of an international network is to translate these developments into concrete opportunities for its members.

Preparing the ground

The business world is experiencing a push for culturally diverse leadership. It first started in industries like oil and gas. Others sectors including consumer goods and professional services were quick to spot the opportunities in emerging markets and to recognize the need to adjust to their clients' requirements. They appreciate the importance of having staff who can do business in regions like Asia and the Middle East.[24] They are therefore encouraging people from their European and North American offices to gain exposure to emerging markets. This trend is resulting in an increasing number of leaders likely to find themselves working in unfamiliar cultures. International networks can help corporations prepare their staff for these daunting assignments.

Values rather than geography

What members want these days from an international network is an experience. The principle is similar to the one that drives consumers to enjoy their morning coffee at Starbucks. It is the bundle of feelings that makes them feel good and gives them a sense of belonging.

The leadership challenge for a network is to help members establish an empathic connection to each others' motivations and behaviours. This can be achieved by looking beyond national stereotypes, such as 'Germans are too formal' or 'Southern Europeans are too unstructured', and by focusing on common values. It is the search for common values that turns a task force meeting into a productive exchange, or committee work into a rewarding experience. It requires a delicate balancing act. The members' cultural backgrounds need to be taken into consideration. What the network wants to achieve is a climate of trust and openness. This is likely to take time and considerable effort given the baggage and past experiences every member brings to the table.

Co-author Cambié was once moderating a meeting of an international network whose mission was to promote education about human rights and democracy. The purpose of the meeting was to identify common projects to be carried out by the different NGOs and philanthropic foundations which were part of the network. This was a first for its members whose interactions had always been limited to the development of joint statements and the production of publications. However, international cooperation on development projects between NGOs is quite common and one would have expected little resistance from the members. The issue, nevertheless, turned out to be trust. And in particular the way in which part of the membership perceived trust. A number of NGOs from former Yugoslavia had just experienced the Balkan war of the 1990s and were operating in a difficult post-conflict environment. The mistake of the network had been to meet far too seldom face-to-face for these NGOs to be able to develop a relationship with the other members and decide whether to trust them sufficiently to enter a closer cooperation. What would have been considered standard practice under normal circumstances turned out to be a test in cross-cultural proficiency.

Endeavor: Changing cultural attitudes

The new knowledge-based society and its climate of openness have led to the rise of new types of networks. Endeavor is an international community of like-minded entrepreneurs. Its mission is to link the know-how of international business leaders with high-potential entrepreneurs in developing countries. Established in 1997 by Yale graduate Linda Rottenberg and venture capitalist Peter Kellner, it specializes in emerging economies that are beginning to attract international investment. These include Argentina, Brazil, Colombia, Mexico, South Africa, Chile, Turkey and Uruguay.

Endeavor screens these countries for entrepreneurs with interesting ideas and submits them to an panel of international business leaders. In the course of a decade, the network has supported 264 entrepreneurs, chosen from 17,000 applications. Over 90 per cent of the businesses backed are still operational and have generated more than 80,000 jobs worldwide as well as annual revenues of US$2 billion.[25]

Endeavor provides its members with resources that range from pro-bono consultancy services and mentorship to access to capital. It functions like a peer group and plays all the roles that we can expect from an innovative community of interests in era 3.0. Its work helps to put entrepreneurship on the agenda of governments, multilateral organizations and other policy makers. It has contributed to changing cultural attitudes towards risk and innovation in the countries in which it operates.[26]

Endeavor also offers role models that fledgling entrepreneurs can use as points of reference. And these aren't necessarily from the global North. Endeavor's board of directors includes Naguib Sawiris, Chairman and CEO of Egypt's Orascom Telecom, Lorenzo Zambrano of Mexico's Cemex and Ali Koç of Koç Holdings, Turkey's top industrial conglomerate. This cultural diversity provides the leadership of the network with a unique perspective. It also gives entrepreneurs in emerging economies the confidence they need by demonstrating that other cultures' approaches to business are just as viable as models from North America or Europe.

By creating new employment opportunities in their local markets, Endeavor's members help to overturn the brain drain that has been affecting many developing countries. In Turkey, the organization has been supporting AirTies, a wireless network technology company whose founder has been leading a team of Turkish engineers from Silicon Valley back to Turkey and is tipped to become the leading provider of wireless technology for small businesses in Europe, the Middle East and Africa. In Mexico, a country where health insurance is a problem, one of Endeavor's members is Imagen Dental, a network of clinics that provides affordable dental treatment. Imagen Dental has become the largest private employer of dentists in the country.

Endeavor has also been establishing connections between its member enterpreneurs and potential investors in other parts of the world. One of its most successful Argentinean members is Mercado Libre, Latin America's answer to the online auction website eBay. It was also the first Endeavor entrepreneur to be listed on NASDAQ, the American stock exchange. eBay has acquired a 19 per cent stake in the company.

Desperately looking for a new leadership style

We are moving beyond the paternalistic internal communication methods of the past towards a more integrated vision of employee engagement. We are currently witnessing the dawn of leadership com-munication. The communication challenges of the new era include highly informed employees, unprecedented market forces and the need to integrate different cultural elements. A new communication style is needed. Companies are dealing with increased globalization, while at the same time their workforce is becoming more ethnically and culturally diverse.

It is the attitude to employee engagement that needs to change. The top-down approach of the past implied looking at employees as a uniform group to align behind decisions taken by senior management. The culture of collaboration and sharing created by Generation Y calls for more inclusive decision making. Business leaders will have to put processes in place designed to actively search for employees' point of view. In our globalized business arena, companies need to explore their employees' cultural models and utilize their background as a resource. The world is changing and keeps presenting them with complex situations. In order to deal with such complexity, corporations need a constant flow of ideas and creative solutions. And what better source for alternative ideas than a multicultural workforce?

However, employees will only come forward and share their experience if they feel that their cultural background is respected. This can only happen if a genuine climate of openness is in place and if corporate leaders have a multicultural mindset. Culture has often been described as the tapestry people use as their point of reference. It tells them how things should be, how people should behave, how places should look, how work should be organized. In their mind, any element that is different from what they are used to gets categorized as 'foreign'. What global business now needs are enlightened leaders able to replace their cultural tapestry with an open canvas large enough to contain all the cultures that contribute to the company's success.

In this chapter, we have explored a number of innovative leadership models. We believe that cross-cultural leadership is a mindset. It might seem too progressive and difficult to implement in companies addicted to the ways of the past. However we are convinced that it will become business as usual in a not too distant future. Nurturing cross-cultural leadership requires constant effort and genuine commitment. So where do we start?

- Develop top-of-mind awareness of other cultures. Promote the study of other cultures within the company not as a way to satisfy intellectual curiosity but as a tool for professional and personal development.
- Encourage employees from different cultural backgrounds to share their knowledge and experience. Introduce processes able to convert this exchange into an integral component of the company's decision making.
- Create an inventory of your employees' cultural experiences. This could take the form of an internal social networking platform, similar to Facebook, where employees can upload information about the countries they have lived in, the cultures they have studied, the languages they speak, etc. This kind of tool serves to promote cross-cultural dialogue and could be used as a source of information every time internal talent is needed for a new project or team.
- Use 'integrative thinking' as a way to conduct meetings. Create a climate in which employees are comfortable to explore opposing

cultural models. When you call a meeting to find a solution to a problem, encourage dialogue rather than advocacy.

- Educate senior management about the need to transform the internal communication function. Globalization 3.0 calls for internal communicators to graduate from internal journalists to leadership strategists. Corporations are no longer able to operate as a lodge with secrets and dominant hierarchies. These days, information is easily available and easily distributed. The workforce is less willing to believe in myths.[27] Therefore, the role of the internal communicator is shifting from brokering knowledge to brokering access to cultures and new complex environments. This is an integral part of leadership communication. The role of the internal communicator will be to assist corporate leaders in their efforts to connect strategically with a diverse workforce.
- Stretch yourself and explore leadership models from other cultures. Use cross-cultural mentoring to integrate new elements into your management style.

Notes

1. Natasha Nicholson, Empower the Next Generation, *Communication World*, March–April 2008, p. 14.
2. Jennifer James, Urban Cultural Anthropologist, in discussion with co-author Cambié via e-mail, June 2008.
3. Michael Green, Senior Consultant and Managing Director, Pertec Global Leadership, Finnish–British Chamber of Commerce, London, 24 April 2008.
4. Roger Martin, *The Opposable Mind*, Harvard Business School Press, Cambridge, MA, 2007.
5. Roger Martin, Dean and Professor of Strategic Management, Rotman School of Management, University of Toronto, in discussion with co-author Cambié, May 2008.
6. Roger Martin, *The Opposable Mind*, Harvard Business School Press, Cambridge, MA, 2007, p. 6.
7. Roger Martin, *The Opposable Mind*, Harvard Business School Press, Cambridge, MA, 2007, pp. 6, 9.
8. Roger Martin, *The Opposable Mind*, Harvard Business School Press, Cambridge, MA, 2007, p. 157.
9. Roger Martin, Dean and Professor of Strategic Management, Rotman School of Management, University of Toronto, in discussion with co-author Cambié, May 2008.
10. Roger Martin, *The Opposable Mind*, Harvard Business School Press, Cambridge, MA, 2007, p. 77.

11. Michael Spencer, Managing Director, Sound Strategies, in discussion with co-author Cambié in London, UK, May 2008.
12. Tatas Demand Apology from Orient Express, financialexpress.com, 4 June 2008, http://www.financialexpress.com/news/Tatas-demand-apology-from-Orient-Express/252442/#.
13. Geoff Dyer and Richard McGregor, China's Champions, *Financial Times*, 17 March 2008, p.11.
14. Professor Paul Collier, Economist, Oxford University, *The Bottom Billion: Why the Poorest Countries are Failing, and What Can Be Done About It*, The Ismaili Center, London, 7 October 2008.
15. Harry G Broadman, China and India Go to Africa, *Foreign Affairs*, March/April 2008, p. 97.
16. Dr J J Irani, former CEO of Tata Steel, and currently Director, Tata Sons, interviewed at Bombay House on 5 April, 2002, by Dr (Col) Rajeev Kumar, currently Senior Practice Consultant at the Tata Management Training Centre, Pune, India.
17. Ramon Ollé, former Chairman of Epson Europe and currently Executive President of La Salle Business Engineering School, How Values Play the Most Important Role, Meeting of IABC Europe/Middle East at ABN-AMRO, Amsterdam, 22 May 2007.
18. Ramon Ollé, Die richtigen Worte finden, in *Engel bei der Arbeit – Führen mit Werten*, Athena, 2006, p. 53 (free translation by co-author Cambié).
19. Ramon Ollé, Die richtigen Worte finden, in *Engel bei der Arbeit – Führen mit Werten*, Athena, 2006, p. 58 (free translation by co-author Cambié).
20. Ramon Ollé, Die richtigen Worte finden, in *Engel bei der Arbeit – Führen mit Werten*, Athena, 2006, p. 88 (free translation by co-author Cambié).
21. Leah Reynolds, Elizabeth Campbell Bush and Ryan Geist, The Gen Y Imperative, *Communication World*, March–April 2008.
22. Mentorship, Wikipedia.org, 20 October 2008, http://en.wikipedia.org/wiki/Mentoring.
23. Marijo Bos, How to Set Up a Mentoring Programme and How to Participate Successfully: Why Be a Mentor? *Women@Work No. 7, Mentoring A Powerful Tool for Women*, EuropeanPWN, France, 2007, p. 96, http://www.amazon.fr/Women-Work-No-Mentoring-Powerful/dp/2952270368/ref=sr_1_1/402-7436757-0568121?ie=UTF8&s=books&qid=1173776246&sr=8-1.
24. Alicia Clegg, The Lure of Overseas Opportunity, *Financial Times*, 26 August 2008, p. 14.
25. Beyond Start-ups: Entrepreneurship in Emerging Markets, commons.princeton.edu, 21 October 2008, http://commons.princeton.edu/ciee/2007/10/beyond_startups_entrepreneurship_in_emerging_marke.html.

26. Spreading the Gospel, *The Economist*, 2 August 2008, p. 72.
27. Jennifer James in conversation with co-author Cambié via e-mail, June 2008.

5 The day after

'Can you see it burning?' Co-author Cambié was attending a function in September 2008 on the roof terrace of the Blue Fin Building , the London headquarters of magazine publisher IPC Media, on the south bank of the River Thames. Another guest was pointing at the City, the financial centre of London, which that day had been the stage of an unprecedented meltdown in the banking sector. After 158 years, the investment bank Lehman Brothers had filed for Chapter 11 bankruptcy protection, the largest bankruptcy in US history. Bank of America had announced its offer to take over Merrill Lynch, which in the spring had reported losses of nearly US$2 billion. What had once been the world's largest insurer with assets of US$1 trillion, American International Group (AIG), had to be rescued from total collapse by the US government with a US$85 billion loan.[1]

The economic downturn that followed the financial crisis has made the public rethink their definition of corporate success. The focus has shifted from quarterly results to the way a company conducts its business. It is the sum of a company's behaviours: 'how it communicates, how it works, how it treats others, how it makes decisions, how it interacts in the marketplace and how consistently it acts'.[2] This will be the new source of competitive advantage.

According to Kemal Dervis, administrator of the UN Development Programme, the world economic crisis has shown people just how interconnected we are, 'with the Indonesian farmer depending on good regulation of the financial sector to improve his standard of living'.[3] The economist Hyman Minsky wrote in his book *Stabilizing an Unstable Economy,* 'Economic issues must become a serious public matter and the subject of debate if new directions are to be undertaken. Meaningful reforms cannot be put over by an advisory and administrative elite that is itself the architect of the existing situation. Unless the public understands the reason for change they will not accept its cost; understanding is the foundation of legitimacy for reform.'[4]

The global conversation that is developing around the world thanks to technology is giving people the means to understand complex realities. The financial crisis has added another layer to this new consciousness. The public feels a need for transparency and new rules of the road. The guiding principles of business have to change to create social benefit for all the constituencies it has an impact on. To principles like thrift and economy we have to add a new one: inclusiveness. To use the words of Annette Verschuren, President and CEO of The Home Depot for Canada and Asia, the business secret of the future will be about including and inspiring people who in the past we thought did not belong.[5]

The public is thirsty for engagement. We believe social entrepreneurship to be one of the most powerful answers to this search for meaning. It is the product of the spirit of the time. It is the expression of a sea change in human behaviour.

Social business depends on transparency and inclusiveness to reach its goals. It needs effective communication to keep its many stakeholders engaged. We believe that social entrepreneurship will be one of the main sectors of choice for the 3.0 communicator.

Social business: A new equilibrium

Social entrepreneurs have the ability to spot an area that needs positive social change and provide a model able to produce that change. They challenge the collective thinking that a single individual with an idea cannot solve humanity's most entrenched problems. Social entrepreneurs are also defined as:

> someone who targets an unfortunate but stable equilibrium that causes the neglect, marginalization, or suffering of a segment of humanity; who brings to bear on this situation his or her inspiration, direct action, creativity, courage and fortitude; and who aims for and ultimately affects the establishment of a new stable equilibrium that secures permanent benefit for the targeted group and society at large.[6]

Social business is really:

> like other businesses, it employs workers, creates goods or services, and provides these to customers for a price consistent with its objective. But

its underlying objective and the criterion by which it should be evaluated is to create social benefit for those whose lives it touches. The company itself may earn a profit, but the investors who support it do not take any profits out of the company except recouping an amount equivalent to their original investment over a period of time.[7]

Social entrepreneurs are not a new phenomenon. Had they lived in our time, Florence Nightingale, the founder of the modern nursing profession from the 19th century, and Maria Montessori, who in the same period revolutionized children's education, would have been given this label.

The difference is that these days, thanks to the internet, ideas for systemic change travel at incredible speed. Technology makes us more aware of the fate of the other two-thirds of humanity. According to the Ashoka Foundation, one of the major advocates of social entrepreneurship, more than two billion people don't have access to financial services, one billion live in inadequate housing, two billion lack electrical power and 100 million children grow up without attending primary school.[8]

The Skoll Foundation is another organization for the advancement of social entrepreneurship. Founded by Jeff Skoll, first president of the online auction website eBay, it provides support to social entrepreneurs. It has selected a series of areas where it believes action is urgently needed:

- tolerance and human rights, such as religious and racial tolerance, women's rights, sexual exploitation and human trafficking, torture and wrongful imprisonment, immigration, and general tolerance and human rights issues;
- health, such as disease control, access to health care and system problems, pollution and toxins, population control and lifestyle;
- environmental sustainability, such as biodiversity and depletion of natural resources, global warming, water, oceans and waste (general and nuclear);
- peace and security, such as war, nuclear weapons, terrorism, arms and drug trafficking, government involvement, conflict resolution, and sustainable development and education in conflict zones;
- institutional responsibility, such as unethical labour practices, bribery and corruption, unethical government (eg executive pay), shareholder activism, business and the environment, irresponsible marketing, unethical sourcing and procurement, and global media integrity;

- economic and social equity, such as poverty and distribution of wealth, drugs, crime and violence, microfinance, homelessness and affordable housing, and education.[9]

Communication is an important part of the social entrepreneurship equation. You need to capture the attention of the public by showing concrete examples of the change introduced by social businesses in communities around the world. The Skoll Foundation has been supporting the production of *New Heroes*, a TV series hosted by the actor Robert Redford and aired on the American station PBS. *New Heroes* tells the stories of twelve social entrepreneurs from different parts of the world, from Zambia to Laos. The Foundation has also entered a partnership with Redford's Sundance Institute, which promotes independent film-making, with the purpose of exploring the role played by film in spreading the message about social entrepreneurship. Another project is Social Edge,[10] an online community for social entrepreneurs, set up by the Foundation as a space where people interested in the sector can exchange information and gain access to resources. Its blogs, podcasts and video interviews provide a powerful port of call for anybody who would like to get a flavour of what social entrepreneurship is all about. The blog Global X,[11] for example, features social entrepreneurs talking about their professional and personal lives. It tells stories like that of Bart Weetjens, a Belgian Buddhist monk who lives in Africa and trains rats to detect mines in the fields of Mozambique.

The art of storytelling is one of the many ways in which communication can contribute to the success of social entrepreneurs. It is the multifaceted character of social business that makes this new area such a natural choice for talented communicators. The advocates of this sector complain that the social entrepreneurship phenomenon has gone largely unnoticed by opinion makers and the media. This is a challenge more and more experienced communicators will be drawn to in the future. Communicators know how to promote underreported issues by framing them in a way that creates an emphatic connection. Social business is about the confluence of many global challenges. Communicators have to help audiences understand that, in our complex time, all issues are intertwined and the stability of their lives is bound to suffer if no sustainable solution is found for the most urgent problems of the developing world.

Organizations like the Ashoka Foundation and the Skoll Foundation are eager to develop the body of knowledge around the innovations and models used by social entrepreneurs. They also recognize the importance for social businesses of reaching out to their equivalents in other countries and creating informal as well as formal networks. These networks help to strengthen the public voice of social entrepreneurship. Communicators can help in this process.

In an innovative area like social entrepreneurship, the communication function has to encompass much more than press relations and speech writing. It has to include relationship-building, fundraising and donor relations management. It is up to an enlightened business entrepreneur to recognize the contribution of communication and put it to good use.

There is another aspect of social business where communicators can play an important part. Social enterprises don't have shareholders like for-profit businesses; they have stakeholders with complex expectations that go beyond financial performance. Their bottom line, positive social change, is difficult to put in a spreadsheet. Skills different from accounting are needed when reporting back to supporters and donors. These groups want to know that the organization they have put their trust in is really making a difference in the lives of a certain part of humanity. This kind of reporting requires strong communication skills as well as cultural and emotional awareness.

Communication has always been used to tell the story of humanity, to spread ideas and connect people. Now that a new consciousness is surfacing and humanity is confronting many urgent challenges, communication is finally being given the chance to come of age and prove its real value.

The 'social entrepreneurial version of Google'

The Institute for OneWorld Health (iOWH) is the world's first non-profit pharmaceutical company. At the core of its mission is the fight against the unequal distribution of the world's health resources, which results in the diseases affecting the world's poorest being largely ignored. Traditional drug makers have been investing less than 10 per cent of their research and development resources in the cure of diseases of the developing world.

According to the World Health Organization (WHO), infectious diseases are responsible for the death of six out of ten of the world's poorest. Diarrhoea kills two million children every year. Malaria remains one of the most feared killers in sub-Saharan Africa. World-wide, it infects more than half a billion people annually. Ninety per cent of the two million victims claimed by tuberculosis every year live in developing countries.[12]

iOWH's founder Victoria Hale came up with a new business model. She likes to think of iOWH as a bridge between research and the production of affordable drugs for the developing world. The Institute conducts the clinical trials and develops the drugs. It then partners with companies and hospitals in the developing world to manufacture and distribute the medicines.

The first fight Hale took on was against visceral leishmaniasis, or Black Fever, the world's second worst parasitic disease after malaria. In India, where the disease is called kala-azar, a quarter of a million people fall ill every year. There are approximately 500,000 new cases of visceral leishmaniasis annually worldwide. Black Fever occurs in 62 countries, with over 90 per cent of the cases in India, Bangladesh, Sudan, Brazil and Nepal. The north-eastern state of Bihar is one of the most severely affected areas.

iOWH knew of an antibiotic, paromomycine, which had proved effective in fighting kala-azar, and found the money to test it. With US$47 million from the Bill & Melinda Gates Foundation and the support of the WHO, the organization was able to conduct clinical trials and file successfully for the drug's approval. It then got an Indian pharmaceutical company to produce and sell paromomycine at a cost of US$10–15 for a full course of treatment.

iOWH's most recent cause is the treatment of diarrhoeal diseases. More children die of diarrhoea than of AIDS, tuberculosis and malaria combined.[13] With a further grant of US$46 million from the Gates Foundation, One World Health is looking for new ways to treat diarrhoeal diseases.

Many sides to a hot story

iOWH's story is one of the hottest in the social business sector. It has many aspects; each of them appeals to a different audience.

In the United States, it is One World Health's maverick spirit and its courage to create what was previously considered an oxymoron, a non-profit pharmaceutical company, that fascinates the public. 'We are the social entrepreneurial version of Google', says James Hickman, Vice President of External Affairs at iOWH. Then there is

Victoria Hale's charisma and her own personal story. She has a PhD in pharmaceutical chemistry from the University of California at San Francisco and began her career reviewing new drug applications at the US Food and Drug Administration, where she was famous for her investigative approach and her ability to spot weaknesses in the arguments of drug companies. This reputation landed her a job at Genentech, the world's leading biotech company. In 1998, Hale had an awakening while sitting in a taxi. The driver happened to be from Africa. He asked what her job was. When he heard that she was working for a pharmaceutical company, he roared with laughter: 'You all have all the money.'[14] This was a cathartic moment for Hale, who decided to quit her job and use US$100,000 from her savings to launch a business model never explored before. She was given *The Economist* Innovation Award for Social and Economic Innovation and was made a fellow of the Ashoka Foundation. In 2005, *Esquire* magazine named Hale Executive of the Year.

In Europe, iOHW uses a different message. Audiences in this part of the world are more conservative when it comes to the development of drugs, and are mostly interested in the Institute's scientific pedigree. It is its scientific credentials and unprecedented work in the field of tropical infectious disease that make Hale's cause attractive to Europeans.

The conversation iOWH has been having in the developing world is of a more delicate nature. The danger there is being perceived as a paternalistic organization from the global North quick with theory and good at promising solutions. Local stories are the antidote. In India, the Institute has been talking about its success in curing kala-azar through the story of Dr Shyam Sundar, a country doctor who spent 20 years fighting the disease. The story became the subject of a BBC World documentary, *Kill or Cure? Kala Azar 2*, which was voted best documentary of the year in 2008 by BBC World viewers.[15]

Dr Sundar is portrayed in his clinic in Bihar, one of the few in India that treats patients free of charge. He is standing by a small child who is lying in one of his 60 iron beds. The child's mother is watching over him with a concerned look, wrapped in her red sari. Children from the region often suffer from malnutrition and are the most vulnerable to kala-azar. The disease destroys their blood cells and weakens their immune system. Death can then be caused by severe diarrhoea or pneumonia. Black Fever is spread by the sandfly, a tiny fly that grows in warm, organic matter and tends to prey on its victims at night while they are sleeping. Farmers in Bihar use dung to coat the floors and walls of their huts. That's where the sandfly breeds. Whole families are often infected as they sleep together on the floor of their hut.

The little boy at Dr Sundar's clinic became ill while his mother was being treated with the disease. The documentary shows the toddler receiving his first injection of paromomycine. Next to him, a beaming Dr Sundar talks about the hundreds of lives the drug can save. He has hope that, for the first time, kala-azar can be controlled. Over the years, Dr Sundar has conducted a survey of over 26,000 people. For every case reported to the authorities, eight go unreported. People die in their huts unable to afford treatment.

Dr Sundar's story provides the sense of drama and the human connection that iOWH needed to bond with its Indian audience. Storytelling is used as a unifier. It creates an emotional connection between iOWH's work and the lives of the many kala-azar victims it is trying to save. Through the universal art of storytelling, the individual fate of Dr Sundar and that of his patients become the story of India.

Hale believes that initial contact with the local communities and beneficiaries of iOHW's work has to be personal. She uses one-to-one communication to establish trust. She often has meals with the people she visits in the field or brings her children along to meet them.[16] 'It's all about respect,' she says. 'You have to meet the mothers of babies who have died of diarrhoea [if you want to be able to develop a cure for the disease]. The ultimate goal is to ask questions and serve the people who are in need.'

When communicating with donors, iOWH's priority is to explain the value of its work and the impact it has on people's lives in the developing world. Apart from the Bill & Melinda Gates Foundation, the Institute has received grants from the Skoll Foundation and the Chiron Foundation, among others. The geography and the scope of the diseases iOWH is committed to fighting are daunting. Millions of people in the world want access to cheap drugs. This is why donors need to be kept informed throughout the process. They need to feel that each step One World Health makes is a step towards saving lives. iOWH does this through research papers, newsletters, e-mails, personal calls and its website.

Calling iOWH

iOWH employs over 50 people in the USA and 25 in India. Its internal communication message is simple. It keeps reminding employees that their work matters because it saves lives. Employees need to become aware of this context.

Giants from the for-profit pharmaceutical sector work together with iOWH for the development of new drugs. The Institute has signed an agreement with Roche and has been screening components from Roche's library in search of a new drug for treating diarrhoeal diseases. It has also entered into an agreement with Sanofi-Aventis, a company with a strong track record in Africa, for the development of new treatments for malaria. The traditional pharmaceutical sector appreciates iOWH's ability to act fast and scope problems that have been neglected in the past. They look at this social enterprise as an awareness builder, an entity that can create markets where they don't exist. 'If a social gift is going to go to other parts of the world, they call iOWH', says Hale, and adds that it is the employees of big pharmaceutical companies, and in particular older employees, that want their employers to get involved in the developing world.

iOWH's role stretches beyond conducting research and developing drugs. It has an important advocacy role. One of its tasks is to engage stakeholders from industry and the public sector and to raise awareness of the impact of tropical diseases on the life and economic growth of many communities in the developing world.

It is the multiple roles of social enterprises that make their communication work so fascinating. They need to talk about their work, its quality and the solutions they are finding for societal problems. But they also have to raise awareness among individuals, organizations and governments about the transformation they want to bring about in society.

This means nothing less than creating a new sensibility among the public. In the case of iOWH, the mission is about introducing a new attitude to the distribution of the world's health resources. But first, the story of the many millions of people suffering from infectious diseases in the developing world needs to be told. It needs to be told in a powerful and compelling way so that audiences around the world begin to relate to the situation of this part of humanity and realize that the system has to change. Never before has the role of communication been so crucial in guaranteeing the success of a business venture.

Notes

1. What next? *The Economist*, 20 September 2008, p. 13.

2. Inspirational Leadership in Difficult Times, howsmatter.com, 17 November 2008, http://www.howsmatter.com/inspirational-leadership-in-difficult-times/.

3. Andrew Jack, A Race to Prevent Disaster, *Financial Times*, 25 September 2008, p. 14.

4. Hyman P Minsky (2008), Introduction to Policy, in *Stabilizing an Unstable Economy*, McGraw-Hill, Maidenhead, 2008, p. 321.

5. Annette Verschuren, President and CEO, The Home Depot, Canada and Asia, Building an International Brand, The International Alliance for Women Global Partnership Forum 2008, Toronto, Canada, 10 November 2008.

6. Roger L. Martin and Sally Osberg, Social Enterpreneurship: The Case for Definition, *Stanford Social Innovation Review*, Standford Graduate School of Business, Spring 2007.

7. Muhammad Yunus, Social Business: What It Is and What It Is Not, in *Creating a World Without Poverty*, PublicAffairs, New York, 2008, pp. 21–22.

8. Full Economic Citizenship, ashoka.org, 6 June 2008, http://www.ashoka.org/fec.

9. Glossary of Terms Used in Application Materials, skollfoundation.org, 18 July 2008, http://www.skollfoundation.org/skollawards/glossary.asp.

10. By Social Enterpreneurs, for Social Enterpreneurs, socialedge.org, 23 October 2008, http://www.socialedge.org/?gclid=CNXfjJr9vJYCFRqH1QodOUmlxw.

11. Global X, socialedge.org, 23 October 2008, http://www.socialedge.org/blogs/global-x.

12. The Global Burden of Infectious Disease, oneworldhealth.org, 6 June 2008, http://www.oneworldhealth.org/global/global_burden.php.

13. The Pipeline, oneworldhealth.org, 6 June 2008, http://www.oneworldhealth.org/media/e_newsletter_spring08.php.

14. Victoria Hale, Developer of Affordable Drugs for the World's Poor, glamour.com, 6 June 2008, http://www.glamour.com/news/woty/articles/2007/11/victoria_hale.

15. BBC World Film Featuring OneWorld Health Voted Year's Best Documentary, findarticles.com, 23 October 2008, http://findarticles.com/p/articles/mi_m0EIN/is_2008_Jan_4/ai_n27489190.

16. Victoria Hale, founder of the Institute for One World Health, in discussion with co-author Cambié, July 2008.

Part 2

The role of social media in international communications

6 The cultural landscape of social media

The present

For many of us around the globe today, our daily activities include at least some time engaging online, whether we are checking e-mails, shopping for books or groceries, accessing our online bank accounts or sending someone a hatching egg on Facebook.[1] We 'skype'[2] our friends and business contacts to talk for free online. We 'chat' by text using instant messaging. Some of us send video messages via our social network profile page. We 'google'[3] instead of looking things up in books or directories. 'Googling' people we know or whom we've just met is the new social pastime.[4] We send files and documents electronically online and collaborate on projects from all corners of the globe using internet-based project management tools. We sign online petitions, and in some countries we can now vote online in local and even national elections.[5] Increasingly, many people are online and available every minute of the day, wherever we may be, thanks to multi-media, multi-tasking mobile devices like the Blackberry.[6] The internet and the world wide web are becoming as ubiquitous and essential in our modern urban lives as water from our taps and electricity for our lighting.

As social media such as blogging, photo-sharing, video-sharing and social networks like LinkedIn, Facebook and Cyworld extend the ways we can engage via digital means, internet communications are evolving the way we do business as well as the way we relate to each other in our private lives. In the way that there is a cultural element of etiquette whenever human beings come together for business or pleasure, we suggest that there is a cultural aspect to online communications. We suggest that cyberspace is a landscape in and of itself, where there are accepted ways of behaviour that have a cultural rather than legal basis. With the rise of social media and online networks being used by hundreds of millions of people around the world, these online behaviours are evolving rapidly and with powerful effect. As part of the cross-cultural communications explored in this book, we want to examine the culture of the internet and web itself and look at how it is relevant to businesses and PR professionals who wish to engage online, particularly through social media. Just as it is useful for enterprises doing business in another country or continent to understand something about the culture they are coming into, there are advantages in understanding online culture when we come into cyberspace. While local and national cultures will inevitably permeate the way that those cultures use the internet and social media, this book also explores cross-cultural communications with a focus on cyberspace as another, diverse – and if not geographical, then virtual – cultural landscape.

Much as a guidebook to a particular cultural region will orientate us with a history of the region we are visiting to help us understand its cultural and historical roots, the temperament and values of its peoples as well as the social norms of communication there, we set off on our journey through the online cultural landscape with a brief look at the history of the internet, computer technology and digital delivery infrastructure, as these are key foundations for the rise of social media.

A brief history

Technology moulds communications media. If you can understand its evolution, it can put you in a good position to use the technology available today, and also to keep an eye on ongoing technological developments that are likely to shape the world of communications tomorrow.

Although the world's first website was launched on 6 August 1991,[7] the internet had been around since the 1960s. While it was at the time of no interest to the public in general, it was being used widely by researchers, developers and military communities primarily in the USA and United Kingdom for daily computer communications.[8]

Its development had begun with defence and the military back in the 1950s and 1960s during the Cold War. Over the next 20 years, computer-based communications networks were developed across university faculties and research facilities, connecting first universities in America and then including those in Europe.

During the late 1980s, Tim Berners-Lee and Robert Cailliau, were two scientists working at CERN (the European Organization for Nuclear Research). Berners-Lee was working in the European Particle Physics Laboratory and his target community for developing an information sharing application for computers was the High Energy Physics community.[9] With his colleague Cailliau, he developed Hypertext Mark Up Language (HTML) and HyperText Transfer Protocol (HTTP) in 1989, the building blocks of dynamic web pages. Using these building blocks, they created the world's first website in 1991 and you can still see it today at http://www.w3.org/History/19921103-hypertext/hypertext/WWW/TheProject.html.

That first website explains what the 'WorldWideWeb' is – initially the phrase was conceived without spaces and referred to as W3 for short – and in a bold statement set out the founding ethics of the web: 'The project is based on the philosophy that much academic information should be freely available to anyone.'[10] That core statement set the standard for an online culture that encourages the free exchange of information.

But how did this small rather unimpressive 'web' thing come to have such a profound impact on the world? A number of commercial factors had to fall into place first. In the early 1990s, the computer processes and technology needed to access online information and communicate electronically were still highly complex and time-consuming, requiring an understanding of commands in software programming language.[11] What was needed to access the web came to be known as a web browser, and during the early years of the world wide web various browsers were developed at research and academic institutions across America and the United Kingdom.[12] The first commercial browser, Netscape, was developed in 1994 and in that year Bill Clinton's White House launched the first White House website.[13] By the end of 1994, over 20 million users were accessing the internet. By 1996, Microsoft's Internet Explorer 4.0 had overtaken Netscape as the clear winner of the browser wars with a third of the market share.[14]

The evolution of technology is a mega-trend today that no business can ignore. A brief tour of the evolution of computers illustrates the importance of keeping your eye on technological developments.

In 1948, IBM's Selective Sequence Electronic Calculator, which was to calculate the position of the moon for the 1969 Apollo mission to the moon, took up floor space of 25 feet by 40 feet. In 1976, Steve Wozniak and Steve Jobs created Apple 1, which sold at just over US$600.[15] In 1984, the first Apple Macintosh appeared, with a graphical interface – ie the data could be accessed by activating icons on the screen and navigation was by way of a device called a 'mouse'.[16] At around the same time, Microsoft released the first version of Windows, its own graphical interface. By the mid-1990s, you were also getting more bang for your buck when it came to computer processing chips, with Intel unveiling its Pentium chip at under US$1,000.[17]

The need for speed

Connection speed is the other significant factor in the online revolution. Connecting to the internet from the mid-1990s to around 2003 was generally via a dial-up modem and a telephone line. Connection speed was slow and the cost meant that most people used it for e-mail primarily and only surfed during off-peak periods. For the average user, sustained video and audio interaction was practically impossible.

And then along came broadband. The broadband story is similar across the globe, with the amount of take-up by consumers being directly linked to availability and cost. Across the European Union 25 per cent of all households were connected to the internet via broadband by 2006.[18] In Asia (excluding Japan), a survey of internet usage in 2006 revealed that 'broadband access continues to have a major impact on consumers' lives' with the highest broadband usage being in Korea, closely followed by Taiwan, Hong Kong, Singapore, Thailand and China.[19] In 2007, Hong Kong came top in a survey of the best cities in Asia for getting a broadband connection due to robust competition and web-enabled mobile phones.[20] In India, the home broadband market is growing while internet café access is slowing, with 23 million home users accessing the internet via broadband during 2007.[21] 'One of the reasons for this is due to the teledensity in these areas,' Tudor Aw, Digital Convergence Partner at management consultants KPMG, says. 'It is, of course, much more economically attractive for a service provider to invest in high quality broadband where teledensity is high than in rural areas. This is one of the perennial issues facing telecoms companies and governments – how do you address universal access in less dense regions?' A case in point is South Africa, where business leaders and communicators there have indicated to us that the lack of cheap, universal broadband is a factor in the slow growth of online engagement.

As we will see, there is a close correlation between the growth of broadband in the Asia-Pacific region and the rise of social media engagement in that region, with a number of countries such as South Korea, China, Singapore and Malaysia topping the charts of worldwide blog readers and blog creators.[22]

Which brings us to the rise of social media.

The rise of social media

Newsgroups and forums

Before the world wide web, scientists and researchers communicated over the internet via newsgroups (or forums). These newsgroups are online spaces where you can discuss particular subjects of mutual interest by posting questions and answers in a 'discussion thread'. Usenet,[23] established in 1980, was the forum on which Tim Berners-Lee announced in 1991 the project that became the world wide web.[24] Another historic announcement made on Usenet that year was the first mention of an open-source software project that was to become Linux,[25] posted by its creator Linus Torvalds:

> Hello everybody out there using minix –
> I'm doing a (free) operating system (just a hobby, won't be big and professional like gnu) for 386(486) AT clones. This has been brewing since april, and is starting to get ready. [26]

The characteristic of newsgroups and forums is that they facilitate discussion between peers around a common topic. Torvalds was sharing information with his research colleagues and asking for feedback.[27] He was not issuing a press release about his 'product' that would change the world.

For anyone coming new to social media, this principle of peer-to-peer communication is an important one to bear in mind. Blogs, the mainstay of social media today, evolved out of newsgroups. The ethic of peer-to-peer discussion is also woven into the culture of blogging and other social media. A top-down, hierarchical and formal tone when engaging in social media does not work and will not be well received.

Forums continue today and are used by many businesses as an extension of their websites' help pages, especially to address users' questions about a product. For example, on the Apple discussion forum, you can 'search for an answer, post your question, or answer other users' questions in the Apple Discussions community.'

Does your business or product need a forum section on its website? Some thoughts to consider:

- Just because you do not offer them a space to do that on your website does not mean that they are not already talking about your product elsewhere.
- You need to search online to see if your customers are discussing your product on the internet.
- If they are, then you need to monitor what they are saying and engage with them in whatever space they may be to address their issues.
- There would be advantages in drawing these customers to a forum on your website where your technical experts could actively participate.
- It would be important to train as well as empower those technical experts in the art of forum discussion – a skill which combines problem-solving and in-depth knowledge of technical details with a strong customer service ethic. This is especially important bearing in mind that your forum is able to offer added value to the customer's experience of your brand while bringing them back to your website to engage with your business.
- Forums need to be seen as a source of valuable customer feedback and a space to add value to products. Businesses that fail to monitor and participate positively in online forums about their products are missing an open invitation from their customers to engage and develop an ongoing relationship of trust and support.

Blogs

Justin Hall started writing online about his life and sharing his reflections in 1994 while he was an intern at *Wired* magazine and a student at Swarthmore College, Pennsylvania. He wrote about his alcoholic father and his sexual relationships with different partners. Every detail of his life appeared on his site, Links.net. Several years before Jorn Barger coined the word 'weblog',[28] Hall set the tone for what most people think blogging is all about and is credited by the *New York Times Magazine* as 'the founding father of personal blogging'.[29]

A blog is a website where individuals or groups can publish a running log of events, personal insights or other content which appears in reverse date order on the site. It is very easy to use and content can be published in a matter of minutes. It is different from a forum in that each contribution to a discussion thread in a forum is given equal weighting – you will see each contribution in equally weighted font and text styles – whereas on a blog, the main author's 'article' or post is given priority weighting through layout, design and text formatting – others may add their comments to the main post but those comments will be seen as subsidiary to the main item. In this way, blogs tend to have an 'authored' feel to them whereas forums are equivalent to discussion groups.

In 1999 Blogger.com launched its free blog creation platform.[30] Blogging exploded, and by 2004 there were 5 million blogs online, with 15,000 being added every day.[31] There are numerous free online blogging platforms including Wordpress.com and Live Journal as well as many self-hosted options. In 2007, a survey by Universal McCann[32] reported 170 million blogs worldwide with a global readership of 340 million people.

What kind of people blog? Well, blogging is about making a human connection. The blogger writes to share their lives and thoughts or knowledge with their readers. Their audience may be small – just their friends and family – or it may reach 10,000 unique visitors or more a day. The readers come back to read more because that blogger 'speaks to them'. While there are many blogs written by teenagers and tech geeks, blogs are increasingly written by women, professionals, experts, business people, literary types, political activists, financiers and more on topics that may range from eyewitness accounts[33] of events in the news through anthropology and psychology to the implications of the global financial crisis.

We will be exploring how and why ordinary people and businesses are using blogging in more detail in later chapters. For now, the question to consider is: If there are 340 million blog readers worldwide, many of whom are in the powerhouse economies of Asia and the leading first world economies – and likely to be within the demographic of the target market of your business – can you as a communications professional or business leader afford to ignore them?

Wikis

Wikipedia,[34.] the free online encyclopaedia[35] that can be edited by anyone in the world, is probably the most famous use of wiki technology. It was founded by Larry Sanger and Jimmy Wales in 2001. It is worth pausing to look back a few years to the origins of wiki technology. In 1995, Ward Cunningham, a computer programer in Portland, Oregon, developed the WikiWikiWeb,[36] an online site where he and his programing colleagues could share and edit information. He explains on his company's website 'I chose wiki-wiki as an alliterative substitute for quick and thereby avoided naming this stuff quick-web.'[37]

Cunningham discusses his design principles[38] online, including the importance of user participation, peer-to-peer engagement and information sharing: any reader may edit the wiki; it is about sharing 'information, knowledge, experience, ideas, views'; visitors to the wiki may interact and collaborate and also observe changes and updates; content may be reviewed by readers (developing from the peer review process in research fields). All these principles continue to permeate the culture of engagement in wikis but also throughout all the various social media platforms.

In particular, Cunningham writes, 'trust is the most important thing in a wiki. Trust the people, trust the process, enable trust-building. Everyone controls and checks the content. Wiki relies on the assumption that most readers have good intentions.' In other words, we assume that participants will act in good faith. The issue of trust will be coming up time and again throughout our journey through the cyberworld.

The world of social media is not much different from the world of social human beings in real life. As there are fraudsters and con artists in the real world, there will be those who play with trust and reliability online. Similarly, there will be those who like to pick a fight or an argument in any social setting, whether at the pub or on a wiki. Wherever 'we' are, there 'we' are also. How we manage such behaviours in the real world has relevance to the processes that can be set up to manage such behaviours online.

Multimedia

We explore online multimedia channels in more detail in Chapter 11. For now, we want to introduce you briefly to a handful of key players that have broadened the user's experience of social media beyond written text to images, video and audio.

Flickr was developed by a Canadian husband and wife team, Stewart Butterfield and Caterina Fake, almost by accident while developing another web-based project.[39] The site enables users to share their photos with the world or just their friends and family – and you don't even have to interface with a computer. Wherever you are in the world, you can upload photos to Flickr straight from your camera-phone via e-mail or MMS,[40] which will also automatically be published on your blog simultaneously.

Similarly, on the video-sharing site, YouTube – launched in 2005 – you can e-mail a video recorded on your video-enabled mobile phone straight onto the site, with simultaneous upload to your blog. Taking the sense of immediacy one step a further, in 2007, web start-up entrepreneur Justin Kan launched Justin.tv by spending several weeks with a portable webcam and batteries strapped to his head, streaming live video of his every moment (with toilet exceptions) onto the Justin.tv site.[41] Viewers could watch him sleep (126 people were logged on at one point) and they could chat to each other via a chat board on the site. Later the same year, a video-streaming site Qik.com launched, facilitating live, streamed video from your mobile phone onto your video 'channel' on the Qik site. Shortly afterwards 'Naked Conversations' author, Robert Scoble used Qik to stream live cellphone video interviews with technology leaders at the World Economic Forum 2008 at Davos, Switzerland. This technology is already having an enormous impact on journalism as well as business communications, as we shall see later.

On the audio front, podcasts are audio files that are uploaded onto a website and are useful in a business context for distributing audio interviews and talk radio-style programmes to your stakeholders. These can be hosted on your own website or on podcast hosting sites like Jellycast[42] in the United Kingdom. For immediacy, there are some sites like Gabcast.com where you can create a podcast by dialling a telephone number from any phone and leaving a voicemail message that will be automatically published as a podcast and uploaded onto your blog – for example, on The Amazing Outdoors Radio Network[43] a weekly Gabcast podcast, Nancy Seamons[44] phoned in her report while whitewater rafting in British Columbia, 2,300 miles from home.

A large part of the appeal of social media is its ability to connect you directly and immediately to your audience. The evolution of these multi-media tools is coming at a time when mobile phones are becoming more web-friendly in terms of functionality and cost. Watch this space – and when considering a social media strategy for your business, it is imperative that you consider multimedia and also, the implications of the shift towards mobile content delivery and creation.

Social networks

In 2007 Facebook, the social network for college students, opened up to the public in general. Older users in their 30s and 40s joined in droves, led by Silicon Valley high-tech professionals.[45] The social networking site was so successful that its founder Mark Zuckerberg, then 23, was offered US$1 billion by Yahoo! for the site – but famously, turned it down in order to retain control.[46]

Where a blog can be likened to an individual taking centre stage and giving a presentation at a conference, then responding to questions from the audience, a social network is more like the networking break after the session. You all mingle down on the floor, discussing topics of particular interest, exchanging business cards, introducing colleagues to new contacts, sharing snippets of your personal life like a snapshot of your kids from your wallet. A social network enables you to interact in a similar way with many other individuals from all over the world through online tools – your page shows who your friends are on the network, you can engage in discussions, display your contact details, upload photos, send multimedia messages and more.

The business social network, LinkedIn, has a purpose that is obvious to a business person. You can see who your contacts know and you can ask for an introduction. There is a section where users can upload their CV, so you can search for specialists who may be able to help you with a project. Giles Colborne, Managing Director of UK-based cxpartners, the web usability professionals, reports that when they were recruiting for a design specialist, his e-mail to his LinkedIn contacts brought in more relevant candidates in a shorter time than the company's regular specifications via recruitment agency.

But what about Facebook, where you can 'tickle' someone online, challenge someone to online Scrabble or take a movie quiz? What's the point of that? Well, what's the point of stopping for a quick chat about last night's football game as you pass a colleague on the way to the photocopier? At work, we are not just automatons who are there solely to work – we engage in human interactions, make friendships, share a joke. Through these small interactions, rapport and friendships are established and maintained. Social networks like Facebook help us make connections across physical space. Sometimes, you may not have anything meaningful to say to a friend or business colleague that would make it worth an e-mail or a phone call but sending them a virtual growing plant with a few words on Facebook may make them smile and let them know you're thinking of them. In the same way that you do not always discuss work with work colleagues or business associates, light-hearted social networks like Facebook enable light-hearted interactions which nonetheless can build rapport and strengthen real world relationships. All these small digital interactions have an incremental value in building and maintaining friendships online that can add to those relationships back in the real world – just like insignificant exchanges in our daily lives have been building human relationships and community for generations.

Instant messaging, VoIP and audio/video interaction

We would include instant messaging (IM) or chat and VoIP (voice over internet protocol) tools like Skype.com within the broad category of social media as such tools facilitate group as well as individual communication and can be integrated within blogs and social networks. IM allows real-time online communication between two or more users through typed text. Many businesses, especially those with global reach, are using IM as a productivity tool to complement e-mail – for example, IM can be more efficient than numerous e-mails for scheduling a meeting quickly.

Skype is probably one of the best known of the VoIP tools, offering free computer calls. You can make yourself available on your blog or social network profile page by showing your Skype status there.

Text-based chat boards can be embedded onto blogs so that users who are on the site at the same time can chat with each other on this publicly displayed board. There are audio tools such as MyChingo. com, which gives you the code to create a public audio message board on your site for visitors to leave an audio comment.

People want to connect – whether it's by text-based chat, sending a photo, singing a birthday greeting into their webcam or 'tickling' someone online: there is a tool that suits everyone. Their exponential popularity and the frivolous as well as serious ways they are being used points to the multi-layered way that we develop connections and friendships. Businesses and communicators who stay away from these tools and platforms are staying away from nurturing human connections with colleagues and customers and missing opportunities to build relationships.

Twitter

Once you've signed up at Twitter.com, you can send SMS text messages of up to 140 characters from your mobile phone to the Twitter platform, to be read on the public 'stream' or by only your friends and contacts. You can also update your Twitter stream from the web. Rather like a multi-group text messaging system, you can similarly receive your friends' updates on your mobile phone – whether they were sent from phones or the web. Twitter was developed by friends Biz Stone and Evan Williams (who had also co-founded Blogger.com a decade earlier), initially as an inhouse tool for their technology start-up team to keep in touch.

Multimedia is also converging on Twitter. You can send your Flickr photos and an audio message to your Twitter stream via TwitterGram. com. Silicon Valley-based French entrepreneur Loic Le Meur has lauched Seesmic.com, a video mashup with Twitter that posts your short webcam videos to Twitter. But the key to Twitter is that it is 'permission' based – people 'subscribe' to follow your 'stream' – so that from a communications perspective, it is a relationship-building tool rather than a 'push' marketing tool.

Later in the book, we will see how one travel company, 71miles. com, has made Twitter integral to its business model. For now, you might consider using Twitter in your business communications in a number of ways:

- Alert your Twitter subscribers to your relevant offline activities such as when you attend conferences – for example, 'I'm manning our stand at the Trade Journals Fair – come and say hello.'
- Share your blog posts with your subscribers as soon as they are posted online. 'Check out my article on car design on our blog – just posted!'
- Maintain your standing as an expert in your field. 'I've just been invited to speak at the Finance Conference in Seoul next month. The conference website is at XXX.'

- Twitter offers an opportunity to connect in real time with your subscribers on a peer-to-peer basis. '@johnreed Yes, I saw that article on house prices too. I agree that…', etc.

RSS feeds and Google Juice

RSS (really simple syndication) has revolutionized our interactions with social media – and, it might even be said, made social media possible. David Robertson, a web designer and partner at Out of the Trees,[47] explains 'It is a group of standardised formats for publishing content[48] and makes it easy for content aggregators to request the RSS feed from the site. The aggregator can then notify anyone who has subscribed to that feed that new content has appeared on your site.' Feed aggregators[49] are similar to your e-mail application but instead of e-mails coming into your Outlook or Hotmail inbox, you receive into your aggregator inbox fresh posts from the blogs and social media sites you have subscribed to.

RSS feeds give social media sites (whether text, audio, photos or video based) an edge over traditional, static HTML-based websites which are less frequently updated after the web designer has completed the job. Regardless of how well search engine optimized traditional websites may be, the problem is that the content is not refreshed regularly – for most businesses, once their website is up with brochure-style information about what they do and who they are, that's it for the next few years. If you are one of those businesses, this means that search results will rank your site highly based on only those specific keywords you've chosen.

Search engine optimization (SEO) is still relevant for helping your blog or social media site get noticed by the search engines, but social media optimization can add substantially to the results. By blogging regularly, for example, you are creating that fresh content loved by search engines. Fresh content on a range of issues around the area of your business means that people will find your site more easily even if they are not specifically searching for your target keywords – they may stumble on your site via one of your blog posts that may only be indirectly relevant to your business. In this way, you don't have to be slavishly tied to keywords as the only method to draw visitors to your site. Blogs also automatically archive your posts so that you can build up an online history of your company's achievements and events – so someone searching may find that old news item and remain on your site in order to explore what else you have to offer. The key here is in using social media to create a dynamic, regularly updated part of your site that links back to your main website in order to draw visitors into what your business has to offer.

Also, Robertson says that RSS feeds offer a number of advantages over the more traditional 'e-mail newsletter' approach, including greater privacy for your subscribers while enabling the business to gather reliable statistics about the number of subscribers as well as visitor behaviour on the social media site. Finally, Robertson adds, 'Whereas e-mails may well be viewed with images blocked or in plain text, RSS feeds enable multimedia elements to be included in the message, including images, audio and video.'

Is social media for everyone?

Social media is not for everyone, nor for every business. There may be good business reasons not to blog. Co-author Ooi gives an example: 'I consulted with a business that provides high-value, data-focused industry knowledge through a premium subscription monthly newsletter. The data is what is important for their clients. We concluded that there is very little that a blog with the personal opinions of those analysts could add. In fact, it might actually devalue the premium service. So although the CEO was keen to blog, I recommended that he should not.'

There may be practical issues, such as lack of time and uncertainty about your audience. If you do not have the time to engage in the social media space regularly and you are likely to have a dead blog on your site with the last entry dating back to last year, that looks even worse than not having a blog at all. You may not be sure who would want to read your blog or listen to your podcast and this is likely to give what you say an unfocused and uncertain quality, which could detract from people's perception of who you are and what your business is about.

As for social networks, many business people are starting to carry on conversations and connections online. Co-author Cambié was contacted via her Facebook profile after a presentation she gave in South Africa – it was one of the delegates who had heard her talk and wanted to discuss future speaking opportunities with her. A presence on a social network can make you more accessible, even if you don't spend a lot of time there.

So if social media is not for some people, who are the communicators and which are the businesses most suited to taking advantage of these tools? We think that social media can add a competitive edge to you and your business if:

- you enjoy discussing your views and ideas;
- you are passionate about your business, industry or area of expertise;
- you know who your customers and clients are and want to engage with them;
- you enjoy engaging with people anyway;
- you are curious about what people are talking about that is relevant for your business or industry;
- you are committed to improving your services or products and want user feedback;
- you value networking and take care to develop business and personal relationships.

Social media is an extension online of what you would normally be doing to grow your business or brand in the real world. It adds value by extending your normal reach to a much wider audience and can be a means for you to build up an easily accessible archive of what you and your business stand for.

Notes

1. Facebook Hatching Egg application, http://www.facebook.com/applications/Hatching_Eggs/6702295930.
2. Derived from internet-based telephony application Skype, see skype.com.
3. Derived from internet search engine Google, see google.com.
4. Googling Oneself is More Popular, *New York Times*, 16 December 2007, http://www.nytimes.com/aponline/us/AP-Personal-Internet-Searches.html?ex=1355461200&en=9190da8e36b78507&ei=5088&partner=rssnyt&emc=rss.
5. Estonia, UK, France, Holland and the US State of Hawaii, *Wired*, 3 February 2007, http://www.wired.com/politics/security/news/2007/03/72846.
6. blackberry.com.
7. Tim Berners-Lee entry on Wikipedia, http://64.233.183.104/search?q=cache:q-wZqPvqnZcJ:en.wikipedia.org/wiki/Tim_Berners-Lee+WHEN+was+the+first+website&hl=en&ct=clnk&cd=1&gl=uk&client=firefox-a.

8. Barry M Leiner, Vinton G Cerf, David D Clark, Robert E Kahn, Leonard Kleinrock, Daniel C Lynch, Jon Postel, Larry G Roberts and Stephen Wolff, A Brief History of the Internet, The Internet Society, 10 December 2003, http://www.isoc.org/internet/history/brief. shtml#Transition.

9. Tim Berners-Lee, The World Wide Web: A Very Short Personal History, World Wide Web Consortium, http://www.w3.org/People/Berners-Lee/ShortHistory.

10. World Wide Web Summary, World Wide Web Consortium, http://www. w3.org/History/19921103-hypertext/hypertext/WWW/Summary. html.

11. What is a Web Browser?, wisegeek.com, http://www.wisegeek.com/ what-is-a-web-browser.htm.

12. Some examples include ViolaWWW, developed by Pei Wei at the University of California, Berkeley in May 1992, Lynx at the University of Kansas and Arena by Dave Raggett at Hewlett-Packard in Bristol, UK, in 1993, as well as Cello by Tom Bruce at the University of Cornell.

13. The Clinton Presidential Library and Museum website archive, clinton library.gov, http://www.clintonlibrary.gov/archivesearch.html.

14. Web Browser History, livinginternet.com, http://www.livinginternet. com/w/wi_browse.htm.

15. The Obsolete Technology Website, oldcomputers.net, http://old computers.net/applei.html.

16. The Obsolete Technology Website, oldcomputers.net, http://old computers.net/macintosh.html.

17. Chronology of Personal Computers, University of Brighton, burks.bton. ac.uk, http://burks.bton.ac.uk/burks/pcinfo/hardware/comphist /comp1995.htm.

18. European and Broadband Telecom Survey Released, govtech.com, 25 August 2006, http://www.govtech.com/gt/100718?topic=117671.

19. Home Networking Trend Among Internet Users in Asia, internetworld stats.com, 30 January 2007, http://www.internetworldstats.com/ usage/use010.htm.

20. Lawrence Casiraya, HK Tops Broadband Survey of Asian Cities, Manila Ranks 19th, Inquirer.net, 21 June 2007, http://newsinfo.inquirer.net/ breakingnews/infotech/view_article.php?article_id=72591.

21. Swati Prasad, Broadband Flows into Indian Homes, zdnetasia.com, 17 August 2007, http://www.zdnetasia.com/news/communications/0,3 9044192,62031023,00.htm.

22. Power to the People: Tracking the Rise of Social Media – Wave 2, Universal McCann survey, May 2007.

23. http://www.usenet.com/newToUsenet.htm.

24. http://groups.google.com/group/alt.hypertext/msg/395f282a67a 1916c.

25. Linux is an operating system that is freely distributed and known for its functionality and robustness. It is used in computer systems around

the world, including those of the governments of Switzerland and Japan, the Swedish Armed Forces, BMW, Hyundai and Qantas. See http://www.linux.org/info/.

26. http://groups.google.com/group/comp.os.minix/msg/2194d2532 68b0a1b.

27. See Torvald's posting, complete with spelling mistakes and personal messages, http://groups.google.com/group/comp.os.minix/browse_thread/thread/e3df794a2bce97da/2194d253268b0a1b? #2194d253268b0a1b.

28. Robert Wisdom on the Street, *Wired*, July 2005, http://www.wired.com/wired/archive/13.07/posts.html?pg=6.

29. Jeffrey Rosen, Your Blog or Mine? *New York Times Magazine*, 19 December 2004, http://www.nytimes.com/2004/12/19/magazine/19PHENOM.html?_r=1&oref=login&pagewanted=all&position=&oref=slogin.

30. Clive Thompson, Timeline of the History of Blogging, *New York Times Magazine*, 13 February 2006, http://nymag.com/news/media/15971/.

31. Jeffrey Rosen, Your Blog or Mine? *New York Times Magazine*, 19 December 2004, http://www.nytimes.com/2004/12/19/magazine/19PHENOM.html?_r=1&oref=login&pagewanted=all&position=&oref=slogin.

32. Social Media – Power to the People, Universal McCann, May 2007, http://www.universalmccann.com/page_attachments/0000/0017/Social_Media_-_Power_to_the_People.pdf.

33. For example, Baghdad Burning, http://riverbendblog.blogspot.com/, which was published as a book by Feminist Press and went on to win the third prize of the Letter Ullyses Award for the Art of Reportage and was shortlisted for the Samuel Johnson prize for non-fiction, http://www.feministpress.org/book/?GCOI=55861100869560.

34. http://www.wikipedia.org/.

35. http://en.wikipedia.org/wiki/Wikipedia.

36. http://c2.com/cgi/wiki?WikiWikiWeb.

37. http://c2.com/cgi/wiki?WikiHistory.

38. http://c2.com/cgi/wiki?WikiDesignPrinciples.

39. Flickr of Idea on a Gaming Project Led to Photo Website, *USA Today*, 27 February 2006, http://www.usatoday.com/tech/products/2006-02-27-flickr_x.htm.

40. Multi-media Messaging Service.

41. http://www.fusionview.co.uk/2007/04/live-tv-show-all-about-the-life-of-justin/.

42. http://www.jellycast.co.uk.

43. http://www.amazingoutdoorsradio.com/.

44. http://www.gabcast.com/index.php?a=episodes&b=play&id=7266&cast=37927.

45. Fogeys Flock to Facebook, *BusinessWeek*, 6 August 2007, http://www.businessweek.com/technology/content/aug2007/tc2007085_051788.htm?campaign_id=rss_as.
46. How Mark Zuckerberg Turned Facebook into the Hottest Platform, *Wired*, 6 September 2007, http://www.wired.com/techbiz/startups/news/2007/09/ff_facebook.
47. http://outofthetrees.co.uk/.
48. If you are interested in the details of the coding and the history of the development of RSS feeds, you can read more at the site of the Berkman Center for Internet & Society at Harvard Law School, http://cyber.law.harvard.edu/rss/rss.html.
49. Check out Bloglines.com and Google Reader.

7 Social media as a part of life

Shopping

Over 75 per cent of consumers surveyed by BurstMedia[1] in 2005 use the internet as a shopping resource. The majority of them use it as their primary source of information when evaluating and comparing products. This is true across all income brackets, with greater usage amongst those of a higher-income bracket.

Nielson's Global Consumer Survey[2] in 2007 reported that:

- Recommendation by other consumers is the most powerful selling tool, especially in the Asia-Pacific, particularly in Hong Kong (93 per cent) and Taiwan (91 per cent).
- Consumer-generated media such as blogs were found to be a reliable source of information in this region as well as in the USA, with 81 per cent of South Korean and 76 per cent of Taiwanese respondents trusting online consumer opinions.
- Globally, online consumer opinions ranked third (61 per cent) in the list of most trusted media, following on the heels of personal recommendations (78 per cent) and newspapers (63 per cent).

The smart move for any business is to be there engaging online with these consumers in the trusted medium of blogs and consumer-generated sites and to do so in an authentic way. Social media strategy consultant B L Ochman[3] illustrates these statistics nicely with a story on her blog, whatsnextblog.com, about her sister shopping for a Miele vacuum cleaner:

My sister called this morning to say 'Help! My vacuum died... what kind of vacuum do you have?' she asked. 'A Miele,' I told her. While we were talking, she read vacuum ratings on ePinions.[4]

'Wow!' she said, several Miele are top rated. Two of my friends recommended them also. But they're really expensive.'

Actually, I told her, they're not. Some of the best models are under $400. They're a hell of a lot cheaper than Electrolux, which isn't so great any more. Sure enough, when she compared prices online, she said she'd read more online reviews, checked more price comparison sites, and then order a vacuum.

By the time she went to Miele's website, she was very close to a decision. She didn't go there first because, like most customers, she didn't expect to find credible information there. She thought the company website wouldn't be objective. She looked at it because she wanted to be sure she'd seen all the vacuum models they make so she could go find information about them on other sites. Like so many people shopping online, she trusted the word of strangers far more than she trusted the company.'

Millennials

In the 1980s it was Generation X, and the 1990s had Generation Y. The generation in their twenties during the first decade of the 21st century have been dubbed the Millennials. Studies[5] on the Millennials refer to a number of defining characteristics of this generation: they have grown up in the information age, and for them using online and social networking tools is second nature; they are highly tolerant of others' diversity and expect the same broad view of others; they value fairness and truth and are concerned about ethical and environmental issues; they prize their individuality and want to be heard.

These twenty-somethings (and also some early thirty-somethings and young adults – the nickname bleeds over the borders of the twenties) are fully engaged online and conduct their personal and business relationships via:

- IM (instant messaging or chat) and social network messaging systems (like writing on someone's Facebook wall)
- e-mail and mobile text messaging;
- phone calls and F2F (face-to-face) get-togethers.

Social media and social networking are not options for this generation; they are a part of life.

Ernst & Young, the global accountancy firm, have a Facebook page[6] to help them fill the 5,500[7] annual intern vacancies. Among the postings on the page, we found a video about the qualities for success at the firm; a weekly poll (this week: 'When considering whether to accept a new job, which is most important to you? Fun colleagues/ interesting work/high salary/career path/lifestyle'); answers to key questions about what it is like to work at Ernst & Young; comments on the Wall from applicants, recruits, Ernst & Young staff – and anyone else.

Dan Black, the firm's Director of Campus Recruiting, explained on BBC Radio 4's *World of Business* that the Facebook page was a space for new recruits to ask questions but also to get to know each other before they started their jobs. They have also organized house shares and social events via their Facebook connections independently of input from Ernst & Young. This is a smart move in more ways than one:

- By fostering a community even before the new recruits start on their first day at work, the firm gives their new staff some powerful messages about helping each other, teaming up, networking and being part of the Ernst & Young cultural family.
- As for negative comments on the Wall, Black says in a *Business Week*[8] interview, 'We knew going in we would get feedback that wasn't exactly positive.' Not censoring comments also works in their favour in another way: it gives their site integrity so that it is known as a place to go for real information, not spin, about the firm.

The third age

Every morning in a quiet suburb of Adelaide, 87-year-old Mrs Hoh[9] sets off after breakfast for her walk down to the local library. She migrated to Australia to live with her son and his family after her husband died a few years ago, leaving her home town in Malaysia where she had had a network of relations and friends. She likes the pleasant walk in the subtropical cool, and when she arrives at the library she logs on to one of the many public computers there and catches up with e-mails from her family and friends back in Malaysia. She signs on to the family site on Yahoo! Groups, set up by one of the extended family in Sydney. There on the group, she exchanges recipes with her sister in America and picks up news that a cousin in New Zealand is going in for an operation on his gall bladder. It is through this family group site that news of births, marriages and deaths has been shared with the extended family network of around 200 members, living in different parts of the world.

Of over 215 million social networkers, 20 million would be over the age of 50 by the end of 2007, according to research by Deloitte as reported in a *Newsweek* article on baby boomers and online networking.[10] Deloitte sees them as the 'future of networking' and *Newsweek* predicted 'Silver surfers could prove to be an even more coveted online group than their teenage predecessors.' It is not just the baby boomers[11] in the USA, but also those of the same age in other parts of the world, especially the Asia-Pacific, who have the time and the money to spend online.

Eons.com was created by Jeff Taylor, founder of Monster.com, the online job marketplace, shortly after his 50th birthday. As *BusinessWeek*[12] puts it, 'Anyone 50 and over can sign up for Eons and share post-retirement dreams with other members, blog about their dating experiences or trips to Africa, and page through and contribute photos and memories to a database of 77 million obituaries.' Another website, Boomj.com, calls itself the lifestyle and social network for Baby Boomers and Generation Jones. In addition to the usual pages for shopping, finance and health that many baby-boomer-focused websites have, there are also member-generated blogs and videos as well as a space for members to create their own groups.

Co-author Ooi has found that many of the active readers of her cross-cultural blog FusionView.co.uk are over-50s with connections in the Asia-Pacific region, especially Malaysia and Singapore. 'They have a global outlook, whether they are still based in Asia or have migrated to the West. There is particular interest in cross-cultural issues and also heritage stories from the past, such as the childhood reminiscences of my father who has written about life during the war years in Malaya', Ooi says.

Some seniors are encouraged to share stories about the past by younger members of their family who want to learn more about their family and cultural heritage. There are enough of these blogs for them to be known collectively as 'legacy blogs'. One example is 'The Life of Riley'[13] by Olive Riley, who was aged 107 in 2007, and which records stories about her younger days in Sydney and the outback.[14]

While many businesses are hotly pursuing the Millennials, it is worth remembering the quiet trend of silver surfing:

- This group, especially those with connections to Asia, are not necessarily only interested in the stereotypical 'old age pensioner' topics like health, travel and finance.
- They have a global perspective and have a diverse range of interests in art, culture and society as well as the time for philosophical musings. Through personal blogging and social networking as well as the time and resources for global travel, today's seniors are connecting naturally with an international network of friends and family as a matter of course.
- Engaging with them online will require tapping into wider global and cultural resources than may have been the case for previous generations of seniors.

News and politics

According to data from the Audit Bureau, the downward trend of newspaper circulation in the USA is largely due to readers preferring to find their news and entertainment via the internet.[15] The data show a 2.6 per cent decline in a six-month period during 2007. In the past 20 years, newspaper sales have been on the decrease anywy, owing to other media such as cable television, but the trend has accelerated since the rise of the internet as a source of information. For example:

- During the US presidential campaign that began in 2007, a Pew survey found that the number of Americans who regularly learnt about the campaign from the internet had more than doubled since the previous campaign in 2000.[16] The numbers of those who followed the campaign via local TV and daily newspapers were down by up to 13 points.
- In particular, more young people than older groups are going online to find information about the campaign, with the video sharing site YouTube and social networking sites such as Facebook and MySpace playing a notable role.
- Significantly, more than half (52 per cent) of web users 'came across' campaign news while online doing something else – that is, they did not go online with the intention solely to seek out political news but happened across the information while they were in the online space.

The picture in Asia and Africa is slightly different – for now. Growing prosperity and better education in these regions have led to an increase in newspaper circulation, according to a survey by the World Association of Newspapers.[17] This survey also indicates a growth in newspaper titles, apparently contradicting the surveys finding a downward trend in circulation. But dig a bit deeper and you will find that the proliferation of new titles is a sign of fragmenting audiences and that it is free newspapers that are driving this growth, while paid-for papers are declining. Roy Ma of Pure Media in Hong Kong commented in *Asia Sentinel*[18] that Asia's high-tech cities such as Hong Kong and Singapore are three to five years behind the West in internet growth. According to *Asia Sentinel*:

- These Asian cities are already seeing an increase in free daily newspapers threatening paid-for broadsheets.
- Anxiety about the increasing migration of readers and advertisers online is driving some international papers like the *International Herald Tribune* to develop multiple channels of news delivery including a mobile platform as well as an online presence.

Note also that:

- Mobile distribution is likely to become increasingly relevant, in particular as technology enables faster and more affordable web browsing and data reception.
- Most significantly, the younger generations who have always lived with computers and the internet are growing up and their habits of looking to the internet as a resource are already driving the shift away from old ways of news and information distribution.
- For communicators, whether in the field of business or politics, being able to tap into this growing demographic through online engagement is going to become increasingly essential.

Celebrity through personal expression

We have seen from a survey by Universal McCann[19] that there are 170 million blogs worldwide with a global readership of 340 million people. The survey reports that:

- China is the leading market for social media adoption, driven by the desire for personal expression and consumer-generated media.

- Blogging is growing in Asia overall, with South Korea following close on China's heels, while Thailand, Malaysia and the Philippines show fastest growth for blogging.
- In Asia the focus of blogs is on personal content, whereas in the USA and Europe blogs have tended to discuss cultural, lifestyle and political issues.
- The reasons for the huge take-up of personal blogging in China are that it is the safest topic (as discussion of political and social issues is disapproved of); blogging is a way for a generation of only children to connect with their peers; and it is an opportunity for self-expression never before experienced in Chinese culture.
- Overall in Asia, social networks such as Cyworld and Bokee are built around blogging, encouraging blogging as an essential part of online engagement on these platforms. These virtual spaces and the internet in general facilitate a freedom of self-expression and non-conformity in contrast to the hierarchical structure of Asian society, and many Asians are enjoying this new-found liberation.

We cannot hope to give a full account of 170 million blogs in this short book but a sampling of bloggers who have come to prominence include (in no particular order):

- In Iraq, the anonymous Baghdad Burning[20] blog, chronicling daily life in Baghdad in postwar Iraq, shot to international fame and has been published as a book.[21]
- In Tanzania, photo-journalist Issa Michuzi is known as the country's top blogger, writing in Kizaromo, his mother tongue.
- In Singapore, 'mr. brown', the pseudonym for journalist Lee Kin Mun, is famed for his satiricial podcast, the 'mr. brown podcast', and blog.[22]
- In the United Kingdom, London-based paramedic Tom Reynolds became known when his blog Random Acts of Reality[23] was published in book form as *Blood, Sweat and Tea.*[24]
- In Malaysia, Kenny Sia[25] has become a celebrity blogger while still maintaining his day job in IT management. He blogs about his personal life and satirizes Malaysian life and politics with a crude humour that is typically Malaysian and just this side of bad taste. In 2008, he was one of the judges on a Malaysian online reality TV show, *Malaysian Dreamgirl,*[26] alongside other local 'A-list' celebrities. All this within three years of starting his blog 'to chronicle the drastic changes over [a] tumultous period of his life'.[27]

- In the USA, 'A-list' bloggers – the celebrities of the blogosphere – who have gained their status through their blogs being amongst the Top 100 blogs as ranked[28] by Technorati have generally tended to be the early adopters from the IT or marketing world or based in Silicon Valley such as Robert Scoble (Microsoft), Steve Rubel (Edelman) and Jason Calacanis (Silicon Valley Reporter). Their blogs focus on social media and technology trends and their opinions lead the cutting edge debates on these issues.
- In France, blogger and entrepreneur Loic Le Meur came to greater prominence after being invited to join Nicolas Sarkozy's team,[29] advising on how to use social media for the presidential campaign.
- Tila Tequila[30] was just a small-time model before she arrived in MySpace in 2003. Since then, she has gathered over 2 million[31] 'friends' (as at 2007, and counting) and launched a career on the back of those millions of 'friends' as a singer (you can buy her self-published music via iTunes), actress (a cameo in a movie) and entrepreneur (selling Tila memorabilia). MTV signed her up in 2007 to host her own bisexual dating show.

So, how might personal expression through social media work for business? One way to approach this question is to look at an example of how NOT to do it. A corporate communicator shared this story with us. She admitted from the start that she had little experience of social media and had a fairly low opinion of it as a corporate communications tool. She was dismayed that the chief executive of her company wanted to blog. She was convinced that he had nothing to say and would not be able to sustain a regular blog. So she told him to write a personal paper-based journal daily to try out how he might like it, since in her mind writing a journal was exactly like writing a blog. He tried it for three days and gave up, proving to both of them that blogging was not for him. However, here's where we think she missed a great opportunity:

- Blogging is not at all like writing a journal, and in our view she had set her boss up to fail. Blogging is a personal expression in public and it is the feedback from a blogger's audience, whether in the form of comments on the blog or through personal interaction, that gives the blog energy and momentum.
- The relevance of a blog comes from writing for an audience and responding to what that audience is interested in.

- There is no imperative to blog daily or when one has nothing to say – consistency and regularity (eg once a week or once a month) can be as effective as high frequency.
- For this communicator, she lost an opportunity to leverage her CEO's enthusiasm to increase his public profile as a thought leader in his industry. Through the personal expression of his expertise and passion for his business made in public he could have created a fresh and authentic way of communicating with his business's stakeholders.

Is a social media strategy part of your business's life?

Someone told us a great story. There was this guy who had dropped his wallet in the street. It was late at night and very dark. But luckily, there was a street lamp glowing in one part of the street just by the corner store so he was able to look for his wallet. Only he couldn't see it within the pool of light even though he searched for ages. The owner of the corner store, as he was closing up for the night, said to the guy, 'You've been looking for something here for hours now. Haven't you found it yet?' The guy replies 'No, I haven't. I dropped it over the other side of the street but it's dark there. I'm looking over here 'cos the light is over here.'

If many of your stakeholders and customers are engaging in social media, then you need to be over on their side of the street, too. If that part of the street is a dark void for you, then it's time to up your skills or bring into your team those with experience of that side of the street to help you integrate social media into your overall marketing and PR strategies.

Looking ahead at the changing landscape of communication:

- Social media may not be for everyone but you need to have an understanding of it to be able to offer your business a full assessment of whether it is for that business.
- Even if, after a 360 degree review, you decide it's not for your business, you need to keep a watching brief to monitor new developments in the social media landscape so you can include its impact in regular reviews of your overall communications strategy.

- With the rise of social media engagement globally in both East and West, it is becoming more and more relevant for businesses that wish to engage with their international stakeholders to monitor trends and opinions in these social media spaces at a worldwide level.
- You want to be the communicator who is ahead of the curve, positioning your company as a trusted voice, engaging in a relevant way with the Millennials or capturing the imagination of well-off seniors and developing your CEO's stature as an opinion leader in his or her industry.

Notes

1. Burstmedia Insights, burstmedia.com, 1 September 2007, http://www.burstmedia.com/assets/newsletter/items/2005_09_01.pdf.
2. Word of Mouth the Most Powerful Selling Tool, Nielson Global Survey, 1 October 2007, http://www.nielsen.com/media/2007/pr_071001.html.
3. How Real People Shop Online, whatsnextblog.com, February 2008, http://www.whatsnextblog.com/archives/2008/02/how_real_people_shop_online_now.asp.
4. Epinions, http://www.epinions.com/Vacuums/skp_~1/dl_~1/adv_search_~1/sort_~rating/pp_~1/sort_dir_~des?search_string=vacuums.
5. http://www.merrillassociates.com/topic/2005/05/call-them-gen-y-or-millennials-they-deserve-our-attention/; http://www.onrec.com/content2/news.asp?ID=15922; http://www.nasrecruitment.com/TalentTips/NASinsights/GenerationY.pdf.
6. http://www.facebook.com/group.php?gid=2204439307.
7. Ernst & Young Becomes First Employer to use Facebook, College Recruiter.com, January 2008, http://www.collegerecruiter.com/web log/2007/01/ernst_young_bec.php.
8. The Best Places to Launch a Career, *BusinessWeek*, 13 September 2007, http://www.businessweek.com/careers/content/sep2007/ca2007 0913_595536_page_3.htm.
9. Her name and personal details have been changed for privacy reasons.
10. Emily Flynn Vencat, Netting Friends Online, *Newsweek*, 15 January 2007, http://www.newsweek.com/id/56570.
11. The generation born between 1945 and 1960.
12. MySpace for Baby Boomers, *BusinessWeek*, 16 October 2006, http://www.businessweek.com/magazine/content/06_42/b4005117.htm?chan=smallbiz_smallbiz+index+page_technology.

13. http://www.allaboutolive.com.au/.

14. Julia Harris, The World's Oldest Blogger, ABC Western Queensland, 27 March 2007, http://www.abc.net.au/westqld/stories/s1881943. htm?backyard.

15. Newspaper Circulation off 2.6 Per Cent; Some Count Web Readers, *USA Today*, 5 November 2007, http://www.usatoday.com/tech/ webguide/internetlife/2007-11-05-newspaper-circulation_N.htm.

16. Internet's Broader Role in Campaign 2008, Pew Research Center, 11 January 2008, http://www.pewinternet.org/pdfs/Pew_MediaSources_ jan08.pdf.

17. Newspaper Growth Defies Conventional Wisdom, World Association of Newspapers, 6 February 2007, http://www.wan-press.org/article12949. html.

18. Are Asian Newspapers Under Siege? *Asia Sentinel*, 9 February 2007, http://www.asiasentinel.com/index.php?option=com_content&task =view&id=370&Itemid=32.

19. Social Media: Power to the People, Universal McCann, May 2007, http://www.universalmccann.com/index.html?_porousLink=_ regionStr*global$_idStr*knowledge___news_social_networking.

20. http://riverbendblog.blogspot.com/.

21. http://www.amazon.com/Baghdad-Burning-Girl-Blog-Iraq/ dp/1558614893.

22. http://www.mrbrown.com.

23. http://randomreality.blogware.com/.

24. http://www.amazon.co.uk/dp/1905548230?tag=randomactsofr-21&c amp=1406&creative=6394&linkCode=as1&creativeASIN=1905548230 &adid=1ATX704FESKVKWQQZZ7J&.

25. www.kennysia.com.

26. http://www.malaysiandreamgirl.tv/.

27. http://en.wikipedia.org/wiki/Kenny_Sia.

28. The ranking, briefly, is based on the number of other sites and blogs that link to a blog, which indicates its 'authority' – the more blogs link to that one blog, the more that blog is considered an authority and the higher it goes in the ranking. The premise is based on the way that academic capital is ranked by the number of citations that a thesis appears in – the more a paper is cited, the more it and its author are considered authorities: Noam Chomsky's works are more likely to be cited by other academics than an essay by an undergraduate, so Chomsky is considered the greater authority.

29. http://www.loiclemeur.com/notes/2007/04/loc_le_meur_bio.html.

30. Tila Tequila, *Time* magazine, 26 December 2006, http://www.time. com/time/magazine/article/0,9171,1570728,00.html.

31. http://techdigest.tv/2007/09/myspace_star_ti.html.

8 Authenticity and trust

Who can you trust?

The Edelman Trust Barometer 2008 shows that despite global economic uncertainty, war and terrorism, there is a 'generally improving mood of trust'.[1] The Edelman Trust Barometer is an annual survey by the global public relations firm, Edelman, on trust and credibility. In the context of social media, the key issues the survey covers are:

- In spite of financial scandals, trust in business remains high – tying with trust in non-governmental organizations (NGOs) and coming in higher than trust in governments. However, in China trust in companies is at an all time low at 54 per cent.
- At the same time, people trust people like themselves – 'people like me' remains high on the trust barometer around the world together with experts like academics and industry analysts. Such trusted peers are defined by common interests and common political beliefs, rather than geographical location.
- Word of mouth was found by the survey to be a credible source of information as well as influential in sharing perceptions and emotions about such information.[2]

The trust survey also found another critical factor in the changing face of influence. People around the world share information about companies, first and foremost with their friends and family and only then with their professional networks and co-workers – for example, friends came in first in Asia (73 per cent) and Europe (75 per cent), while in North America family was first (82 per cent) whereas in Latin America, business and personal connections were more evenly distributed at around 73 per cent each. Many of these people are online much of the day and comfortably use e-mail and peer-sharing social media tools – critical paths of information flow across personal and business networks are sending links via e-mail, sharing bookmarks using social bookmarking sites like delicious and StumbleUpon.com, as well as sharing videos and photos via YouTube.com and Flickr.com. The question for communicators here is: what are you doing to make it easier for people to share information about your company via such means?

The trust survey included 'young opinion elites' – college-educated, high-earning professionals who are media and policy engaged, aged between 25 and 34. This group are on their way to becoming the leaders of the future. Note some of the key characteristics of this group:

- They are likely to use more information sources than the older generation, and they are likely to spread their opinions about companies on the web.
- They also engage throughout the day on blogs, forums, social networks and wikis online as well as garnering information from traditional sources such as print and broadcast media.

The Edelman report advises 'Share your content with your employees, passionate consumers, and bloggers, allowing them to co-create, repurpose, and improve their knowledge through dialogue. Change your tone from one that pronounces to one that invites participation, ceding some control in return for credibility.'

The Edelman survey also states boldly that in Asia, new media is no longer new and is now part of the mainstream media. Consider the following:

- Broadband access, as we have seen, has been instrumental in this evolution and social media in China in particular has taken off as a new forum for self-expression and social commentary.
- Traditional media remains highly trusted in Asia and also across the world but trust in social media is also very high, especially in countries like China where other media is tightly controlled.
- For businesses aiming to engage with Asian consumers and markets, a presence in the world of social media is going to become an essential part of their strategy to take advantage of this development.

Tim Gingrich, marketing services executive at Weber Shandwick Asia Pacific, says 'Chinese society places a strong emphasis on relationships. It may be some time before a poke on Facebook replaces a pot of green tea as the preferred method of establishing relations. But the convenience and novelty of social media is nevertheless making powerful inroads among Chinese, especially youth. The internet, as it is doing for young people all over the world, is allowing Chinese youth to socialize with peers who share the same interest rather than the same geography.'

Our view is that where blogging and other social media are being used in Asia primarily for personal expression and informal social connection, there are prospects for those companies who can step into the social media landscape in Asia to engage authentically in culturally appropriate ways. Business blogging has not yet taken off in the same way as it has in the West, and the lack of competition in Asia, in our view, leaves this arena wide open for well-conceived social media engagement to succeed and for any such businesses to gain first-mover advantage.

Being one of us

A Malaysian blogger who blogs for personal enjoyment as well as for professional reasons illustrates how social media can be used successfully in Asia. Eric Forbes is the personable young editor at MPH Group Publishing, one of Malaysia's leading local publishers, which is affiliated to MPH Bookstores, a chain of established bookshops throughout Malaysia. MPH Publishing was set up in 2006 to encourage local writing and homegrown authors. He started his blog Eric Forbes' Book Addict's Guide to Good Books[3] a year before joining MPH, mainly for personal pleasure as he wanted to share his love of books and good writing. In addition to book reviews, he gives advice about writing and getting published in the Malaysian market as well as blogging about bad writing and the talentless but ambitious 'wannabe' authors he comes across. He told us, 'I had no idea that a blog could actually be a vital component in the overall marketing plan of a company. When I joined the MPH, I decided to see how my blog could be part of a formal business strategy. That's when I started organizing the MPH Breakfast Club for LitBloggers to engage Malaysian bloggers with a passion for books and the reading life.'

Co-author Ooi was invited to speak at the inaugural Breakfast Club in February 2007, alongside local poet Sharanya Mannivannan. Ooi recalls, 'The invitation grew directly out of the friendships I had made with Eric and with blogger and creative writing teacher Sharon Bakar through our blogs. We had been reading each other's blogs and commenting as well as e-mailing each other, discussing books and writing for some months and when I told them I was going to be visiting Kuala Lumpur, they invited me to the LitBlogger event.' Many of the prolific local literary bloggers attended as well as a number of Malaysian writers, including Man Booker Prize longlisted author Tan Twan Eng. The event was publicized beforehand on the blogs as well as in the print media, with blogger Kenny Mah[4] spontaneously designing a banner for the event that was virally distributed across the Malaysian blogosphere. Banners and posters for display on blogs have since become a regular feature of the literary and arts scene in Kuala Lumpur, many designed voluntarily by local bloggers. After the event, reviews of it appeared in numerous blogs around Kuala Lumpur.

Forbes says that since that first event, 'the Breakfast Club is now a monthly fixture on the Malaysian literary landscape and the MPH Group of Companies has definitely experienced a surge in book sales and brand recognition. However, it is vital that we are always on our toes because every false move will be observed and discussed on blogs.' He views return on investment for this active engagement with local bloggers as long term in nature but adds 'We found that the returns on investment are also quite immediate. You do get immediate feedback from the blogging community on how they perceive the company and every move it makes.'

At the event, Ooi was able to observe first hand the power of authentic social networking online and offline. Forbes' blog is well respected and enjoyed by the local litbloggers as well as the reading public. He is clearly regarded as a local expert on publishing, writing and high-quality literature and has become widely known through his blog. In person, he is approachable and unpretentious, reflecting the style and tone of his blog, and he makes himself available to the writers and readers attending the events. He is 'a person like them', a passionate book lover, but also acknowledged as a literary authority, in part because of his blog. You can see the respect for him in those attending the events, but at the same time they value his being 'one of us'.

An interesting by-product of Forbes' and also other litbloggers' enthusiasm for literature and writing is the boom in local Malaysian literary publishing in the last few years. When Ooi's UK-published novels came out in 1998 and 2000, she was only one of a handful of Malaysian-born writers published overseas and the literary scene in Kuala Lumpur was virtually non-existent. Since then, blogging has taken off in a big way in Malaysia, with the literary bloggers forming a real offline network as well as socializing via their blogs online, as we have seen. The LitBlogger events have kick-started a vibrant debate about the quality of Malaysian writing as well as issues around postcolonial literature. Other literary events, such as 'Readings' run by Sharon Bakar, have also been thriving both on the blogs and in trendy venues around Kuala Lumpur. Would-be writers encourage each other and enterprising young publishers have been forming new imprints to showcase local short stories and essays. Many new young writers have added their works to the body of Malaysian writing and a few more have been published overseas.

The key to success here has been strong personal networks, as has always been the case in Asia, further strengthened by social media. Learning points from this litbloggers' case study might be:

- The Malaysians mix personal stories and animated debate in their blogs and you will find literally hundreds of comments to many bloggers' posts, mostly from people they already know. When there is a malicious comment, many of the community rally round to defend the blogger, much as friends would do in a real-world dispute.[5]

- To engage in such a social media space, businesses need to focus on building their personal networks through trusted representatives prepared to engage in the way that Eric Forbes has done.

- Using offline events also builds trust and relationships, especially if they offer opportunities for direct involvement by those in the network – many litbloggers have been invited to read and speak at the KL events, signalling their status alongside established and published authors.

- The artwork for publicizing the events grew up spontaneously and such energy can most likely be harnessed and rewarded in the long term through commissions or competitions.

- Most importantly, MPH and Forbes treat the litbloggers as an essential part of the publicity, events and literary scene – it shows in how they engage with them and it shows in the results.

The Goliath problem

When you find things written in a public space about your company that you consider to be untrue, inaccurate or heavily biased against you and you have the opportunity to freely edit it to correct these problems, you should just go ahead and make those corrections, right? Wrong.

This is what happened to Microsoft in 2007 when it found an article on Wikipedia which it considered to contain inaccurate information about one of its software applications and which they suspected was strongly influenced by a rival technology giant.[6] According to Wikipedia's About page,[7] 'With rare exceptions, its articles can be edited by anyone with access to the internet, simply by clicking the "edit this page" link'. One of the rare exceptions is writing or editing an article about yourself – this goes against the ethic of authenticity and trust that the Wikipedia project is built on because what you say about yourself is most likely to be biased in your own favour. Most people would agree that this makes sense. But then, the problem comes when someone else writing something about you on the site may not be telling the whole story or may themselves be biased. In such a case, you are supposed to raise your objection in the discussion or talk pages rather than carry out the dispute on the actual content page itself. This seems fair and is in the spirit of academic discourse, while preventing the content page becoming a morass of heated argument. However, many casual visitors looking up a topic are most likely to glean their information from the main content page and move on, rather than take the time to read through the debates in the discussion pages. The policy of removing the dispute off the main page may in itself, arguably, be creating a bias of sorts by giving greater credence to the disputed issue merely because it remains on the main content page while the person or company that the article may be about has to raise their objections in the sidelines. Technology writer and author of 'Does IT matter? Information Technology and the Corrosion of Competitive Advantage', Nicholas Carr,[8] summed up the problem neatly on his blog Rough Type,[9] 'It seems like we're getting to the point where anyone who has gained deep enough knowledge of a subject to have developed a point of view on it will be unwelcome to edit Wikipedia.'

Accordingly, Microsoft felt they could not edit the offending article themselves. Instead, they offered to pay Australian blogger Rick Jelliffe to 'provide more balance' on Wikipedia. Microsoft were publicly open about it and Jelliffe blogged about the offer on the O'Reillyxlm.com blog,[10] saying,

> I am hardly the poster boy of Microsoft partisanship! Apparently they are frustrated at the amount of spin from some ODF stakeholders on Wikipedia and blogs.
>
> I think I'll accept it: FUD [Fear Uncertainty and Doubt] enrages me and MS [Microsoft] *certainly are not hiring me to add any pro-MS FUD, just to correct any errors I see.* [our emphasis]

Microsoft nonetheless came under fire from the Wikipedia community and across the blogs for what was perceived as a 'bribe' to a blogger to get its views onto Wikipedia. Subsequently, other instances of corporate editing of Wikipedia were outed by means of the Wikipedia Scanner, software that had been developed to identify the originating source of the edit – those outed included voting machine company Diebold, the supermarket giant Wal-mart and the CIA.[11] The kerfuffle about Microsoft and these other instances of corporate editing comes out of the general perception that big business and big brands are only out to sell you their corporate spin. This takes us back to the results of the Edelman Trust Barometer and the fact that 'people trust people like themselves'. Wikipedia's kudos lies in its being a volunteer project, run by a community of individuals for the community. For corporations to wade in and seemingly try to mess with that ethic has been viewed as an enormous breach of trust. The consequence is that those corporations have reinforced the image of themselves as untrustworthy and only looking out for their own interests.

Reputation management expert Alan Lane of Vasgama,[12] who has advised international corporations, governments and multilateral groups, explains 'Big corporations are expected to be responsible and a stabilising force, no matter how irresponsible the other guy may be. If a corporation gets overly loud and vocal, it becomes the Goliath to the other guy's David and everyone always roots for David.' In his experience, companies cannot control what is said about them online – and in reality they have never been able to control what is said about them whether online or offline. What they can do is set out their position on a given issue for consideration and Lane recommends that they do so on their own terms and in their own space, such as on their own website, through face-to-face engagement, or by traditional media briefings. If corporations consistently engage with issues around their products or services in an authentic and trustworthy way in their own space, rather than rushing in to fight fires wherever such forays may occur, they are likely to gain more trust in the long term. 'The two worst things you can do', Lane says, 'is to ignore a potential reputation problem or to rush around in a panic trying to get rid of it. You need to assess whether the situation merits a response – and in some cases, it may not. For example, the person raising the issue may have no credibility. Where the issue needs a response, you need to make sure that your response is appropriate and does not create a David and Goliath set up.' In Lane's view, Microsoft would have done better by refuting the inaccuracies in the Wikipedia article through dialogue on its own website via, say, a chat room.

In terms of social media tools, the company has a raft of employee blogs at Microsoft Community Blogs[13] which they could have tapped into to discuss the Wikipedia inaccuracies, disputing them through discussions focused on the technical programming issues. Engaging in the discourse from an expert perspective within their own space in this way, Microsoft could have turned the situation to their advantage – one or more technical experts blogging the issues at the factual level in terms of programing and software specifications and functionality, linking to the Wikipedia article and inviting comments: all that would have shown us the smart tech guys who do the programing at the big corporation, who are the human faces of an otherwise faceless Goliath. These guys – and every individual employee that makes up a big corporation – are 'people like us' and they are the most valuable assets any business has when engaging in today's trust-focused climate.

Trust can only be built up over time through consistent action. In the real world, someone who you see behaving authentically over time is going to be someone who you are more likely to trust. Think about times when you've said 'I know X, she's not the kind of person to do that sort of thing' – or of yourself, you might have said 'You know me, I like a good laugh/I don't do camping/I'm always up for a challenge.' We trust people we know, and as we've seen this is backed up by Nielson's Global Consumer Survey.[14] Similarly, in social media spaces, a long-term consistently authentic presence is going to gain you more trust and respect than a SWAT-style approach to blogs and wikis only when you perceive a problem. Lane says that major international companies do well to have websites that include a lot of information about their corporate responsibility policies and articles discussing hot issues around their industry. 'They are engaging with the issues but it's dignified and responsible', Lane says.

In a similar vein, US Democratic preside,ntial candidate Hillary Clinton set up a Fact Hub[15] during 2007 to counter inaccurate reporting about her and her campaign in the press and on the blogs. It was built on a blog platform and has RSS feeds. Each post has a matter of fact, neutral tone, focusing on correcting facts – for example, 'There is a rumor online that the Hillary campaign "scrubbed" Elliot Spitzer from our website. This is untrue.'[16] It makes rather dry reading but serves its purpose of presenting Clinton's side of story, based on 'the facts'. It is decorous and dignified while engaging with rumours, accusations and other claims against her.

When dealing with online accusations, gossip or inaccuracies about your organization, it is worth remembering that wading into the fray may not be the best tactic. Instead, consider:

- You have to react quickly but it may be best not to do so on the other's terms but rather to engage on your own terms. This may mean that you need to consider incorporating into your business's website an area that can be used to address issues head-on, whether it is a fact hub or resource of articles.
- If you already have a blog, that blog could be used judiciously to address such issues.
- For the best impact, such a blog needs to build up a trusted reputation over time – if it is nothing more than corporate spin, it won't cut the mustard.
- Whoever blogs on that blog needs to be prepared to be open with their readers – it is more effective if they reveal their full names and their place within the organization rather than hiding behind just a first name and fudging their corporate role. Think about it: in the real world, would you trust someone whom you only know as 'John' and who is 'something in import/export' – or would you prefer to deal with John Green, Director of Sales?
- Just as in the real world, consistently authentic engagement in social media will stand you in good stead on the occasions when you have to deal with a potential hazard to your reputation.

Inauthenticity

How you conduct yourself in promoting your blog or social media site also matters. Blog consultant Debbie Weil landed herself in a controversy over the blog she helped her client Glaxo Smith Klein (GSK) set up, AlliConnect.[17] In the early days of the new GSK blog, she wrote a post on her own blog BlogWrite for CEOs[18] and sent out an e-mail to her contacts, encouraging her readers to go over the AlliConnect and add a comment, adding, 'No need to say that you know me, of course.' A number of marketing professionals and bloggers came down on her like a ton of bricks, accusing her of 'pimping for comments'.[19]

In our view, the furore was disproportionate to her 'crime'. In her e-mail and blog post, she had stated clearly that people seemed shy to leave comments and she was asking her contacts/readers to add comments in the hope of 'jump start[ing] the... conversation'. She also disclosed that she worked for GSK. The error that provoked the strong reaction was her suggesting that people should not mention that she had asked them to leave a comment – that was the one whiff of inauthenticity that tainted her otherwise upfront approach to her colleagues and blog readers. Weil herself writes in her follow-up post[20] during the drama 'It looked as if I was asking colleagues to conceal that they know me. Those who know me – and know my tone of voice in an e-mail – understand that I didn't really mean it. I regret using the phrase. It was a mistake.' She goes on to give examples of marketing professionals e-mailing contacts to tell them about client blog projects and asking for comments. She argues that her use of e-mail was a standard backchannel, which is used regularly by most marketing professionals.

While Weil's reputation has not been seriously damaged by this incident, it is an object lesson in always conducting yourself with the utmost integrity – as well as not asking others to conduct themselves in otherwise than a spotless manner. Co-author Ooi recalls having to rein in the enthusiasm of a client for this very reason, 'I'd just explained the power of adding comments to other people's blogs – that by commenting you can build relationships with bloggers and also encourage them to come and look at your own site. One of my client's senior team said "Great, we can get all our people going to all these blogs and forums and leave lots of positive comments about our organisation – we won't say who we are, of course..." I had to stop him right there! I took care to explain the problems with that less than honest approach. He was a decent, all round great guy and I don't think he meant to be deceitful – many people are just not used to the new culture of social media and the principles of behaviour that go with it.'

So, authentic engagement means:

- When considering implementing a blog as part of a corporate communications strategy, especially if the corporation concerned is a giant, well-known brand, whether loved or otherwise, transparency and authenticity must be at the core of that strategy.
- When otherwise engaging in the landscape of social media (adding comments or even using e-mail as part of your marketing plan), be aware of how what you say and do may be – or may be interpreted as – less than honest. Anyone can 'out' your mistake or 'crime' to a very wide audience in moments.
- The emphasis on trust and authenticity online reflects current trends in the real world where trust is a global issue for individuals, governments and business. Successful social media engagement will depend on how your online actions reflect your role within this trend.

Fictitious blogs

The Delicious Destinations[21] blog is a fictitious blog created by Toby Bloomberg of Diva Marketing for GourmetStation, a US company which delivers gourmet food to your home.[22] At the very top of the blog, there is a clear statement, 'Through *the character of T. Alexander* and occasional real-life guests, our aim is to share with you light-hearted fun ideas about food, gift giving, entertaining and culture' (our emphasis). However, in spite of that, when it first came to the notice of marketing bloggers, it came under fierce attack for the conceit. According to INC. magazine,[23] communicator Robert French of the blog Blogthenticity.com[24] asked his readers 'What value do you find in this tactic? Is it authentic?' and marketing professional Hugh Macleod, who blogs at GapingVoid.com, awarded Delicious Destinations the Beyond Lame award. Both Bloomberg and GourmetStation owner Donna Lynes-Miller contacted their critics by e-mail and via the comments function on their detractors' blogs to explain the reason for their use of a fictitious character – 'We are a small pioneering food company and we see the blog and its content as a way of adding value to our patron's experience. What T. Alexander has to say about food is not as important as what our patrons have to share about their culinary adventures.'[25] The result was to cool the flames of criticism and the blog continues to thrive. What was important here was that the beleaguered creators approached their critics in an open and calm way, rather than responding with equal ire – by acknowledging the criticism and explaining what they were trying to do on Delicious Destinations, they were able to disarm the opposition.

The success of Delicious Destinations is unusual in terms of fictitious blogs used for marketing purposes. Others have failed, such as Captain Morgan's blog (for Captain Morgan's rum) and Wrigley's Juicy Fruit blog, both of which have been replaced by non-social media websites after heavy fire from critics. McDonald's Lincoln Fry blog was a fiction about a couple who found a fry at McDonald's that looked like Abraham Lincoln – the blog also no longer exists after being ridiculed across the blogosphere, but details can be found on the Museum of Hoaxes site,[26] which reports 'none of it is real, not even the comments'.

Fictitious blogs generally work best as satire. Jeremy Blachman started a blog called Anonymous Lawyer[27] in 2004, the online diary of a senior partner in a US corporate law firm. Its tone is just on this side of believable – we've all come across people like this one, who writes in December 2004:[28]

> The week between Christmas and New Years is always a slow one, but it's now when you can tell which associates really have their priorities straight. We don't mind if our associates have families. We tolerate it. But it's nice to see them in the office this week, so we know the firm is really what matters. I see people leaving at 3:00 and I start wondering whether their heart is in it, and whether they'll stand for it come crunch time when we really need them. This isn't just a job, its a career.

At that time, Blachman was still at Harvard Law School. He graduated in 2005. By then, Anonymous Lawyer was a cult success and in 2006 he cut a six-figure deal to publish the blog as a book.[29] As of 2007, the blog continues with even sharper writing:

> My daughter had a birthday last week. I forgot. My wife thought it would be fun to see how long it would take me to remember. It took four days… It was only when I saw she updated her Facebook profile with pictures from the party that I realized what I'd missed. So I put a message on her Wall and hopefully that'll take care of it. I'm going to text her later just to see if she'd logged in yet to read it.

As of 2008, Blachman is working on a potential adaptation of the book/blog for television.[30]

We would caution against going the fictitious blog route for marketing purposes. Even the very experienced blogger and communications professional Toby Bloomberg came under fire and although Delicious Destinations was rescued and thrives, the path of fictitious marketing blogs is strewn with more disasters than successes. On the other hand, fiction can work well in blog form and in itself can be a great marketing tool alongside the book once it has been published. However, co-author Ooi has been observing would-be writers in the blogosphere for some time and comments, 'There is a lot of competition out there from unpublished and unpublishable novelists hoping to make a mark with the novel-in-the-form-of-a-blog so if you are hoping for Blachman's kind of fame, your writing and your concept better be pretty damn brilliant.'

Authentic voices

KiaBuzz[31] is the official blog from South Korean car manufacturers, Kia Motors, developed for the company by Edelman Korea. The look of the blog reflects the Kia Motors online brand presence, featuring the company logo and the corporate rust-red colour against white. It has a slick, professional visual feel, much like the main Kia Motors[32] and Kia Global Network[33] sites. As we mentioned earlier in this chapter, a corporate blog that is closely associated with the main business website runs the risk of being seen as just another space for corporate spin – and far from being a vehicle for authentic conversation, it can become yet another display from an untrustworthy behemoth. While KiaBuzz generally maintains a positive view of Kia and its products, we were struck, however, by the real voices that blog on the site.

Juny Lee, account manager at Edelman Korea, explains 'Kia prepared its business blog for three months from July 2006 and Edelman Korea provided social media coaching for Kia internal bloggers. The bloggers are 13 experts from Kia's various working groups, including the research and development, overseas communications and overseas sales teams. President and CEO of Kia Motors Corporation, Euisun Chung, also occasionally writes a post.' He emphasizes that the CEO writes his own posts, adding 'KiaBuzz's management team is well aware of the negative and disastrous effect resulting from ghost blogging in the blogosphere in the era of web 2.0.'

Most of the posts discuss design and technical aspects of Kia cars as well as wider automotive issues. This is the blog's main strength as this is where the bloggers can speak as experts and share their excitement about cars, engineering and design. Their readers seem to be car fans and engage enthusiastically with these issues through the comments section. For example, Jung Ae-Hwang in the trends research team discusses green consumption in the 21st century[34] and Chil-Young Kwon in the production management team offers a behind-the-scenes view of rolling out a new model:

> Our plant is busy with the facelift (F/L) version of Lotze (also known as Optima or Magentis). (I was captivated by this car at first sight and wanted to claim it as my own design!) Much cooperation and effort goes into producing a new car after it is developed in the R&D center. First, new equipment must be installed on the production lines. Discussions are held with line workers about assembling the new parts. In addition, test vehicles have to be made and examined to ensure that quality problems do not arise during production. Production management serves as a liaison function throughout this process.[35]

Mixed in are general, newsy items such as one from Cor Baltus, the general manager of Kia Netherlands about the Kia ice skating team.[36] These have a more corporate feel to them but still manage to maintain a personal voice. And there are the occasional posts that are not afraid to acknowledge the not-so-rosy – for example, James Kim, deputy general manager of the overseas policy research team, writes 'with the merger of Hyundai and Kia almost a decade ago, the Kia brand seems to have lost a few of its eager fans. Personally, I thought Kia used to project an image of spending more time coming up with ideas and conducting more tests than Hyundai',[37] and Panu Vainamo, general manager of marketing and PR, Kia Europe, reports 'Well, the final tally is in and unfortunately the cee'd came up a bit short in the voting for the 2008 European Car of the Year (COTY) award – finishing just outside the podium in 4th place out of seven finalists.'[38]

As to the reason for starting a blog, Kyuah Oh of Edelman Korea explains 'Kia Motors wanted to find an alternative online communications tool to overcome limited effect of online communications tool and provide extra compared to what existing marketing tools have to offer, especially online. Homepage, Press Releases, C-level speeches, advertising and PR are no longer as effective as they had once been in the past, now that the consumers are "smart".' One of the challenges of entering the social media space is the interactive nature of that online culture, with comments being open to anyone. Some business bloggers close off the comments function so that their blog becomes a one-way discourse from them to their audience – this is generally frowned upon in the blogosphere as it shows a lack of willingness to engage fully in a peer-to-peer discussion, relying instead on the 'old school' model of top-down, one-way public statements.

KiaBuzz has a published comments policy on its site and the editorial group monitor and manage any comments that are received. Oh says 'The Group would usually accept all kinds of negative comments, provided they abide by the policy. It takes great interest especially in productive criticisms and bloggers' suggestions on Kia issues and related posts. Kia understands that not only positive comments and encouragement but also valid criticism and "reality checks" from visitors help Kia to grow. Writers are always answering bloggers' comments and questions to actively engage in two-way conversations and to build relationship with them. Such interaction leads to genuine discussion and promotes mutual understanding.'

The hallmark of a successful, authentic blog then would be:

- A personal voice, genuine engagement with reader feedback, both positive and negative, 'keeping it real' and content that is relevant to their audience.
- Incorporate multimedia in the form of videos and striking photographs helps to engage the visitor more deeply.
- Blogging works the best for those organizations and individuals whose business culture is one of openness, mutual respect and a strong sense of customer or stakeholder engagement. It works least, as we have seen, for businesses whose approach to others tends towards the defensive and authoritarian.
- Although the Kia Blog features bloggers primarily based in Korea, it is written in English. Oh explains, that the company 'is currently exporting to more than 150 countries and sales rate resulting from the export is reaching as high as 80 per cent. We concluded that for Kia to continue to grow in the global market, it is necessary to provide ceaseless and new information on Kia brand directly and fast to international automobile bloggers. And thus, Kia decided to use English, the global language and bloggers from more than 150 English speaking or English proficient countries are visiting KiaBuzz.'

South Africa: Joining the conversation

In South Africa, political engagement is beginning to take place online. The hot political issue of 2007 was the African National Congress (ANC) succession with the current ANC President (and president of the country) Thabo Mbeki and Deputy President Jacob Zuma as the main contenders. The succession debate was argued out online as much as elsewhere, with, reportedly, around 59 Facebook groups on the subject. The Facebook group 'Help us stop Jacob Zuma becoming South Africa's next president'[39] had 31,529 members at the time of writing. Its wall had over 5,000 postings. To promote the group, they was even an official Zuma Group ring tone but for all the heated anti-Zuma feeling online, Jacob Zuma was elected in December 2007 as leader of the ANC.[40]

Helen Zille, the Mayor of Cape Town in South Africa's Western Cape province and leader of the Democratic Alliance political party (DA), South Africa's official opposition, has a blog on the landing page of her official website, HelenZille.co.za.[41] Anthony Hazell,[42] head of relationship management for the DA, explains how the blog is managed: 'The posts tend to be a team effort, done by support staff, but in consultation with Helen. She does a regular weekly post, which is republished from the main DA website, called SA Today.' Each post has the relevant byline, clearly indicating who the author is.

One of the concerns of most communications managers is negative comments, and the political arena is especially full of strong opinions and heated tempers. On Zille's blog, Hazell says, 'Generally, we just respond – put our point of view across. We'll publish negative comments provided it's not anonymous or racist or discriminatory or hate-speech of any kind, and provided it plays the ball and not the man (to borrow a sporting metaphor).'

The DA also engage on Facebook to 'join the conversation' started by their supporters. Hazell tells us in an e-mail 'There are several DA-related Facebook groups, which we keep an eye on and participate in. We've met with the creator of one of those groups – he and his fellow admins are keen to be recognized as the "official" DA group. The DA didn't start any of the groups. We merely try and add value by posting links, sharing news and participating in debates. This is where the most engagement with younger supporters happens.'

As a keen social media explorer himself, Hazell blogs and is also on Twitter. He adds 'We're using Ning.com (a social networking platform) for an internal staff network, and we're considering creating a broader DA social network under the URL my.da.org.za to provide a DA platform for interaction with and among supporters and members.'

As for the South African social media landscape in general as of 2008, Hazell's view is that 'Bloggers aren't particularly influential on

South Africa's (SA's) politics at the moment, because our internet penetration is still pretty low, and social media penetration even lower. From my point of view, I see them as another media channel to broaden our reach. The biggest blogs in SA are overwhelmingly about sport, and then probably about marketing and media. It's not so much about interacting with political bloggers to get them to write positive stuff about the DA. My focus is to do interesting stuff online, and then to get 'A-list' bloggers to write about what we're doing – not because they necessarily support the DA, but because we're doing stuff that no other political party (and few businesses) are doing.'

The key points that are relevant for public affairs communicators are likely to be:

- The cultural history of different nations will dictate the level of open discourse in both the offline world and on the internet. However, internet access and social media are changing the ability of citizens to engage in debate and dissent and this is likely to influence the political arena there in the future.
- There may be a lot of online noise and satire on sites such as Facebook about a political issue or candidate, but the effect may not be as influential in real terms as it might seem at first sight.
- On the other hand, the Zuma Facebook example highlights the opportunities social media offers for those of minority views to gather online.
- Authenticity is particularly important on politicians' blogs so the Zille blog's clear bylines are essential to build trust. The openness to negative comments adds to this.
- Taking the time to engage in others' online conversations can build relationships online – much like the usual real world networking activities that politicians engage in such as walkabouts, community meetings and talking to constituents.

Malaysia: The bloggers decide

'Malaysia is not used to having a real opposition,' says journalist and blogger[43] Zahara Wan. It is a week after the shock results of the 2008 Malaysian election and the country is reeling from the message sent by the voters. Wan, who has been watching the election closely, explains 'Ever since Merdeka (Independence from British rule) fifty years ago, there's only ever been one ruling party, Barisan Nasional

(National Front). They usually win all the 13 states with maybe one state going to an opposition party. For the first time, this year the opposition won control of five states.'[44]

Barisan Nasional (BN) are still in the majority and by no means overwhelmed by the coalition of opposition seats but the results have shaken the status quo and stirred up some soul-searching. The results were considered so abysmal that there were calls for the resignation of the party leader, Prime Minister Datuk Seri Abdullah Ahmad Badawi.[45]

What's more, Malaysian politics has historically been divided along racial lines with UMNO (United Malays National Organisation), the Malay party, heading up Barisan Nasional, and other political parties representing Chinese and Indian interests. In 2008, the opposition wins went primarily to parties such as DAP (Democratic Alliance Party) and Gerakan, which are multi-racial alliances. That the opposition wins went to these multi-racial alliances is as significant as the fact that the opposition gained so many seats at all.

What was the reason for the historic political change in Malaysia that saw huge opposition gains by parties representing common rather than racial interests?

'It's the bloggers', Wan says. 'Definitely. For the first time, in the last couple of years before the election, people were talking about all kinds of political issues online through the blogs. They criticize government policies. They talk openly about corruption and cronyism. The political bloggers like Jeff Ooi (Screenshots[46]) and Rocky (Rocky's Bru[47]) have a huge following and people go to the blogs for the latest news and views.'

Malaysia is a democracy based on the British model but is uneasy about complete freedom of speech. However, Malaysian bloggers have so far been protected by a guarantee of non-censorship. Asohan Aryaduray, new media editor at *The Star*, a Malaysian national newspaper, explains 'When former Prime Minister Tun Dr Mahathir Mohamad launched the ambitious Multimedia Super Corridor (MSC) project in 1996, to attract the world's leading IT companies, the government came up with the MSC Bill of Guarantees, which included a commitment that the Malaysian government would never censor the internet.' However, this commitment has not led to an entirely smooth ride for Malaysia's bloggers. In 2007, two bloggers were sued by a government-controlled national newspaper,[48] a cabinet minister called bloggers liars and cheats, other bloggers were arrested[49] and/or investigated by police.

Incidents such as these 'usually lead to a vigorous reaction in the online world before the current Prime Minister or Deputy Prime

Minister has to go on the record again to remind everyone that there will be no censorship', according to Aryaduray. However, in August 2008, ZDNet Asia reported[50] that the blog Malaysia Today was blocked by the Malaysian Communications and Multimedia Commission, which has been interpreted by observers as a breach of the 'no internet censorship' guarantee.

During the election, Wan followed updates every few minutes online via the websites of press publications such as the *New Straits Times* and *The Star* as well as via the blogs. She says 'Sometimes, the blogs beat the traditional press to the news. Rocky got hold of a politically sensitive letter before the media. He wrote on his blog that he'd heard there was this letter in existence and asked his readers to send a copy to him. He got it within 24 hours and posted it on his blog.' Rocky is the pseudonym for Ahirudin bin Attan, a journalist, the former president of the National Press Club and former editor of the newspaper that brought the lawsuit against him – blogging in his personal capacity. In addition to Rocky, other prominent political bloggers include Jeff Ooi, initially blogging his personal views but then as a member of opposition party DAP alongside other opposition MPs such as Lim Kit Siang.[51] The opposition has taken to the blogs more keenly than those in the ruling party for the simple reason that the blogosphere more readily offers them direct and immediate access to an audience than mediated channels such as newspapers and television.

In the lead-up to the election, according to the *New Straits Times* website, NST Online, aware that the web was the new battleground for votes, the political parties set up websites to provide updates of their activities and provide information about the issues. There was also concern about rumours and false information spreading across the blogosphere and some political parties had members on standby to post replies and counter-arguments. UMNO Youth had a team of 30 volunteers – or cyber troopers – tracking gossip on the internet. The team also used SMS to counter rumours spread by SMS. DAP and Gerakan similarly tracked blogs and also uploaded party political videos onto YouTube.[52] According to *The Star*, 'Some Barisan candidates also turned to blogging, hoping to connect with the young, but they gave up because the number of visitors was just too low.'[53]

In the aftermath of the election, Malaysian media analysts share Wan's view of the influence of blogs on the outcome. *The Star* comments 'The bloggers and alternative media... inflicted serious wounds onto the Barisan', and also reports that SMS text messaging was 'the most effective weapon in helping the Opposition knock out the Barisan Nasional.' SMS had the advantage or reaching rural voters, whereas blogs and other online media were primarily used by urban Malaysians. However, traditional outlets such as newspapers and television and old-fashioned face-to-face campaigning remained a strong factor in these elections, notwithstanding the influence of online and mobile communications. The internet also raised online donations of over RM 100,000, primarily for the opposition parties, a new development in Malaysian electioneering.[54]

Azmi Sharom, writing in *The Star*, says 'A democracy needs dissent as long as it is peaceful' and goes on to add 'The country is on the cusp of a new type of politics. It is perhaps no accident that amongst the Opposition in Parliament, the one with the largest number of seats is a multi-racial party that calls for a non-racial method of affirmative action.'[55]

In another first for Malaysia, political blogger and outspoken critic of the government turned politician Jeff Ooi has put his money where his mouth is and taken on a new role as politician, winning a seat as DAP member for Penang. He writes on his blog 'OK, am I the first blogger in the world who is elected into Parliament through the democratic process? I am feeling the heat now.'[56]

Following the election, newly appointed Information Minister Datuk Ahmad Shabery Cheek announced plans to meet the bloggers during March 2008 and was reported in *The Star* as saying 'The alternative media, like bloggers, play a role in nation building. It is the most direct and simple channel for people to voice their opinions. Sometimes, they can bring about a negative effect but it is mostly positive.'[57] But with the arrest of prominent blogger Raja Petra Kamarruddin in August 2008, this truce between politicians and bloggers remains fragile.[58]

The broad points we would like to draw out of this case study are:

- While politicians in Asia may continue to distrust bloggers, bloggers can be influential among their citizens, and in many cases may voice the concerns of the populace.
- The media in countries like Malaysia is being forced to examine their role and structures in the light of bloggers scooping news and becoming increasingly trusted by the people for political news and opinion.
- Short of outright censorship and interference with the infrastructure that delivers the internet to private citizens, nations all over the world will need to face the rising use of social media channels for political expression, criticism, debate and protest.

- While traditional meet-the-people campaigning and print and broadcast media will always have strong roles in Malaysia and globally, blogs and social media provide an expansive online space for influential discussion beyond physical boundaries. Increasingly, mobile communications such as SMS text messaging are also playing a key role, especially in reaching rural communities and those who do not have cheap or easy access to broadband-based communications.
- One of the key factors in the influential role of Malaysia's political bloggers is that they had been blogging their outspoken views for many years before this election, and despite interference through lawsuits and arrests they have continued boldly to speak their minds.[59] This has added to the bloggers' authenticity – and a testament to the trust gained by one blogger, Jeff Ooi, is his election to parliament as a representative of the people.
- In contrast, politicians from the ruling party did not engage in the social media landscape other than to criticize bloggers through reported statements in the mainstream press. So, it is not surprising that when the ruling party's candidates tried to blog late in the day, they 'gave up because the number of visitors was just too low'. The lesson here is that blogging is about building up trust over time, being authentic and, in the case of political blogging in Malaysia, standing up for what you believe in whatever the consequences.

The USA: Land of the YouTube video and home of the bloggers

The attitude towards social media by the candidates in the US race for the presidential election 2008 contrasts dramatically with the attitude of the politicians in Malaysia. Comparing the two approaches gives us an insight into the different cultural approaches to not just social media but the relationship between authority and 'ordinary people' and the principles of democracy and free speech.

In the USA, the blogosphere is a landscape where free speech and the democratic process can be played out on a scale beyond physical boundaries. From the early days of the race in 2007, many of the candidates included social media in their campaign strategies. Every single one of the major candidates had a blog,[60] of which most were written by campaign bloggers and some included posts personally written by the candidate. For example, Democrat Hillary Clinton's campaign site had a blog[61] as well as Hillcasts,[62] videos of Hillary speaking directly to her audience about what Hillary as President would mean. There were also a range of videos of her campaign trail, speeches, photographs, press releases and a section where supporters could contribute to her campaign as well as take part as volunteers. The byline of the blogging team, led by Crystal Patterson and including a volunteer, Michael Brasher, and also her Chief Strategist Mark Penn, was clearly evident at the top of each post. This transparency is a good move in the interests of authenticity.

Another Democratic hopeful, John Edwards, in addition to a blog, was one of the first candidates to use Twitter[63] to keep supporters updated on his campaign trail. 'Tweets' (posts on Twitter) posted by his staff were clearly labelled 'from staff' but there were also those that appeared to be from Edwards himself. The overall impression was of a busy campaign schedule: arriving at a range of cities across America, meeting different members of the community, appearing at numerous events and some attempt to engage in short 'tweet' conversations.

However, it was Democrat Barack Obama, of all the presidential candidates, who used social media with the most innovation and panache. He had a website, a blog, a Twitter[64] stream, a page on Facebook,[65] a profile on MySpace[66] and his own social networking site MyBarackObama.com.[67] His campaign also used SMS text messaging and ringtones to capture voters and there was an exclusive Obama application for the iPhone. According to the *Boston Globe*, 'More than any previous presidential campaign, Obama's effort is transforming politics with its use of technology.'[68]

Of all the Obama tools, the MyBarackObama social networking site stands out above the rest. It was created with the help of Chris Hughes, one of the original founders of Facebook, and boasted over a million members by the time Obama won the election in November 2008, many of whom were the young and tech-savvy Millennials. Through online self-organizational tools, members could organize local events, debates and fund-raisers. Uniquely, there was an online phone-banking tool that enabled supporters to make calls to voters, encouraging them to vote Obama, available in both English and Spanish,[69] with the ten people making the most calls getting the chance to meet Obama himself. Hughes explains the success of the self-organizing tools in the *Boston Globe*, 'People in the country are excited about change in general, and when you combine that with organizing tools that allow them to do stuff without someone looking over their shoulder, they can get a lot done.'[70] This illustrates neatly the issue of trust – not just building the trust of your audience in you but trust that allows you to let go of control and empowers other individuals to take action, perhaps more effectively that you could, in their local contexts. These campaigns at grass-roots level combined with centrally orchestrated events so that when Obama arrived in a city, many local supporters were guaranteed to turn up through online word-of-mouth.

Obama won the campaign in a landslide victory to become the first African-American President of the United States of America and there is no doubt that social media played its part in this historic election.

- As we saw in the previous chapter, young people engage online as part of life. It is not surprising, then, that by using social media strategically (as reported by the BBC[71]) 'Mr Obama had an unprecedented level of support among young people and new voters in the 2008 election. He won the votes of those under 30 by an impressive 66 per cent to 31 per cent, much higher than in any previous election.' On the power of the youth vote and Obama's social media strategies, *The Washington Post*[72] says 'The Millennials may have found their first president – one who engages them in their own space.'

- Online engagement also helped the campaign raise a huge war-chest of funds that outstripped the Republican campaign budget. The BBC[73] reports that Obama's internet fund-raising activity attracted more than three million donors and raised 'about $650m (£403m) – more than both presidential contenders in 2004 combined'. This meant that Obama had the resources to maintain more campaign offices in more locations than the Republican camp and could also buy more broadcast media airtime than his opponent, enabling his campaign to reach more voters than the Republicans.

- Supporters, fans and followers were encouraged to take action to show their support for the campaign – whether by organizing local events or giving a donation, however small or large, or by raising funds. This 'crowdsourcing' approach to campaigning harnessed the energy of individuals to give their time and resources towards an Obama win in the same way that the online crowdsourced encyclopedia Wikipedia and other social media projects harness individuals' energies towards shared objectives.

Obama's road to social media front-runner was not always smooth, as evidenced by a kerfuffle on MySpace. A keen supporter, Joe Anthony, had started a MySpace page in support of Obama back in 2004, and by 2007 that profile had 160,000 'friends' [74] – valuable capital for the Obama campaign. The official campaign team developed informal working relations with Anthony and as the online campaign took off the MySpace site exploded, resulting in Anthony's workload increasing exponentially. He asked for payment for his time and negotiations led to the campaign seeking control of the site. As discussions broke down, the campaign went to MySpace to require it to shut down the URL used by Anthony – www.myspace.com/barackobama – and restart it under the control of the official campaign, which MySpace did. These Goliath tactics prompted searing criticism from online supporters[75] but in the long term did not seem to hurt the Obama campaign. In particular, Obama made a personal call to Anthony which seemed to help bring the temperature of the whole incident down. The campaign built up their network from the ruins and later in 2007 Obama reached out to his MySpace community by selecting a handful of MySpace users to have dinner with him to discuss political issues. The video of the dinner played on MySpace after the event and the lucky few blogged about it on their MySpace pages.[76] By the time of the election in November 2008, Obama's MySpace profile had 872,021 friends.

It was not only the presidential candidates who understood the importance of social media as a communications tool but also the mainstream media. Twitter has been used by journalists following the campaign trail to report in brief, real-time spurts on the road.[77] There are journalists' blogs on news websites following the campaign. The most interesting mainstream and social media collaboration, however, was the CNN-sponsored YouTube presidential debates. Ordinary people could upload questions posed in home-made videos to specially dedicated debates pages on YouTube, one for the Republicans[78] and one for the Democrats.[79] The candidates gathered at the television studio on the night of the debate and took the YouTube questions, their responses in turn being uploaded onto YouTube as well as playing out over the airwaves.

From this very brief tour through the social media landscape of the 2008 US presidential race, some key points emerge:

● The candidates established blogs alongside their websites from the outset, aiming to build trust and an online relationship with their supporters from the beginning.

- They used a range of multi-media and mobile platforms to reach out to a range of supporters across a range channels from real world events to online engagement.
- Bloggers were courted by the political parties and treated like the press with, for example, presidential candidates turning up to address the Yearly Kos bloggers convention.[80]
- Traditional face-to-face events still played an important role and were leveraged, especially by Obama, in conjunction with social media to make influential personal connections that could then be played out further on social network sites such as MySpace.
- The Goliath problem reared its head for Obama on MySpace and will undoubtedly dog any large organization, whether political or otherwise, in its online engagement – the key is to resolve it effectively, and in Obama's case he used a simple but valuable tactic to diffuse the ill-feeling: a personal phone call from the man himself.
- For the Hillary campaign, they were able to avoid the Goliath problem in the context of correcting misinformation by setting up the Hillary Fact Hub (as discussed in a previous chapter), which enabled them to dispute misrepresentations on their own ground rather than wading into an online fight on other social media spaces.
- The Obama campaign's use of social media was strategically integrated with the traditional methods of real world interactions – phone calls, doorstepping, town hall meetings, kissing babies – and broadcast media airtime. Social media in itself did not win him the election. Traditional strategies remained the foundation of his campaign. What social media contributed was a widening of Obama's reach to a different demographic of voters and also an ability to raise huge additional funds through an accumulation of small donations.

Notes

1. Edelman Trust Barometer 2008, Key Findings, http://www.edelman. co.uk/trustbarometer/files/trust-barometer-key-findings.pdf.
2. Edelman Trust Barometer 2008, Full Report, http://www.edelman. co.uk/trustbarometer/files/trust-barometer-2008.pdf.
3. http://goodbooksguide.blogspot.com/.
4. http://kennymah.wordpress.com/.

5. Kenny Mah's Life for Beginners was Spammed by Someone Pretending to be Him, http://kennymah.wordpress.com/2007/03/08/i-am-woman/.
6. Michael Arrington, Techcrunch, Battleground Wikipedia, 24 January 2007, http://www.techcrunch.com/2007/01/24/battleground-wikipedia/.
7. http://en.wikipedia.org/wiki/Wikipedia:About.
8. http://www.nicholasgcarr.com/info.shtml.
9. Nicholas Carr, Experts Go Home, roughtype.com, 24 January 2007, http://www.roughtype.com/archives/2007/01/experts_go_home.php.
10. Rick Jelliffe, An Interesting Offer: Get Paid to Contribute to Wikipedia, oreillynet.com, 22 January 2007, http://www.oreillynet.com/xml/blog/2007/01/an_interesting_offer.html.
11. John Barland, See Who's Editing Wikipedia – Diebold, the CIA, a Campaign, *Wired*, August 2007, http://www.wired.com/politics/onlinerights/news/2007/08/wiki_tracker?currentPage=2.
12. www.vasgama.com.
13. http://www.microsoft.com/communities/blogs/PortalHome.mspx.
14. Word of Mouth the Most Powerful Selling Tool, Nielson Global Survey, 1 October 2007, http://www.nielsen.com/media/2007/pr_071001.html.
15. http://facts.hillaryhub.com/.
16. Fact Check: Spitzer Not Scrubbed from Hillary Website, The Fact Hub, 11 March 2008, http://facts.hillaryhub.com/archive/?id=6470.
17. http://www.alliconnect.com/.
18. http://www.blogwriteforceos.com/.
19. Shel Holz, A Shel of my Former Self, Earn Comments For Your Blog the Organic Way, 12 July 2007, http://blog.holtz.com/index.php/weblog/earn_comments_for_your_clients_blogs_the_organic_way/.
20. Debbie Weil Blog, Write for CEOs: Using the Backchannel of Email to Invite Comments on a Blog, 12 July 2007, http://www.blogwriteforceos.com/blogwrite/2007/07/using-the-backc.html.
21. http://www.gourmetstationblog.typepad.com/.
22. http://www.gourmetstation.com/cgi-bin/gourmet/index.html?id=GHTSyrNc.
23. Jory Des Jardins, When Blogs Go Bad, inc.com, November 2005, http://www.inc.com/magazine/20051101/handson-technology.html.
24. www.blogthenticity.com, but the site seems no longer to exist.
25. As reported by INC.com – see footnote 25 above.
26. http://www.museumofhoaxes.com/hoax/weblog/comments/2450/.
27. http://anonymouslawyer.blogspot.com/.
28. http://anonymouslawyer.blogspot.com/2004_12_01_archive.html.
29. *USA Today*, 20 July 2006, http://www.usatoday.com/life/books/news/2006-07-19-bchat-anonymous-lawyer_x.htm.

30. *The Wall Street Journal*, 31 August 2007, http://blogs.wsj.com/law/2007/08/31/jeremy-blachman-welcome-to-the-law-one-ls/.
31. http://www.kia-buzz.com/.
32. http://www.kiamotors.com/.
33. http://www.kia-global.com/.
34. http://www.kia-buzz.com/?p=119.
35. http://www.kia-buzz.com/?p=133.
36. http://www.kia-buzz.com/?p=113.
37. http://www.kia-buzz.com/?p=139.
38. http://www.kia-buzz.com/?p=63.
39. http://www.facebook.com/group.php?gid=2391058928.
40. Mbeki Faces Lame Duck Term, Mail & Guardian Online, 19 December 2007, http://www.mg.co.za/articlePage.aspx?articleid=328053&area=/breaking_news/breaking_news__national/.
41. http://helenzille.co.za/new/.
42. Hazell's personal blog is at Ant's World, http://antsworldsa.wordpress.com/.
43. http://kakteh.blogspot.com/.
44. http://thestar.com.my/election/.
45. Wrong to Ask PM to Step Down, *New Straits Times*, 16 March 2008, http://www.nst.com.my/Current_News/NST/Sunday/National/2187931/Article.
46. http://www.jeffooi.com/. No relation to co-author Ooi.
47. http://www.rockybru.blogspot.com/.
48. Malaysian Bloggers' Suit Kicks Off, Al-Jazeera, 25 January 2007, http://english.aljazeera.net/news/asia-pacific/2007/01/200852513457585310.html.
49. Malaysia: Blogger Detained by Police, Global Voices, 13 July 2007, http://www.globalvoicesonline.org/2007/07/13/malaysia-blogger-detained-by-police/.
50. M'sia Govt Breaks Promise, Censors Net, ZDNet Asia, 29 August 2008, http://www.zdnetasia.com/news/internet/0,39044908,62045527,00.htm?scid=rss_z_nw.
51. http://blog.limkitsiang.com/.
52. Nurris Ishak, Cyber Troopers Battle for Voters, nst.com, 17 February 2008, http://www.nst.com.my/Current_News/NST/Sunday/National/2160084/Article.
53. Wong Chun Wai, Denial Syndrome Must End, *The Star*, 14 March 2008, http://thestar.com.my/news/story.asp?file=/2008/3/14/election2008/20637966&sec=election2008.
54. Wong Chun Wai, Denial Syndrome Must End, *The Star*, 14 March 2008, http://thestar.com.my/news/story.asp?file=/2008/3/14/election2008/20637966&sec=election2008.
55. Azmi Sharom, Time to Act as Statesman, *The Star*, 20 March 2008, http://thestar.com.my/news/story.asp?file=/2008/3/20/focus/20674089&sec=focus.

56. JEFF for Malaysia, Screenshots, 15 March 2008, http://www.jeffooi.com/2008/03/jeff_for_malaysia.php.
57. Shabery to Hear Out Bloggers, *The Star*, 22 March 2008, http://thestar.com.my/news/story.asp?file=/2008/3/22/nation/20725852&sec=nation.
58. Kamaruddin was arrested under the Internal Security Act as he was deemed a threat to security, peace and public order – as reported by *The Star*, Malaysia on 12 September 2008, http://thestar.com.my/news/story.asp?file=/2008/9/12/nation/20080912135857&sec=nation.
59. When Jeff Ooi and Rocky were sued by the *New Straits Times*, bloggers Susan Loone and Sheif of Kickdefella launched a solidarity network, Bloggers United. See http://kickdefella.wordpress.com/2007/01/19/calling-one-calling-all-defend-your-right-to-free-speech/. Bloggers from Malaysia and around the world could post the Bloggers United badge on their blogs in support of 'Free Speech, No Fear'. This campaign raised the profile of the bloggers, bringing the issue of free speech to the fore, and is likely to have increased the readership of political blogs in the country.
60. http://techpresident.personaldemocracy.com/node/20#youtube.
61. http://www.hillaryclinton.com/blog/.
62. http://www.hillaryclinton.com/video/hillcast/.
63. http://twitter.com/johnedwards.
64. http://twitter.com/barackobama.
65. http://www.facebook.com/barackobama.
66. http://www.myspace.com/barackobama.
67. http://my.barackobama.com/.
68. Brian C Mooney, Technology Aids Obama's Outreach Drive, *The Boston Globe*, 24 February 2008, http://www.boston.com/news/nation/articles/2008/02/24/technology_aids_obamas_outreach_drive/?page=1.
69. Sarah Lai Stirland, The Tech of Obamamania: Online Phone Banks, Mass Texting and Blogs, *Wired*, 14 February 2008, http://www.wired.com/politics/law/news/2008/02/potomac_primaries.
70. Brian C Mooney, Technology Aids Obama's Outreach Drive, *The Boston Globe*, 24 February 2008, http://www.boston.com/news/nation/articles/2008/02/24/technology_aids_obamas_outreach_drive/?page=1.
71. Who Voted for Obama, BBC News Channel, 5 November 2008, http://news.bbc.co.uk/1/hi/world/americas/us_elections_2008/7709852.stm.
72. Kevin Merida, America's History Gives Way to Its Future, *The Washington Post*, 5 November 2008, http://www.washingtonpost.com/wp-dyn/content/article/2008/11/05/AR2008110500148html?hpid=topnews.
73. Richard Lister, Why Barack Obama Won, BBC News Channel, 5 November 2008, http://news.bbc.co.uk/1/hi/world/americas/us_elections_2008/7704360.stm.

74. Micah L Sifry, The Battle to Control Obama's MySpace, techpresident. com, 1 May 2007, http://www.techpresident.com/node/301.

75. Katherine Q Seelye and Sarah Wheaton, Obama's MySpace Conundrum, The Caucus, 2 May 2007, http://thecaucus.blogs. nytimes.com/2007/05/02/obamas-myspace-conundrum/.

76. Kristen Nicole, Obama Launches State Profiles on MySpace, mashable. com, 18 July 2007, http://mashable.com/2007/07/18/obama-myspace-state-profiles/.

77. Patrick Ruffini, The Year of Twitter, techpresident.com, 29 January 2008, http://www.techpresident.com/blog/entry/20767/the_year_of_twitter.

78. http://www.youtube.com/republicandebate.

79. http://www.youtube.com/democraticdebate.

80. Deanna Bellandi, US Bloggers Get Special Political Treatment, iolechnology.co.za, 3 August 2007, http://www.ioltechnology.co.za/article_page.php?iSectionId=2891&iArticleId=5019158.

9 Connecting communities

Many social media tools are available online free or at very low cost, which makes this form of mass communication easily accessible to anyone or any group, regardless of their budget. This means that social media can be a powerful communication tool for those who would otherwise be marginalized within their society or by mainstream-focused traditional media. Through blogs and other online tools, such groups can make their voices heard alongside established 'brands' such as news websites and corporations as well as enterprises catering to majority interests. They can also bypass the gatekeepers of traditional media, and this is especially empowering in societies where press freedom and the freedom of personal expression is restricted.

Social enterprises can also use social media tools to build online communities not just around their business but as their core business itself, developing new services conducted entirely online that would have been unthinkable before.

The tsunami blog

On 26 December 2004, a 9.0 magnitude earthquake deep in the floor of the Indian Ocean created a huge tsunami that devastated the coastline of 11 countries, including Indonesia, Thailand and India. In just one day, a reported 150,000 people were dead or missing and millions were left homeless.[1] Holiday-makers from around the world staying at beach resorts were caught up in the disaster, together with local people living along the coastline. In the immediate aftermath, the task of rescue and recovery was slow and painful. Families in distant countries desperately tried to find out what had happened to their loved ones. Identifying the dead and finding the missing was a mammoth task.

People turned to the blogs to share their stories and feelings – eyewitness accounts and expressions of horror and grief were posted within a week as well as anger at perceived incompetence on the part of the authorities in the aftermath.[2] Within two days, photos of the devastation had been posted onto the photo-sharing site Flickr.com by people who were at the scene[3] – you can still see them on Flickr now, a few years on by searching 'Asian tsunami' and scrolling back to December 2004.

The South East Asian Earthquake and Tsunami blog (the 'TsunamiHelp' blog) was created in the last days of December 2004 on the Blogger.com platform by India-based bloggers Peter Griffin, Rohit Gupta and Dina Mehta.[4] The volunteer team grew to 200 volunteers within a few days and the site was getting over a million visitors before long. The blog posted information about the relief effort, agencies to contact for information and to offer help, reports from the scene from eyewitnesses, and links to media coverage of the disaster – all gleaned from a variety of information sources via e-mail and text messages sent to them from volunteers. *The Guardian* quotes Mehta on how the blog became a hub for information about the tsunami: 'What was it that put my colleagues and me on the global stage answering news requests? It was all viral and we were on a completely "out of control" ride and yet somehow it all worked.' The viral effect was heightened by traditional media as well as well-known, high-traffic blog sites linking to the blog. Later, the team created a wiki, TsunamiHelp,[5] which became a repository for all the information they had collected during the project, including pages ranging from helpline numbers, confirmed dead and fund-raising events to image galleries.

We would suggest that part of the strength of the TsunamiHelp blog lay in its volunteer spirit. People often feel helpless as bystanders in the face of a disaster such as this tsunami. We give some money, we take some clothes to our local charity shop. Beyond that, we watch the news and feel for those who are suffering. The TsunamiHelp blog gave people the opportunity to help in a concrete way, even though some may have been at a distance from the scenes of disaster. People could find out information and send it to the blog – links to media reports or blogs, contact information for aid agencies, anything that would be of help. The core team themselves seemed driven and passionate about the cause they were serving and that gave an authenticity to everything that was on the site. The TsunamiHelp blog is a prime example of people coming together spontaneously and self-organizing into an effective force across physical and national boundaries via the social media landscape. Jane Perrone, writing in *The Guardian*, comments 'Perhaps most importantly of all, the TsunamiHelp blog has left a lasting legacy. The model of communication it forged has set the standard for web coverage of subsequent disasters, including Hurricane Katrina[6] and the Pakistan earthquake,[7] and many of the TsunamiHelp bloggers have used their expertise to launch similar projects on other disasters. And NGOs and academics are interested in using the TsunamiHelp model as a template for communication during future disasters.'

A number of points can be drawn for communicators, not just those working in the aid, relief or disaster management fields – but also for anyone who has to set up disaster recovery for any organization or network where swift, effective communication is key:

- The TsunamiHelp team set up a blog in moments, using free online software. It was then a matter of people coming to them via Google searches and eventually through links from high-traffic sites. For organizations planning ahead for disaster recovery where you have to contact your employees and stakeholders urgently, you could set up an 'urgent communications' blog whose URL and access details are already known to your staff and network. Link that with SMS and e-mail notifications to this internal network and your disaster communications can be live and effective in moments.
- Integration of blogging platforms with mobile phones is becoming increasingly streamlined and cost-effective. Consider implementing that cross-over functionality into your strategy for urgent communications so that incoming information via SMS can be easily accessible via a blog and vice versa.
- The TsunamiHelp team were comprised of volunteers. This is what made it quick and easy to set up. The team did not have to go through any official channels or get anyone's permission to do what they did – often the steps that slow down businesses and other organizations. Whereas an official agency setting up this type of service would most likely have spent time and resources checking and verifying the information it posted on the site, the volunteers took whatever came in and published it, trusting their contributors to be acting in good faith – this accounts for the wide

range of resources made available so quickly. In any event, with an interactive site like a blog, users of those resources can also get in contact to correct or update any inaccurate information so that the project is always a living, evolving creation. This interactive process is most likely the 'checks and balances' needed to keep the information continually reliable and relevant. Here again, as in many social media projects, trust is the foundation stone of success. What is your level of trust when it comes to working with others in such a scenario? Will that help or hinder your communications strategy?

- The volunteer spirit is a powerful one – people do what they do as volunteers because they feel passionate about something or because they believe in what they are doing. Their reward is not money or a pension plan but a satisfaction that they did their bit to help. The results of action taken in this spirit can often win out over similar action done with a 'jobsworth' attitude. How could your organization tap into the volunteer spirit among your staff, stakeholders and network around a communications project, whether social media related or not?

- We've emphasized the volunteer spirit in this case study because it has strong relevance not just in the case of disaster communications but also in the context of social media engagement generally. The volunteer spirit permeates a large part of the internet and social media landscape in the form of open-source software and application development as well as in projects such as the TsunamiHelp blog. When approaching social media and engaging in that landscape for your business, do you do so with an open-source, volunteer spirit or will you be seen as the one player who is all about looking after number one?

Work

India is the home of another innovative social network that has been ethnographically designed for the cultural conditions of a specific subcontinent. Bangalore-based Babajob.com[8] is a social network aimed at connecting India's vast number of clerical and often non-literate manual workers with employers looking for office helpers, clerks, maids, security guards, garment workers and the like. The site explains India's personal networking culture: 'Most people find jobs through people they know – namely their extended social network – and most employers – particularly when hiring employees that work in the home – would like to hire a person who someone they trust can vouch for.' [9]

The account of a job-seeker can be managed by a 'mentor', who is usually a friend, relative or other interested person – this is especially useful where the job-seeker is non-literate or does not have access to a computer or phone. An employer looking to recruit someone can browse the job-seekers' directory for free, but if they wish to contact potential candidates, they need to buy phone number access to an unlimited number of jobseekers or post a job ad for a fee. When a jobseeker is hired through this process, the mentor is rewarded with a commission.

Babajob.com is linked to a full social networking site Babalife.com[10] where members can blog and post photos and videos as well as interact with the site via their mobile phone. Both sites are available in English, Kannada, Tamil and Hindi. The purpose of offering both a job-seeking site and a social networking site together is based on the 'belief that in order to correctly model social relationships in a community and keep the attention of those people that are not hiring nor need a better job, a system should be – or at least leverage – the communication medium of its users.'[11] In other words, in real life people create social relationships or networks first whether or not they are looking for a job, and should the need arise they can then make use of those contacts to find work. The two sites aim to mirror that social functioning – by encouraging anyone to come onto Babalife.com to connect with friends and family for no other reason than fun and friendship, members will eventually use the job-seeking part of the site as a natural part of their social networking.

The most innovative aspect of this project is the text-free job search function[12] that is being developed in association with Microsoft Research India,[13] also based in Bangalore. The text-free user interface minimizes text in favour of pictures, diagrams and video, enhanced by voice annotations when the mouse is rolled over an object such as a picture. This enables non-literate users to access the job listings themselves even when they are coming to a computer for the first time. For example, the job categories are represented by pictures – a woman cooking for the cook category, a woman carrying a child for childcare/ nursemaid, a man clipping a hedge for gardening. Click on a picture and you are taken to the listings, with the pay shown in large numbers on a rupee note, the address in text and a milestone showing the distance from the town centre. Voice annotations are played when the mouse rolls over any of the items to confirm the information by spoken word.

For communicators and businesses looking at implementing a social network, the Babalife.com–Babajob.com network highlights cultural issues and practical solutions with valuable lessons for cross-cultural communications:

- Their focus as a social enterprise is on improving the work opportunities of the low-income, non-/semi-literate. This niche focus drives everything they have developed. A strong focus on a niche can be a powerful driver for innovation. What is your niche? How can you think outside of the box to develop online communications for that niche market?
- The founder and CEO, Sean Blagsvedt, and his management team have a solid background in software program management, digital design and IT research. Although from multi-national backgrounds, they are all based in the locality they serve, Bangalore. Their knowledge of the specific cultural and societal locality gives them a deep understanding of the issues facing the low-income, non-literate workers whom they aim to serve. Their specialist knowledge of IT and background in research grounds their technology-based solution to these social issues. For the social network you are planning, have you dug deeply into the culture of the people you are aiming to serve? In terms of technology, do you have not just the best software developers but also those who have the right approach for the job? Can they think beyond what they already know to apply it to your specialized niche market, taking into account all relevant local factors?
- The site is offered in English and a number of local languages. Offering alternate language options is especially relevant in countries such as India. But with increasing global population movements, even in English speaking countries, you may need to consider whether non-English versions of your site may significantly increase the number of users.
- The specific needs of the people they are aiming to serve have led them to partner with Microsoft Research to develop and trial the text-free user interface. What partnerships do you need to develop the most relevant online tools for your customers or stakeholders? Looking beyond your corporation's boundaries to research centres, universities and other places of cutting-edge design and technology can create new synergies and help position your organization at the forefront of your industry.

Home sweet home

The simplest form of social network can be created using a discussion forum. This was done by Philippines-based Filgifts.com,[14] an online gift shop catering to Filipinos around the world. Director and Managing Partner Gerry Ditchling explains 'We know most Filipinos living abroad miss the Philippines and look forward to coming home. So we thought of getting them together through an online post about their lives abroad and their experiences on their recent visits to the Philippines.' A central part of the site is the Balikbayan Chronicles.[15] '"Balikbayan" is a colloquial Tagalog term referring to Filipinos living abroad who come and visit the Philippines. "Balik" means come back and "bayan" means country. We started Balikbayan Chronicles in 2000 and it has taken a life of its own.' Most of the posts are by Filipino expats, talking about how they miss home and describing their visits back – for Christmas, for a funeral or on business. They hardly mention shopping or gifts or anything related to the main site but are personal stories that are often touching. One chronicler expresses the mood of the postings very well: 'I've read some of our balikbayans' testimonials, and most of them, have the same things to say: The Philippines, *ang sariling atin.* There's no place on earth such as beautiful as ours. Yet, the Philippines, is always been so beautiful. I've been here in the US for 14½ years but my heart would always be a filipina.'[16]

Through the chronicles, the Filgifts brand is transformed from 'a shopping site' to a 'home from home' and a place for Filipinos to connect with their home country and also other Filipinos. Although many postings are one-off stories rather than blog posts developed over time, the feel of the chronicles is that of a community, bound together by a common heritage and love for a distant homeland.

The take-home points here are that:

- You do not necessarily need a complicated social networking site to create a sense of community and connection.
- People like to engage with personal stories from other people like themselves – you do not need to control the content beyond a simple guiding statement such as 'Please feel free to share your thoughts and experiences of your recent visit to the Philippines in the Balikbayan Chronicles. Your first-hand experience will surely help fellow balikbayans see what it's really like!'

- The stories that people write about do not have to relate in any way directly to the product or services you are selling for the interaction to be successful. And in some cases, such as for Filgifts.com., it is more successful because of that disconnect.

Health

Jay Drayer and his wife Terry found themselves becoming the carers, or caretakers, for her dad Joseph after he was rushed to hospital with a serious heart condition. Their lives changed radically. Their days were spent working round the two-hour commute each way to the hospital, answering well-meaning enquiries from friends and family, juggling the times when people wanted to visit with Joseph's fluctuating energy and treatment schedule – and all the while trying to maintain their own busy working lives and commitments to their children.

'If there's anything I can do, let me know.' How often do we hear that good-intentioned question in a time of crisis? Many people in Joseph's 'community' made this offer of help to the Drayers. Speaking to us on the phone from Houston, Drayer reflects 'But how do you respond to that? What is this person really willing to do? You really appreciate their offer but you don't want to put people on the spot.'

When a family member is seriously ill, those who become the caretaker are also conduits of information for the extended network of family and friends. Drayer says 'The caretaker suffers – there's the stress, anxiety, frustration, exhaustion. It can all lead to depression and burn-out. The patient suffers, too – because the caretaker is distracted by having to manage the community and also keeping up with the household chores that the patient cannot handle anymore, like mowing the lawn, paying the bills and so on.'

Out of this personal crisis, Drayer developed an online community, CareFlash, which enables anyone to create a private social network to share their medical circumstances with friends and family, and to update everyone 'in a flash'. The patient or caretaker sets up the network and becomes the 'owner' of the site. They can invite friends and families to join. Health status updates can be posted onto the site via a blog-style function. The patient's community can rally round to give emotional support via message-boards and messaging functions. They can also help in a practical way: the site 'owner' can post tasks that they need help with via task-linked iHelp Calendar™

– eg mowing the lawn, bringing hot meals – and any member of the patient's community can sign up for a particular task. This empowers each member of the community to do what they actually can to help in a real way while freeing up the time and precious emotional and physical resources for the patient and caretaker.

The site also helps the patient and their community to understand the illness by 3-D animated flash images that take you inside the body as well as links to relevant information from established sources such as the National Institution of Health Information. The flash animations, created by medical-imaging specialists Blausen Medical Communications, can be explored by the user through-clicking and dragging to see different views, and is accompanied by an audio narrative.

Drayer says that a large part of the US healthcare economy is driven by people coming for treatment from overseas. These patients may come with family and friends but they will have an extended network back home, and in this age of global connection, they may have friends and family from all over the world. For some of these patients, English is not their first language and they may also come from a culture where they are not comfortable asking questions of their doctor, whom they see as someone in authority. The support network and access to information facilitated by CareFlash is extended to such global communities by the multi-language versions of the site on offer (at the time of writing: Dutch, Hungarian, Spanish and Arabic). It is also integrated with the social networking site Facebook. com, making it a simple step to invite your existing online friends to this care network.

Even if the interest of your business is not healthcare or people in crisis, there are several factors to be drawn from this case study:

- Drayer's personal experience of a family health crisis grounds the project in authenticity. As is often the case in the social media landscape, an authentic vision will be more powerful than a project conceived and implemented for marketing reasons alone. On which end of this spectrum would your social media project fall?
- The site tools empower each member of a patient's community to do what they can and also empower users through the information it channels. How does your social network empower your members? What tools and resources does your site offer that can help people work together, whether it is related to a crisis or otherwise?

- CareFlash came into being to serve a real human need. Many social networks are implemented by businesses because it's the sexy thing to do. Or it's a great marketing tool. But is there a real need for a social network in the context your business? Will it really be useful or enhance the lives of your customers or employees?
- CareFlash is aware of the global potential of their services and cross-cultural issues for their users. Have you considered language issues and other cross-cultural sensitivities for global users of your social network?
- While CareFlash is a business and funds itself through advertising revenue, Drayer emphasizes that the ads are unobtrusive and tasteful. The company also channels 10 per cent of its profit back to healthcare foundations as part of its commitment to the community. How might you include a 'giving back' element in your social network project as a mark of your commitment to the community?

Gay, transgendered and intersexed

'Social media is incredibly important for non-mainstream communities. Being able to come together and get support is fantastic but just knowing there are others out there with the same problems is an incredible boon in and of itself. Knowing you're not alone can sometimes be enough to keep you going when you'd otherwise literally want to just curl up and die.' This is what Zoe Robinson, co-creater of T-Vox, told us in an e-mail.

One community that is marginalized across the globe comprises those who identify as gay, transgendered or intersexed and those questioning their gender. T-Vox[17] is an online space run by volunteers that offers resources as well as opportunities for chat and discussion to this community. The main site is a wiki, powered by WikiMedia,[18] the free platform that was first created for Wikipedia, the global user-generated encyclopedia. The wiki covers advice as well as legal information. Users who have signed up to T-Vox can add to the wiki database and the law section has information on UK, US, Australian and Austrian law. There is a chat room for real-time chat as well as a forum for more in-depth discussions. The site creators, UK-based Zoe Robinson and Jennifer Kirk, also host podcasts discussing transgender and other issues relevant for their community.

Robinson says that while most of the wiki's users are based in the United Kingdom and USA, their other main 'contributors and users [are] from Japan, Australia and Western Europe. We get traffic from all over the world, and we're working on expanding our language base to better accommodate people from countries where English is not a main language.' Feedback from users has been positive. Robinson says, 'Our no-nonsense approach to information (we try to tell people what they need to hear, which may not always be what they "want" to hear) seems to be a big hit.'

However, they have experienced several orchestrated attacks on T-Vox's wiki and one concerted attack on their forum. 'The forum attack seems to have been perpetrated by a lone hacker who wanted to show off to friends,' Robinson says, 'while the wiki attacks have been organized by transphobic campaign groups who don't like us empowering their potential victims. We deal with them firstly by blocking the IP ranges they use so the attack can't continue, then we either roll-back the Wiki or restore the forum from the latest of our regular backups. We've never lost data from any of these attacks because we know they could happen at any time and so keep regular backups.'

From her own personal perspective, Robinson says, 'Community is important when you're transgendered because the experience is a very isolating one. It's important to know that you're not alone, that other people have gone through the same thing and that others are experiencing the same problems you are struggling with.'

A cautionary tale

From a business and marketing point of view, watching the number of members grow on your online social network must be a dream come true – here are the statistics you need to prove return on investment, here is the captive audience you can market to and here is the data you can monetize via advertising on your site. The temptation is to maximize these assets to the hilt via traditional marketing means such as advertising and mailshots and also – this being social media – to find new and innovative marketing techniques to sell stuff to this network.

The social networking phenomenon of 2007, Facebook.com, had a valuable asset base of 42 million users[19] as of September 2007 and was already monetizing it via online banner ads that appear on the Facebook pages that users access. Part of Facebook's draw for users is the mini-feed, an RSS feed that publishes what a Facebooker is doing in that social network's universe. So, for example, when Latifah adds the zombie application, her Facebook friends learn about this in the RSS news feed that shows them what their Facebook friends are doing. Part of the success of the mini-feed has been its inconsequentiality – there are very few real world implications if all your Facebook friends see that you've sent a virtual pot plant to someone: it's just a bit of fun.

Facebook created an application, Beacon, to partner with third-party businesses so that Facebook friends could see what a user was up to on sites outside Facebook. For example, a user may be playing an online game on another site or browsing through a DVD rental catalogue and Beacon would send this information back to the user's Facebook profile. From a marketing perspective, this might seem a stroke of genius in that it appears to apply the best of what social networking is all about – users' interactions are shared with their friends and the application seems to help friends recommend goods and services to each other. The backlash against this 'behavioural targeting' took Facebook and their Beacon partners by surprise.

As a result of the backlash against Beacon, which included an online petition signed by 55,000 people, Facebook backed down from the scheme by making it opt-in rather than opt-out and giving users more control of what items appear in the news feed.[20] There remained nonetheless concerns among the public, civil rights groups and commentators regarding Facebook's privacy policy for its users. In March 2008, Facebook founder Mark Zuckerberg was heckled at the SXSWi (South by South West Interactive)[21] conference in Austin, Texas during his keynote appearance by a delegate shouting out 'Beacon sucks!'[22]

Some learning points might be:

- Facebook hit the headlines when co-founder Zuckerberg was offered US$1 billion for the site by Yahoo.[23] Although he turned it down, perception of Facebook turned from being that of a little David into a global Goliath. The Goliath image was compounded by the Beacon fiasco. People may cut you some slack while you are a David, but once you are perceived as a Goliath, they hold you much more accountable – and rightly so, as your influence and reach extend far more widely. Be aware of where you or your business stands in that spectrum.
- People came to Facebook for fun and personal or community interaction. Beacon was perceived as a cynical manipulation of

the 'word of mouth' recommendation concept and commercial exploitation of the network's users. Check whether what you are doing online has a perceptible whiff of commercial exploitation. People may be willing to reveal aspects of their lives openly online but need to be able to control how much and when they do so. Consider carefully the privacy options that you offer on your social networking site.

Notes

1. The Deadliest Tsunami in History? *National Geographic*, 7 January 2005, http://news.nationalgeographic.com/news/2004/12/1227_041226_tsunami.html.
2. Scenes from a Disaster, *The Guardian*, 30 December 2004, http://www.guardian.co.uk/world/2004/dec/30/tsunami2004.features11.
3. Richard Giles Blog, Flickr Tsunami, 28 December 2004, http://richardgiles.net/2004/12/28/flickr-tsunami/.
4. Jane Perrone, The Coming of Age of Citizen Media, *The Guardian*, 26 December 2005, http://blogs.guardian.co.uk/news/archives/2005/12/26/the_coming_of_age_of_citizen_media.html.
5. http://www.tsunamihelp.info/wiki/index.php/Main_Page.
6. http://katrinahelp.blogspot.com/.
7. http://quakehelp.blogspot.com/.
8. http://babajob.com/home.htm.
9. http://babajob.com/home.htm.
10. http://babalife.com/.
11. http://babalife.com/aboutus.htm.
12. http://babajob.com/tfoverview.htm.
13. http://research.microsoft.com/~indranim/.
14. http://www.filgifts.com/default.asp.
15. http://www.filgifts.com/ffp/chronicles/read.asp.
16. http://www.filgifts.com/ffp/chronicles/read.asp?MonthPage=12/1/2006.
17. http://www.t-vox.org/index.php?title=Main_Page.
18. http://www.mediawiki.org/wiki/MediaWiki.
19. New Members on Facebook, Platform Growth – Inside Facebook, 25 September 2007, http://www.insidefacebook.com/2007/09/25/new-numbers-on-facebook-platform-growth/.
20. Jerome Taylor, Facebook Drops Controversial Opt Out Advertising Service, *The Independent*, 1 December 2007, http://www.independent.co.uk/life-style/gadgets-and-tech/news/facebook-drops-controversial-optout-advertising-service-761683.html.
21. http://2007.sxsw.com/interactive/.

22. Christina Warren, 'Beacon Sucks' Sums Up SXSWi Facebook Keynote, dowloadsquad.com, 10 March 2008, http://www.downloadsquad.com/2008/03/10/beacon-sucks-sums-up-sxswi-facebook-keynote.
23. Fred Vogelstein, How Mark Zuckerberg Turned Facebook Into the Web's Hottest Platform, *Wired*, 9 June 2007, http://www.wired.com/techbiz/startups/news/2007/09/ff_facebook.

10 Encouraging new forms of expression

Social media tools enable almost instantaneous communication online to and from anywhere in the world, provided you have internet or mobile access. The world has speeded up exponentially and anyone with a camera-phone, mobile phone or laptop with mobile internet access can be a citizen journalist, as we have seen elsewhere in this book. And no longer are we passive consumers – using social media, we can take part in what is happening out there in the real world by engaging in discussions, blogging our views, adding our own photos and reports, and organizing together to take action. Business models are also evolving with this new, fast-moving engagement and using social media tools for time-sensitive interactions with their customers.

Immediacy

South Africa: The Newswatch blog

In early 2007, East Coast Radio, the second largest regional station in South Africa, began to explore the world of blogs and social media. Broadcasting from Durban, Kwazulu-Natal, East Coast Radio, also known as ECR, is a commercial radio station with an audience of over 2 million. Diane Macpherson, ECR's News Editor, recalls, 'Blogging was a relatively new concept in South Africa at the time, certainly on the corporate side of things, although since then, there has been an explosion in blogging and more and more companies have been recognising that this is a legitimate source of info and of marketing.' ECR already had a website at www.ecr.co.za and the blog was built on Wordpress and was initially hosted as part of the main site. The design incorporated the corporate colours and reflected the layout and feel of the main website. Once the blog design was ready, Macpherson says, 'From a news perspective, we were poised to launch but felt that the launch needed to coordinate with a major news event that we could cover. We could then use the medium of radio to drive listeners to the blog.'

That major event came in mid-March 2007 in the form of a massive storm around Durban followed days later by huge tides that all but eroded the coastline. Macpherson remembers 'We called for storm photos on air and, boy, did they come in. Hundreds of them – which our web company loaded in galleries on the site. And we were live within hours.'

ECR relied on their main medium, the airwaves, to alert people to the blog and what they could find there. On its launch morning, the Newswatch blog received more than 10,000 unique visitors. By the end of the second day, 35,000 unique visitors had gone to the blog. Listeners, responding to calls to send their photos of the disaster, jammed the server with about 1,000 pictures on the first day alone. The website experienced about 35 per cent of its total monthly traffic in a single morning. The pictures from the blog have also been viewed around the world. Macpherson says, 'The site actually crashed for a few hours due to the traffic. Our ingenious web team had to change the entire parent website to separate the blog hosting from the main website.'

The ECR Newswatch Blog can now be found at www.blog.ecr.co.za/newswatch. ECR also has a number of other blogs, CrimeWatch, Sports, Big Breakfast and Just Plain Darren, which are all offshoots of programmes broadcast on the radio. There is a Facebook group with over 1,000 members and the main website offers a chat forum, which is free but accessed by registration. ECR has clearly embraced social media and is using a cross-platform approach to engaging its audience.

ECR has also stepped into the world of citizen journalism via the Newswatch Blog, extending the familiar radio 'phone-in' format onto the social media sphere. The blog posts regularly on current news stories, adding information that might not have made it into the radio news slots. Listeners can comment on the stories and this seems a popular interactive element with many posts attracting upwards of 100 comments. Additionally, in a section headed 'You be the journalist', there is a call for submissions: 'If you witness an interesting event you think East Coasters would love to see, simply whip out your cell phone or digital camera, take a picture or video clip and e-mail it to diane@ecr.co.za. It may just appear on this site!' Using the comments facility in Wordpress, ECR has also created a space for their listeners to share comments around a news event on a simple page headed 'Something on our mind?' This facility also has the secondary function of providing the news team with potential leads or additional information for their news stories.

Macpherson says:

> We always see a spike when there is some sort of hot button item in the news such as a natural disaster or a controversial human interest story that is playing out. Our audience dictates what we focus on and contributes to the story.
>
> Last year in May 2007, the murder of a young man in a Durban restaurant proved one such catalyst. Marc Joubert was a popular local who loved life and had many friends.[1] He died when armed robbers opened fire one Saturday night at a popular restaurant. The crime was so heinous, it sparked a national outcry. And because we were the radio station his friends and family listened to, our blog became the centrepiece in terms of communication regarding the crime and also for condolences for Joubert's death. Within a few hours on a Sunday, there were almost 200 comments on the blog story we had carried on the incident.
>
> And soon afterwards, a Durban-based parliamentarian who is a member of opposition party, the Democratic Alliance, had printed out the many comments and presented the document in South Africa's Parliament in Cape Town as an illustration of the sentiment of the people, most of whom were angrily calling on government to take harsh action to stamp out crime in this country. It was televised on the parliamentary channel and we were all quite proud to see our blog being named and pages, about 40 of them, being waved around in a bundle by the Member of Parliament.
>
> It was then that we realised the blog was not just a means of depicting in photos what we could never achieve on the airwaves, but also of being a vehicle for social protest and expression.

The Newswatch blog won the South African Blog Award for the Best New Blog of 2007. Macpherson e-mailed us the morning after saying she was 'very chuffed'. She says 'When our disc jockeys began taking about the word "blog", many people had no idea what that was. I would wager that our popularisation of the blog resulted in many off-shoots around our province. I have no empirical data to back this up but it is a good hunch and a recognition of the power of the popular media.'

We don't all have to be a major radio station to use some of the strategies that ECR implemented to make their blog a success:

- ECR held off launching the blog until there was an event that could make the platform relevant to its listeners. Timing was key. This statement is an obvious one. But it is worth remembering that the blog or social media channel that your organization sets up is similar to a publication or a traditional media channel.
- The blog complements the main radio medium and the ease of instantaneous online publication offered by blogs is ideal for this engagement. How might you use your social media platform to offer additional value and resources to your stakeholders?
- ECR's blog has become a focal point for their listeners' responses to news items. How could you position your blog as focal point for your stakeholders?
- ECR's technical team responded quickly to the overload on their systems on the launch day to make sure that the blog was kept up and running in spite of the surge of visitors. What structures do you have in place to troubleshoot your social media channel – especially in a situation where an urgent technical response is needed?
- The ECR news team found story leads in their visitor comments and responses. While it takes resourcing to track comments, this area of a blog can be a mine of information for your business. Do you check your comments sections regularly and actively engage there to encourage visitors to share their views and knowledge?

Mobilization

China: The kitten killer of Hangzhou

The online video shows a woman standing in stiletto heels, her face partially obscured. She is by a river bank, caressing a kitten gently – apparently kindly. She bends down and places it on the walkway at her feet. The creature is docile, trusting. The camera follows her as she bends, focusing in a close-up zoom on the cute little kitten. Her feet in their shiny, stiletto sandals are very close to the animal. She steps on the kitten, hard, killing it.

This is just one of many videos that had been spreading across the internet in China, showing 'dogs, cats, rabbits and toads being stomped to death by a sexy woman wearing stockings and high heels'.[2] The difference is that this video became the icon of a rallying call across China to stop animal abuse. Paul Littlefair, senior programme manager in the International Department of the Royal Society for the Prevention of Cruelty to Animals (RSPCA), explains 'This video caused outrage when it was spread across the internet. Although the woman could not be identified easily, the location was identifiable through various landmarks. People began to network online to try and track this woman down. Journalists picked up the story, adding fuel to the campaign. This became a cause celebre in the media as well as online. Eventually, the woman was found. She was a nurse and had apparently been recruited by the men who had made the film. She was fired from her job and made an online apology.

'This video was a turning point for animal welfare in China. What this woman and the filmmakers had done was not a crime under Chinese law. The police did not – and in fact, could not – get involved. The woman and her actions were in effect tried online through the debate on blogs and on the threads on discussion boards. The incident raised big questions for the nation that were debated in the mainstream media as well as online – questions like: can this be right, what happens in other countries when people do this, shouldn't China have laws to punish this kind of behaviour?'

Littlefair has been travelling to China for the last ten years, liaising with official bodies and animal protection groups there that are working to educate the general population around the treatment and well-being of animals. He has observed the growing awareness of animal welfare in that country over the years and in particular notes the influence of social media in engaging people in the debate through personal stories by animal enthusiasts, tips on animal care and behaviour and stories about rescued animals. These appear on numerous blogs, online networks and discussion forums set up by individual enthusiasts rather than the RSPCA or other formal organizations. The RSPCA itself does not get involved in campaigning among the general populace in China. Rather it works with government departments, academic institutions and local NGOs to promote discussion and raise awareness of animal protection issues. When necessary it registers its concern on specific cruelty matters through formal channels, for example by writing letters of protest to city or provincial governments. It is the locally organized grass-roots campaigning and protests that have made the most impact over time on the attitudes and views of ordinary Chinese people – and this is being slowly translated into the potential for change in the official attitude towards animal welfare.

An example of how forums and blogs have been used in China in relation to animal welfare is the role they play during periodic dog culling by the authorities, often during outbreaks of rabies. Littlefair explains:

> Culling takes place somewhere in the country every few months. This is done by local authorities and action is taken against both stray dogs and owned pets. In one case in 2006, around 50,000 dogs were indiscriminately killed in 10 days. Forums and blogs warn people about those districts where culling is going on and they encourage legitimate forms of protest such as calling or faxing the local government offices to express your outrage. Sometimes, they are used to organise street protests – which are technically illegal without proper permission and individuals do not have the same status to obtain permission as formally organised groups have.

Littlefair goes on to describe what happened during a clampdown on unregistered dogs proposed in October 2006 in Beijing:

> This was not in response to rabies, which is not seen in China's major cities, but an attempt to control the growing number of pet dogs before the Olympics. Chinese journalists were banned from reporting negatively about this campaign, in particular the plans to confiscate and destroy unregistered pet dogs. Owing to the high annual fee levied by the city government, most Beijing dog-owners cannot afford to register their animals. As the deadline for registration approached information was leaked and international organisations, including the RSPCA learnt about it. We protested formally by sending letters to the city and provincial governments and also the Olympic organising committee.
>
> Beyond the usual, accepted routes of protest, Chinese citizens spread the word via blogs and also used online forums to organise street activities to make their opposition known. In an illegal protest of individual citizens, several hundred people turned up outside the city zoo. It was a coordinated but peaceful demonstration with banners and tee-shirts – the participants were mainly dog lovers and their sympathisers. Public security bureau officers photographed them, there were some arrests and one person, who was thought to be the ringleader, was apparently detained for months.

Overall, the outcome was that the clampdown and threatened cull were stopped. The street demonstrations, as well as the attention of the domestic and international press and foreign organisations such as the RSPCA, caused senior Chinese leaders to intervene and call the campaign off. But this was the first time that the internet played a central role in pulling all these factors together – notwithstanding the control that the authorities have over the internet, the leaked news of the culling and the ability to use the forums and blogs to organise protests and spread the word within China and also internationally could not have been done without these social media tools.

There are also internet-based networks organized around animal welfare and rights, comprising groups of people located all over China, some of whom may never have met. Littlefair gives the example of the Chinese Animal Protection Network,[3] which began as a group of informal enthusiasts in the Shanghai area and has grown into a nationwide network with around 50 local and provincial groups. The members use an online network to keep in contact and also to report to the wider Chinese community outside China. It has launched a number of different projects to address different animal issues such as animal ethics, the welfare of companion animals and vegetarianism. According to its website, the network 'is using technology, research, education, artistry, and creativity [to] make our world a better place for all sentience [sic] beings.'

The overall result of this is that animal welfare is being taken seriously now at the highest levels, according to Littlefair. There have been an increasing number of academic papers published in Chinese universities on the morality and ethics surrounding the use of animals, tackling such questions such as whether animal welfare is a Western concept or a universal one that should be embraced by China. Littlefair says 'A search for "animal welfare" in Baidu, the largest search engine in China, yields close to a million relevant pages now compared to 100,000 in 2005. That's almost a10-fold increase in 3 years. While it's by no means a scientifically controlled count, it is a useful way to measure the increase in Chinese-language material on the subject that is out there.' Most significantly, in 2008 the RSPCA and the Chinese Academy of Social Sciences' Institute of Law came together to host an international conference in Beijing to discuss animal welfare legislation for China, an important step towards a change in official policy.

The issues we would highlight here for communicators and PR professionals are:

- The RSPCA themselves do not engage in the online campaigns nor any press-related activities associated with the grass-roots campaigns, always maintaining their independence from these groups – which is critical for the continuing authenticity and trust that is required for their role in that region and globally. It can be tempting to engage online when there is a campaign that you might be able to take advantage of for your business. Consider very carefully the ramifications of such active online engagement. Will it help in the short term but be potentially damaging in the long term? If you do engage, how can you do so in a way that is open and authentic?

- The RSPCA built on the groundswell of local debate and feeling about animal welfare in a way that was appropriate to its activities in the region through engaging in an international conference in Beijing with the nation's legal think tank. This plays to its strengths of engaging in issues at a high level in a discreet and measured way, leaving the vocal grass-roots campaigning to other groups. A successful campaign that truly effects change needs engagement at all levels and through different channels. Where can your organization best position itself to make a difference? It may be through online activities or it may be through traditional methods such as symposiums and conferences. But an awareness of what is going on within social media as much as anywhere else will add to your ability to effect change.

71Miles: A social media travel business

Tools for speedy communications come in useful in many arenas, not just during times of disaster. 71Miles.com is a web-based travel company located in California, specializing in weekend destinations within reasonable driving distance of major cities in Northern California and Washington, DC. Twitter, as we have seen, is the short messaging web/mobile phone hybrid. Subscribers to the 71Miles Twitter feed are notified by 'tweets' of last-minute deals. A link in the tweet takes you to a web page with more details. The bargains are often time critical and available on a first come, first served basis, so there is an advantage for users to receive the tweets on their mobile phone. Adam Rugel, founder of 71Miles, explains 'One user, a former Google employee now semi-retired, told us he's the ideal recipient for hotel deals via Twitter because he can pick up on a moment's notice and book the deals he gets from us over SMS. Text message marketing in the US is still relatively new, and in general, the response has been positive as users seem to respond to the novelty of it.'

What is worth noting about this young company is that in addition to using Twitter as a central part of their business strategy, 71Miles has based its business model around social media tools. The main website is a Wordpress blog written by Co-Founder and Editor John Vlahides, featuring articles on a range of travel destinations – some of which may not have any relationship to the weekend breaks offered by the company. His articles give a flavour of the destination and offer insider tips. For example, Vlahides writes up a day trip that can be made to Angel Island from San Francisco – there is no product that the company can sell here – and he offers the additional personal tip: 'If you're considering going to Angel Island this weekend, make the trip on Sunday. Saturday's weather forecast calls for wind. Pack layers: the weather changes fast. To avoid the crowds, hike up the Sunset Trail and down the North Ridge Trail; most people do the opposite.'[4] The real-time relevance of the tips plus a link to a local weather website are likely to encourage readers to come back to the blog regularly to check out the travel tip for the next weekend. By widening the remit of the blog to travel breaks other than their own travel products, 71Miles can attract readers who are generally interested in things they can do in their local area who may not be in buying mode at the time of reading but who are likely to remember 71Miles when they are next looking to purchase a weekend break. Rugel adds 'Allowing users to interact with John Vlahides within the comments section of 71Miles.com give the site personality and makes it feel alive. It also allows us to acquire great recommendations from users.'

In addition to Twitter and Wordpress, 71Miles also uses Google Maps and sometimes Google Calendar as part of their website to help visitors identify location and special dates for their diary. They have also created online videos hosted by Brightcove.com, which take viewers on a trip to 'drive down one of California's most spectacular back roads; hike atop windswept Bodega Head, and peer down 275 feet to fog-shrouded coves; then explore the dramatic coastal landscape of Sonoma State Beach.'[5] Rugel explains 'These existing platforms make it very easy to develop quickly. Without them, 71Miles would have been much more expensive, and time-consuming, to build. The advantages are time-to-market, reliability, and scalability. The disadvantage is that we can't customize in ways that we wish we could, because the platforms not tailor made for us.' The company also created a Facebook application during 2008 – Trazzler – which is a quiz that helps you 'discover your unique travel personality and builds a fantasy itinerary for you and your friends'.[6] Of their foray into social networks and fantasy applications, Rugel says 'The hottest issue of the day for business like ours is the Facebook newsfeed and its implications for lead generation. Is it a trend, or something thats here to stay? Will other social networks successfully replicate it? Only time will tell.'

What is striking for us about 71Miles is the use of a range of social media tools as a foundation for the entire business. The points of note from this case study for businesses and communications professionals are:

- Do you need to re-invent the wheel when considering social media for your website? Many corporations like to have products tailor-made for their purposes and in many cases that is the most appropriate path to take, especially where their requirements are complex and there is a high premium on branding. However, there are circumstances where using third-party applications like Twitter, Brightcove, Google Maps and Google Calendar can be an advantage – especially if the developers there can be engaged contractually to apply their expertise specifically to your project.
- How might you use Twitter to build real-time engagement with your customers and clients? Twitter messaging differs from straight SMS marketing in that the emphasis with Twitter, as a microblogging platform, is on community and conversation rather than on selling stuff. To receive a tweet, you have to subscribe to the relevant Twitter feed and you can choose to receive it on your mobile phone or via Skype, your instant message application, by e-mail or in a number of Twitter desktop applications. You can unsubscribe very easily via any of these applications. You as the customer are in complete control. In contrast, traditional SMS marketing can often be unsolicited and only transmitted to your mobile phone – and has consequently fallen into the category of junk mail for many people. Twitter can also be used to link users to a blog where the relationship can be developed, thus making the user experience richer and deeper than a traditional SMS marketing text.

Speed

Text has been the front-runner in time-critical blogging for most of the last few years. As we've seen in previous sections, posting written updates to a blog is quick and easy, as is Twittering with short text messages.

Enter social media startup, Qik, in late 2007. Qik is a platform for user-generated videos. What makes Qik different is that users with a mobile phone[7] that has a video function and WiFi or 3G capability can stream live video from their phones to be watched by visitors to their Qik page in real time. Visitors can 'chat' with the video-blogger by typing their comments online – the comments appear on the video-blogger's mobile phone screen. Blogger and social media geek Robert Scoble used his mobile phone to film live interviews with prominent delegates at the World Economic Forum in Davos[8] in early 2008, the first major use of the Qik platform, shortly after the service launched. His audience could send him chat messages during the interview asking him to ask the interviewee about specific issues. This is what makes the real-time video service exciting for communications – an audience from all over the world can participate and interact in real time with the video blogger and the participants in that filmed event. At the Davos event, Scoble's live video interviews probably scooped many journalists who were still working in the traditional way.

Not surprisingly, news journalists are taking an interest in this new video-streaming platform. US-based video blogger Steve Garfield gave a presentation in March 2008 to the New England Newspaper Association for the New England News Forum entitled 'Rebooting Your Newsroom with LIVE mobile video broadcasting', explaining what Qik is and how to use it for news reporting.[9] In the following month, US newspaper *The Sacramento Bee* used Qik to stream live footage of the protests during the Olympic torch procession in San Francisco.

In this fast-moving arena, the points for businesses, organizations and communicators to take into account are:

- How might you take advantage of some of these speedy communication tools for your enterprise?
- And if you do take advantage of the live streaming functionality of sites such as Qik, will production quality be more important to you than edgy, uncut, real-time streaming? Are you going to go for real immediacy or an edited version of it?

- Are you ready to be caught on a mobile-phone video, possibly streamed live to an audience of millions?
- Are you ready to be critiqued in real time by Twitter comments at a conference, or even while you may be unaware that you've been observed by someone quietly tapping into their mobile phone?

The rise of social media has been changing the communications playing field, levelling it out to include the participation of many. We looked in some detail in earlier chapters at the technological and economic factors driving this revolution. Even as we write, new technology is continuing to change the ways information and news is being delivered, primarily in the areas of mobile and video communications. What are you doing to keep abreast of developing technologies that are speeding up one-to-many communications?

Notes

1. See http://blog.ecr.co.za/newswatch/?s=joubert for more stories on Joubert.
2. Cat Stomped to Death in Film Draws Outrage, *Shanghai Daily*, 3 March 2006, http://english.sina.com/life/p/1/2006/0303/67958.html.
3. http://www.capn.ngo.cn/en.asp.
4. John Vlahides, Angel Island Day Trip, 18 April 2008, http://71miles.com/weekly/circling-angel-island.
5. http://71miles.com/company-info/pilots.
6. http://www.facebook.com/apps/application.php?id=5808774727.
7. At the time of writing, only Nokia phones are supported.
8. Robert Scoble, Scoble's Davos Videos, webpronews.com, 4 February 2008, http://www.webpronews.com/blogtalk/2008/02/04/scobles-davos-videos.
9. See Garfield's blog post at http://stevegarfield.blogs.com/videoblog/2008/03/new-england-pre.html, which also has a link to the video of that presentation.

11 The next frontier
Multimedia and beyond

In this final chapter on social media, we explore in more detail the convergence of multimedia, social media and mobile communications. The human instinct for communication desires visual, face-to-face connection in real time – and if we cannot actually be physically close, then virtual proximations are a second best that we flock towards. As digital technology and its distribution infrastructures develop, we are seeing those proximations come closer and closer towards real time anywhere and at any time. When we seem to be glued to the computer screen or endlessly fiddling with our mobile phones, we are not, as some naive observers might consider, bonding with those machines – we are most likely bonding in a very human way to other people on the far end of that digital stream.

If social media can be likened to a cultural landscape, multimedia is the next frontier of the expanding virtual space. Relationship building in this environment moves beyond being good with written text, which is needed for blogging, to involving the whole persona in engaging our voices and visual images – and also in some spaces, avatars or digital representations of ourselves. According to Reuters, a survey in October 2008 across seven Asian countries found that 56 per cent of affluent Asians use their mobile devices to take pictures every week and 30 per cent watched video clips on those devices.[1] The report goes on to say 'Some Asians also used these devices to blog or make Web movies.' Additionally, in many countries around the world where literacy rates are low and broadband infrastructure is patchy, it will not only be the affluent who will be accessing mobile communications and non-text based media. Tudor Aw, Digital Convergence Partner at management consultants KPMG, adds 'People will begin to increasingly use their mobile as a device for converged services, including social media. For example, Nokia are pushing hard in this space and see a world where we take a photo with our mobile, write a blog associated with that photo or video clip and then upload it to Facebook. If this happens, then the implications for emerging markets are profound – people in Africa may access mobile technology as a means for getting on the digital express!'

For professional communicators, understanding how multimedia can be integrated within your social media and wider strategies will increase your tool set for communications in the 21st century and enable you to engage with the increasing numbers of people all over the world and especially those in Asia who are eagerly and comfortably using video, images, voice and text to engage in their daily lives.

Video

The social media sommelier

'I can't write, so I missed the whole blog thing, and I was pissed', US wine retailer Gary Vaynerchuk told *Time* magazine.[2] He started a video blog – or vlog – instead, creating winelibrary.tv as an extension of the family wine store, Wine Library, based in Springfield, New Jersey and also online at winelibrary.com. In May 2008, the vlog had 80,000 visitors a day, according to *Guardian* tech columnist Jeff Jarvis.[3] By then, Vaynerchuk had appeared on national talk shows and *The Washington Post* as well as in *Time* magazine. When he announced the publication of his book *101 Wines* on his vlog his fans rushed to buy it, pushing the book up to No 36 in the Amazon bestseller list. The family store, started by his Russian émigré father, is now a US$60 million a year enterprise.

Sure, the success of the business is due to more than a daily wine vlog but its role in getting the business noticed nationally beyond New Jersey cannot be underestimated. The daily show's tagline is 'Changing the wine world', and that is what Vaynerchuk is all about. Most episodes are no longer than 15 minutes and it's just him tasting different wines and telling you what he thinks of each one. But don't expect a stuffed shirt, talking head wine expert. He is one of the guys, casually dressed in an open-neck shirt, and he reviews wines like one of the guys – or, rather, the funny guy in your gang of friends, the joker, the one you want at all your parties. He is animated, loud and brash. He has been known to suck on a sweaty sock when talking about the earthy flavour of red wines. Vaynerchuck is changing the wine world by bringing in people who would otherwise consider wine culture pretentious and exclusive. Vaynerchuk's vlog breaks down the barriers of entry so that anyone – not just the so-called experts – can express their opinion about wine. You can leave your comment to the vlog in the usual blog comment box or within the timeline of the video.[4]

To take that social conversation side of wine tasting further online, winelibrary.tv has created an associated wine review network at corkd. com. Users can sign up to a free account and review wines, list their favourite ones and create a wish list of wines they would like to buy. They can become each other's Drinking Buddies (like becoming Friends on Facebook) – and of course buy wines from winelibrary. com. Fans can plan Third Thursday Tasting Group meet-ups and there is a Facebook application where you can ask Vaynerchuk a wine-related question. Additionally, you can 'friend' Vaynerchuk on a number of social networks, including Twitter, LinkedIn, Pownce and MySpace. Most innovatively, Vaynerchuk has created a user-generated project combining online networking with the real-world activity of wine-making, the Vayniac Wine Project.[5] This project gives users the chance to take part in the winemaking process – literally. In association with vineyards and winemakers, the Vayniac community can help to sort the grapes and take part in crushing, fermenting and pressing as well as attend barrel tastings and release parties – all coordinated through an online site, Crushnet.[6]

'Don't tase me, bro'

Almost everyone carries a mobile phone with them for most of their waking day. And almost every mobile phone has a video camera. As we have seen with applications like Qik, live video of events can be streamed to the internet in real time. Even without that immediacy, we are all exposed to being videoed with or without our knowledge or consent at any time. The following case study shows some of the pitfalls of this 'citizen surveillance' society and offers some advice on how to minimize them.

In September 2007, a University of Florida student Andrew Meyer made the headlines[7] when police used a taser on him during a scuffle at a campus forum where Senator John Kerry was speaking. Videos of the incident filmed on cameraphones as well as on video cameras were posted on YouTube.com[8], and at the time of writing many are still available on the site for viewing.

Meyer's questioning style is provocative, and the police officers move in to remove him after apparently being signalled to do so by one of the organizers. Kerry can clearly be heard at this point to say 'That's all right, let me answer the question.' Meyer resists, shouting and waving his arms and at one point saying 'Is anyone watching this?' The incident escalates until four officers forcibly shove him to the back of the hall and wrestle him to the floor. He is heard shouting 'Don't tase me, bro' and then shouting 'Ow!' while a number of people in the hall scream.

The University of Florida, the police and John Kerry were all caught up in the publicity aftermath. The police were accused of brutality, the college of using strong arm tactics to gag free speech and Kerry of standing by weakly while all this was going on. Two of the police officers were placed on leave pending an investigation (they were subsequently cleared).[9] The college wrote letters to students and staff, held press conferences, gave regular updates and dedicated a page of their website to responding to the incident.[10] Kerry issued a statement condemning the arrest and saying that he had not been aware of the use of the taser until later.[11] The university, the police and Kerry did everything by the book in handling the publicity fallout to this incident so it is not the crisis management aspect that is of interest in this case. What we want to tease out here are some issues to consider that may help prevent this sort of incident catching you or your organization off-guard in the first place.

Media coach and president of the Professional Speakers Association in the United Kingdom, Alan Stevens, advises 'Small incidents can escalate suddenly. Your security team, whether police or a private firm, needs to be fully briefed about what to expect and how they are expected to handle incidents. The responsibility really falls on the event organiser to make sure incidents are handled in an appropriate manner. At political meetings, you are bound to have hecklers and many politicians like to be heckled. It gives them a good opportunity to deal with a meaty topic and also they are practiced in dealing with hecklers. In fact, being seen to deal effectively with hecklers can increase the speaker's standing.'

The key is not to play into the hands of hecklers. Stevens says 'You can't prevent people filming an incident and in fact, these days, you have to assume at all times that whatever is happening is being recorded.'

In the digital age, where every cameraphone is a fly on the wall:

- It is increasingly important that all players, not just those in the police and other authorities, are trained in media awareness.
- All staff in public or private organizations, whether at executive level or at ground level, can benefit from a increased understanding of the public relations implications of their actions.
- In fact, it is becoming more critical for front-line staff to be properly trained in how to handle themselves and others. They are the ones who are most likely to face unexpected incidents, irate customers and pranksters so they are the ones who are most likely to represent your business or organization in any videoed incident. Media training can help them do their job better and decrease the likelihood of a badly judged incident being captured on video.
- It comes down to a combination of judgement (Is this the right moment to use force? What is the right level of force to use?) and an assumption that everything you do is going to be recorded (Even if I'm within the law in my actions, do I want this spread all over the internet and global news channels by tonight?).

Podcasting

'Anyone can podcast,' says UK-based podcasting guru Neville Hobson, who with business communications associate Shel Holtz produces the twice-weekly podcast on communications and social media, For Immediate Release.[12] 'You just need to have something to say.'

Podcasts are audio files that can be downloaded from the internet via iTunes or other audio application. They are mp3 files, the same format as music files, and can also be listened to online via audio streaming. Most podcasts take the programme style of talk radio, with hosts engaging in interviews or conversation with guests, interspersed with short musical interludes or 'words from our sponsors'.

Wiggly Wigglers is a garden centre with a strong organic focus operating out of a farm in Herefordshire, United Kingdom. They sell vegetable seeds, fruit trees and flowers as well as composting and other gardening equipment. They produce a half-hour weekly podcast[13] from the Wiggly Wigglers sofa in the farmhouse with a mixture of interviews and segments recorded out in the rain and on visits to other farm sites, including a couple in Vancouver and

Indiana. The show is hosted by the Wiggly Wigglers team themselves and they chat about the hedge being laid at the farm, invite a university professor to discuss their carbon footprint, discuss the effects of fertilizer on biodiversity and which end of the cow produces the most methane. They do not focus very much on their own products in the programmes – and in a sense they do not need to. What they are reinforcing is the experience of Wiggly Wigglers brand as one for people interested organic and environmental issues as well as in gardening and vegetable growing. The listeners' feedback segment of the programme adds to this sense of a community of like-minded people. The podcast overall has a chatty, slightly home-made quality, so that you get the sense of hanging out on the sofa with a bunch of your mates.

Neville Hobson, who with Shel Holtz has written a book on podcasting, *How to do Everything with Podcasting*, says that cost should not be an issue for businesses considering creating a podcast:

> All you need is a computer and a microphone – which can cost as little as £30. There is also free audio editing software you can download from the internet, such as Audacity.[14] Once you've recorded your audio file and edited it, you need a place to host it and there are numerous inexpensive hosting packages. You can then deliver it via your blog and also on iTunes. In terms of the recording standard, the podcast does not have to be 'professional sounding' – which is to say it does not have to be scripted. But you do need good sound quality – that's important.

Hobson recommends that you consider the business objective for creating a podcast:

> You need a clear rationale. A good reason to do it is to build a relationship with your customers. A podcast can complement your other communications strategies in this way. You can build a community around a podcast by encouraging listeners to e-mail in or record an audio comment via telephone or their computer. This sort of thing is difficult to do using traditional media which is geared to impersonality. Social media is aimed at an informal, networking style of communication. The show can evolve into one where it's more than just you – it's you and your listeners creating the show through their feedback; you can invite some to be roving reporters and send in short reports to incorporate as part of the show and also, listeners can suggest topics to cover in the show. Listeners can also easily share your show through forwarding a link to it by e-mail, blogging about it on their blogs or adding your show badge to their site.

In terms of measurement, Hobson suggests some metrics that businesses can use to judge success:

> There are tools that allow you to measure how many downloads you're getting and from which countries. Also you can count the number of comments both audio and text-based ones as well as the number of inbound links to your show pages. The number of downloads is of course different from the number of people who actually listen to the show – that is more difficult to tell. You can supplement the basic tools with surveys and asking for feedback. There is no cast iron guarantee of measured success: you need to look at podcasting – and social media metrics in general – on a like to like basis with other communications strategies that fall into the same category. How do you measure financial returns on having a website? Or the financial returns of an employee newsletter? Podcasting and social media measurement are in the same arena.

Virtual worlds

At one moment during 2005–07, it looked like Second Life, the virtual world, had become more than just a niche social media site for geeks and had well and truly arrived in the mainstream of the real world. That moment was on the UK's popular and populist TV chat show, *Richard & Judy*, when an avatar of presenter Richard appeared on the nation's TV screens and flew a few bumpy virtual feet as a demonstration of this 'Next Big Thing' in online entertainment. Now, we look back and wonder where Second Life has gone. Well, it's still there but in the medium term it looks like it did not prove as popular nor as exciting a brave new world as it had been hyped up to be.

At the height of the excitement, shortly after a *BusinessWeek* front cover article, profiled an virtual entrepreneur[15] who had made real millions in real money on Second Life, this virtual space was expected to be the new frontier for business and personal communications, offering fantastic marketing opportunities for businesses. A number of big-name players entered Second Life with experimental marketing projects, such as Coca-Cola's Virtual Thirst competition,[16] which invited submissions for the design of a virtual Coke vending machine – there is some debate about whether it was a great success or not.[17] Wells Fargo Bank was one of the earlier adopters and developed a game, Stagecoach Island, in Second Life, aimed at helping young people learn financial responsibility.[18] Wells Fargo left Second Life in 2007. They cited that the failure to scale in the virtual world meant that when more than a handful of users came to their virtual island, the system slowed and crashed.[19] Also, an event they held for a virtual interview with Second Life entrepreneur 'Anshe Chang' was disrupted by Second Life 'terrorists' who sent flying male genitalia across the virtual interview space.

In July 2007, *Wired* magazine correspondent Frank Roase published a piece entitled 'How Madison Avenue is Wasting Millions on a Deserted Second Life'.[20] The title says it all.

The problem with Second Life is that it takes commitment and time to become adept at all the controls that you need to personalize your avatar and to move around the virtual space. Once you've got the hang of moving around, there is very little to do there if you are looking for a game experience. It is literally a virtual space for you to hang out as you might hang out in real life. So you need to be creative and adept at making a good life for yourself in this space, much as you might aim to create a good life for yourself in the real world. Keen Second Lifers use the space to connect with like-minded others as you might in a text-based chat room, only you can connect visually as well in the virtual body of your avatar – you can be a monster, an alien, another gender, a child, an idealized version of yourself and so on. But to create an experience-rich Second Life, you need to have a lot of technical programming skill. Without the structure of a game or high technical skill, as we might be used to, it is a space where we are left to our own devices – and it can be a challenge to thrive in such an environment as it can be a challenge in one's 'first life'.

While Second Life is no longer the hot property it was some years ago, the promise of virtual environments will continue to inspire web developers so it is likely that in years to come we will see a number of attempts to revitalize virtual worlds. This is likely to be linked closely to developments aimed at creating a 3-D experience of the web. So there may yet be another dawn for Second Life and other similar virtual spaces and while it may not be worth actively pursuing a Second Life presence at this time, it is worth keeping a virtual watching brief for future technological developments and opportunities in this arena.

Mobile communications

A constant companion 24/7

Developments in multimedia mobile communications are evolving rapidly, and discussion of the possibilities for business could fill a whole chapter, and even a book, in itself. For our present purposes, we will focus on some key points to factor into your overall communications strategy.

Simon Liss, Managing Director of welovemobile.co.uk,[21] a creative mobile advertising and media agency based in London, says 'The mobile channel is unique because a mobile phone is the one communication device that you always have with you. In the United Kingdom, mobiles have achieved almost 100 per cent penetration. It's the one item that people won't leave the house without. Mobiles are always on – they keep you in touch with friends, colleagues and family and are live 24/7. Mobiles are always there – always to hand and are used in parallel with other media and channels.'

But for those companies considering taking advantage of this unique channel, there is one major issue to bear in mind. Mobile marketing has a bad reputation among consumers because the consumer experience of it is severely tarnished by spam texts, unsolicited text messages sent to any mobile phone number. Texts which come to your mobile phone without your asking for them intrude into your private space and can cost you money, especially if your user plan charges you to receive texts. A survey in 2008 commissioned by Cloudmark in 2008 found that two-thirds of UK mobile users have received spam text messages on their mobile phones.[22] Not all the messages are sales focused – 10 per cent of them have been attempts to extract personal data, 38 per cent have included links to an unknown website and 45 per cent have tried to lure the recipient to call a premium rate number. According to MediaContentToday reporting on the survey, 44 per cent of respondent mobile phone users said they would consider switching to a different carrier to get away from the unwanted text messages. In the USA, the *New York Times* reports 'American consumers are expected to receive an estimated 1.5 billion unsolicited text messages in 2008, according to Ferris Research, based in San Francisco, which tracks mobile messaging trends. That is nearly double what they received in 2006.'[23] In March 2008, half of China's mobile phone users, amounting to around 200 million people, received advertising spam via text, prompting an investigation by the authorities.[24] According to news reports, China Mobile, one of the mobile phone service providers through which the spam was channelled ,'vowed to block text messages originating from seven online advertising firms'. When planning your mobile marketing campaign, how can you avoid falling into the same category as spammers and advertising firms that need banning from the mobile airwaves?

Simon Liss advises that context is all important. He says,

> Campaigns and communications need to be time relevant (ie the right time of the day) and time sensitive (ie giving an immediate response where necessary). They need to offer content that is relevant to the consumer in terms of location and place and also reflect the mood or attitude of the user – showing an understanding of their interests. Mobile is very good at initiating and continuing dialogues with audiences but because it is such a personal device, it needs to be approached with utmost caution. In addition to appropriateness and context, consumers will demand that any communications on their phones come from a recognized and trusted source and, most importantly, that such communications are invited, anticipated and rewarding. The experience for the consumer needs to be rewarding because this is key to successful mobile PR and communications. People tend to use their phones in short bursts, mostly for personal communication. If you are going to take up some of this precious time, then you had better be sure that you are offering something worthwhile in return.

Understanding the medium

Mobile phones can be packed with a range of applications that enable them to be used for much more than just phone calls and text messaging. Examples include:

- a camera with video and audio recording capabilities as standard;
- players to listen to music and watch videos, including live streaming video;
- live video broadcasting applications, as we have already seen in earlier chapters;
- mobile versions of Windows Office to create and edit Word documents, Excel spreadsheet and Powerpoint presentations;
- mobile e-mail and web browsing;

● and you can even read books on your phone, which can obtained from such sites as BooksInMyPhone.com.

According to *BusinessWeek*, a M.Metrics survey has found that American users use their phones for mobile browsing at the weekends in a different way from how they browse on their PCs on weekdays. *BusinessWeek* reports 'Mobile browsing surged 89 per cent in the past year, with mobile page views increasing by 127 per cent... The increase reflects growing availability of all-you-can eat data plans and increasingly sophisticated handheld devices such as the Apple iPhone.'[25] The top sites being visited by US mobile phone surfers are: Craigslist, the classified ad site that offers a localized focus by region and city; eBay, the online auction site; and the Weather Channel. On top of those activities, according to *BusinessWeek*, 'The fastest-growing mobile-web categories relate to weather, entertainment, games, and music.'

Timely texting

Some examples of timely, user-centric applications of mobile phone messaging include sport, religion, death and crisis communications.

Following the 2008 earthquake in China, the Chinese authorities sent over a million text messages to residents in the Guangxi Zhuang Autonomous Region and Guizhou Province to reassure them that they were not in the seismic zone and to counter false rumours.[26]

The Pittsburgh Penguins, the ice hockey team, has been sending ticket status alerts to their student fans. According to textually.org,[27] the team

> started sending news of available, severely discounted seats to college kids on the mornings of home games. The messages noted how many tickets were unsold, letting students know if they needed to camp out all day to get one of a few available, or if tickets were ample enough that they'd be available at the booth just before the puck was dropped. Messages went out to 2,000 subscribers, and 1,800 replied for a shot at the signed puck within the first hour.

Pope Benedict XVI sent daily inspirational text messages to Catholic youth during the six-day event around World Youth Day 2008 in Sydney, Australia.[28] At the other end of the spectrum, *Hello!* magazine readers can sign up for a daily gossip text with headlines from the magazine for the equivalent of 50 cents or a full multimedia story with photo for US$2.[29]

A Spanish mortuary is offering a service to enable well-wishers to send their condolences by text message. According the UK newspaper the *Daily Telegraph*, 'Each of the deceased has a code number, which must be included along with the text message and a keyword, which can be sent to an automated number similar to the ones used by reality television programmes... Messages are either sent straight to a mobile or go to the mortuary, which hands them on.'[30]

Mobile video

Viewing video and mobile TV on mobile phones is a major trend to watch. In 2007, there were 17 million mobile TV users in Asia, according to *Asia Media Journal*.[31] The two largest markets were Korea and Japan, with Malaysia, the Philippines and Vietnam being rolled out during that year. Upcoming launches are in China, India, Indonesia, Singapore and Taiwan. In Europe, a million Italians can watch up to a dozen mobile TV channels for a monthly fee and 40,000 Swiss can access news broadcasts on their mobile phones.[32] During 2008, France awarded a licence for a mobile video channel, and in Germany Mobile 3.0 launched mobile video services, while Britain auctioned wireless spectrum for mobile TV. In the USA, AT&T Wireless launched AT&T TV, a ten-channel subscription service that includes a movie channel. There are technical and regulatory issues as well as infrastructure considerations that need to be further developed for mobile TV to really take off, but the future has already begun.

In addition, internet-based video-sharing sites such as YouTube have evolved their applications to enable YouTube videos to be watched on your mobile phone – with inbuilt social networking capabilities so you can share the video with your friends from your phone. For those who prefer to watch movies on a bigger screen, CinemaNow announced in April 2008 that it would offer a service for US consumers to watch movie trailers on their mobile phone and then order the full-length version to watch at home on their TV or computer. Juicecaster.com is a social networking site specifically for mobile phone access so that you can share videos and photos 'directly from your mobile phone' – and you can also interact with friends on the network from your phone.

Real world interfaces

QR (quick response) codes are bar codes that can be scanned by mobile phones to enable fast and easy input of data from an external source into the mobile phone. They look like black-and-white abstract patterns and can be captured by the phone's camera via a bar code scanner that can be downloaded onto your phone. Once decrypted by the QR reader application on your phone, the embedded information will be revealed – eg a link to a website or web page with further information or just simple text such as contact details. QR codes are already widely used in Japan and their presence is increasing in the West. While surfing on your PC, you can capture the bar code offered by a website via your cameraphone – then, with one click on your phone, you can be taken straight to the mobile version of the site on your phone: this is a quick way to bookmark a website for later review on your phone.

QR codes also enable an interface with real world objects or experiences. In Japan, a tomb-maker is incorporating them into gravestones for his customers. As C Scout Japan comments, 'Contents can include pictures, video, family information, and other items. While using a QR code for this may actually seem a bit outdated in a country of burgeoning RFID technology, they are simple and will likely be readable by generations of future devices.'[34] In the United Kingdom, Manchester Digital Development Agency reports 'As part of Manchester Art Gallery's Revealing Histories: Remembering Slavery Trail, 2D QR codes have been placed next to selected objects in the galleries. The codes provide links to specially created web pages, set up for viewing on a smaller mobile or PDA screen. Like the more traditional trail leaflet the codes provide an opportunity for visitors to contribute feedback, but in this case it will be by using their phone.'[35] Street artist Banksy has included QR codes in murals he has created in a railway tunnel near Waterloo Station in London, United Kingdom, which link to his entry in Wikipedia.[36] The Harrods store in Knightsbride, London has also used QR codes encoded with information about their Design Icons exhibition on giant billboards.[37]

QR codes are only likely to take off globally when the scanner application comes bundled with mobile phones – at present, tracking down compatible scanners to download for your particular model of phone takes time and persistence and is one layer of inaccessibility that will discourage an average user. However, our view is that this will only be a matter of time – and in particular, as users' curiosity continues to be sparked by the appearance of these patterned codes on various high-profile projects like those we've mentioned.

What next?

Along our journey through the cultural landscape of social media, we have seen a number of the key values of the digital natives that engage in this virtual space:

- A high premium is placed on authenticity and trustworthiness. These values are important in the real world of business and politics too, but on the internet failure to keep to these standards is much more easily identifiable and held up for shaming.
- People want to connect with their friends and family – it is this very human desire that is driving the rise of social media. This is behind the evolution of multimedia modes of communicating, and fast communication.
- People will find ways to speak their minds and deplore perceived injustices, mobilizing and campaigning online.
- People enjoy engaging online for fun and creativity as well as personal expression.
- Many also find a purpose in helping others and creating self-help communities online.
- People want it all right now, right here. Content can appear online instantaneously and video of events can be transmitted live while those events are happening offline. Information sharing now moves at the speed of light.

For professional communicators, businesses and organizations, social media is a cultural and communications landscape that cannot be ignored. As we have seen, rising numbers are engaging on blogs, video-, audio- and photo-sharing sites, social networks, web/mobile hybrids like Twitter and mobile multimedia. More and more people are also turning to the internet for news, shopping, information and entertainment, even if they are not actively seeking out social media spaces. Mobile phones are increasingly bringing that digital landscape to people's pockets so that they are connected 24/7.

We leave you with some final thoughts:

- Social media is no longer a niche activity – you cannot get more mainstream a figure using social media, and using it to great success, than the President of the United States Barack Obama. It is likely we will see more political figures starting to integrate social media into their communications strategies.

- Even if social media is not immediately relevant for your business, at the very least build into your communications strategy a regular review of the social media landscape and how it is impacting your organization and industry.

- There may be business reasons for you not to actively engage using social media – nonetheless, it is prudent to implement active monitoring of what is going on in that medium that is likely to impact on you, your business, your competitors and your industry.

- If you do engage in social media, take the time to explore the space and the tools as they may relate to your industry and business. These are evolving all the time as technology and infrastructure evolve. There will be some tools that fall out of popular use and others that spread virally. Maintain a watching brief on these developments.

- Successfully engaging in social media means that you have to take off your business jacket (and tie, if you wear one), roll up your sleeves and come out from behind your executive desk. You can still be an expert and an industry leader but you also have to be 'one of us' with the people you want to connect with.

- We have included some discussion of the technology and infra-structure in the early chapters of this social media tour because understanding something about the technology can help you use the tools better as a communicator. To implement a great social media project, you will need the input of a good tech team and knowledge on your part as a user will inform the way that you can work with them on the project. Ultimately, however, the project is a communications project and needs to be led by you, not them, so knowing what each tool can do and why will give you an edge in planning and implementing the project.

- There are free and cheap tools available as we have seen, and while they may be appropriate for individuals and not-for-profits strapped for cash, we do not recommend them for businesses and other organizations for whom design and functionality maybe more important.

- Blogging and engaging in social media takes time and commit-ment. You may need to allow time for training and troubleshoot-ing. It is worth assessing your resourcing and time management before embarking on a social media project. You may also want to 'beta test' a project on a small scale before launching it more widely.

- There are risks in using social media, as we have seen. However, there is always risk in any enterprise and any communication channel. The key is to understand the risks of the particular channel and put in place appropriate policies to address problems should they arise.
- There are also rewards in using social media. You can raise your profile as an expert and industry leader; you can engage with your customers and stakeholders beyond physical boundaries; you can increase public trust in your organization by engaging authentically online; you can increase your web presence and thus your search engine ranking; you can connect with those you may not otherwise be able to reach through other communications channels.

And finally, keep an eye on the evolving technology. As the price of super efficient processing hardware keeps falling, and faster broadband connections become the norm, online engagement is becoming part of the mainstream. The iPhone, while not the first phone nor even the best phone for multimedia functionality as well as personal and business communications, has captured the global imagination as a device that can keep you connected 24/7 to the world. It is a sign of things to come. Social media may be the biggest, most influential trend right now. But developers are already creating applications for mobile communications, converging online with mobile even as we write. And if mobile communications is the next emerging trend, after that, what's next?

Watch this space!

Notes

1. Wealthy Asians Use Phone to Blog, Take Photos: Study, Reuters, Yahoo! Tech, 16 October 2008, http://tech.yahoo.com/news/nm/20081016/tc_nm/us_mobiles_asia.
2. Joel Stein, Totally Uncorked, *Time*, 28 June 2007, http://www.time.com/time/magazine/article/0,9171,1638446,00.html.
3. Guardian column: Gary Vaynerchuk – Jeff Jarvis BuzzMachine, *Time*, 5 May 2008, http://www.time.com/time/magazine/article/0,9171,1638446,00.html.

4. The videos are hosted on Viddler.com, which specializes in enabling comments to be inserted wherever you click on the timeline so that you can comment on a specific section of the video.

5. http://tv.winelibrary.com/vayniacwine.

6. http://www.crushnet.com/cms/node/3092.

7. Cops on Leave After Taser Incident, Student's Behaviour Under Scrutiny, CNN, 18 September 2007, http://edition.cnn.com/2007/ US/09/18/student.tasered/.

8. For example, see http://www.youtube.com/watch?v=6bVa6jn4rpE.

9. University of Florida Police Cleared in Use of Taser on Student, wftv. com, 24 October 2007, http://www.wftv.com/news/14413428/detail. html.

10. http://www.president.ufl.edu/incident/.

11. Kerry Condemns Keckler Arrest, Political Radar, 18 September 2007, http://blogs.abcnews.com/politicalradar/2007/09/students-rally- .html.

12. http://www.forimmediaterelease.biz/.

13. http://www.wigglywigglers.co.uk/podcasts/index.lasso?-session=shop per:4F4CB0840ccb816525MWoyA042EB.

14. http://audacity.sourceforge.net/.

15. Virtual World, Real Money, *BusinessWeek*, 1 May 2006, http://www. businessweek.com/magazine/content/06_18/b3982002.htm.

16. Coke Launches Virtual Thirst Promo on Second Life, Marketing Vox, 17 April 2007, http://www.marketingvox.com/coke-launches-virtual- thirst-promo-in-second-life-028917/.

17. Coke Campaign Officially a Success and Not Over, Second Life Insider, 28 August 2007, http://www.secondlifeinsider.com/2007/08/28/ coke-campaign-officially-a-success-and-not-over/.

18. Daniel Terdiman, Wells Fargo Launches Game Inside 'Second Life', CNet News, 15 September 2005, http://business2-cnet.com/Well s+Fargo+launches+game+inside+Second+Life/2100-1043_3-5868030. html.

19. Chris Skinner, Why Wells Fargo Left Second Life, finextra.com, 13 June 2007, http://www.finextra.com/community/Fullblog.aspx?id=290.

20. Frank Rose, *Wired*, 24 July 2007, http://www.wired.com/techbiz/ media/magazine/15-08/ff_sheep.

21. www.welovemobile.co.uk.

22. UK Mobile Users Drowning in Spam, MobileContent, Today, 25 April 2008, http://www.mediabistro.com/mobilecontenttoday/messaging/ uk_mobile_users_drowning_in_spam_83358.asp?c=rss.

23. Laura M Holson, Spam Moves to Cell Phones and Gets More Intrusive, *New York Times*, 10 May 2008, http://www.nytimes.com/2008/05/10/ technology/10spam.html?_r=3&adxnnl=1&oref=slogin&ref=technol ogy&adxnnlx=1210440586-NTMuiSk304slLZz9WrlCFg&oref=slogin.

24. Beijing Investigates Spam Attack, BBC News, 24 March 2008, http:// news.bbc.co.uk/2/hi/business/7311242.stm.

25. Olga Kharif, Welcome to the Weekend Web, *BusinessWeek*, 29 May 2008, http://www.businessweek.com/technology/content/may2008/tc20080528_406846.htm?campaign_id=rss_daily.

26. Gerrit Visser, China Uses Text Messaging to Reassure Public, Smart Mobs, 12 May 2008, http://www.smartmobs.com/2008/05/12/china-uses-text-messaging-to-assure-public/.

27. Penguins Sell Tickets via Cellphone Alerts, textually.org, 21 April 2008, http://www.textually.org/textually/archives/2008/04/019865.htm.

28. John Kullman, Pope Will Text Message to Reach the Youth, mobilecrunch.com, 7 May 2008, http://mobilecrunch.com/2008/05/07/pope-will-text-message-to-reach-the-youth/.

29. *Hello!* Delivers Gossip to Cell Phones, Mobile Content Today, 6 May 2008, http://www.mediabistro.com/mobilecontenttoday/media_deals/hello_delivers_gossip_to_cell_phones__84147.asp?c=rss.

30. Mortuary Allows Condolences by Text Message, *Daily Telegraph*, 1 October 2008, http://www.telegraph.co.uk/news/newstopics/howaboutthat/3114781/Mortuary-allows-condolences-by-text-message.html.

31. Mobile TV Tops 17 Mil Users, *Asia Media Journal*, 22 April 2008, http://www.asiamediajournal.com/mediatrends.php?id=308.

32. Kevin J O'Brien, Mobile TV Spreading in Europe and to the US, *New York Times*, 5 May 2008, http://www.nytimes.com/2008/05/05/business/media/05mobile.html?_r=1&ref=technology&oref=login.

33. CinemaNow to Offer Movie Orders by Cellphone, textually.org, 29 April 2008, http://www.textually.org/picturephoning/archives/2008/04/019955.htm.

34. Michael Keferi, QR Code Graves Give a Memorial Window, C Scout, Japan, 20 March 2008, http://www.kilian-nakamura.com/blog-english/index.php/qr-code-graves-give-a-memorial-window/.

35. Manchester Art Gallery: Data Matrix Project, Manchester Digital Development Agency, 29 February 2008, http://www.manchesterdda.com/article/229/.

36. Banksy's QR Code, 2d-code.co.uk, 15 May 2008, http://2d-code.co.uk/banksy-qr-code/.

37. QR Code on Harrods Poster, 2d-code.co.uk, 22 April 2008, http://2d-code.co.uk/harrods-poster-qr-code/.

Conclusions
The end of the quest

There is no doubt that what we are currently experiencing is the birth of a 'truly global order'. This is the term Fareed Zakaria, the editor of *Newsweek International*, uses in one of his books for the new 'international system in which countries in all parts of the world are no longer objects or observers but players in their own right'.[1]

This phenomenon is having a major impact on the communication profession. We are dealing with an unprecedented shift in momentum. In this book, we have tried to analyse the different components that make this shift so daunting – and at the same time so promising. We have looked at the new skills communicators need to acquire in order to get ahead of the curve and become world class.

Before we began writing the book, we spent a large amount of time studying the changes happening in the new environment. In an effort to understand the universal forces at play behind Globalization 3.0, we spent hours in conversation with practitioners from different corners of the communication profession. Although the general feeling suggested that a new awareness was surfacing, it was often no more than a hunch. People felt that communication is about to make a quantum leap but could not quite pin down the drivers behind it. So we set out on a quest, looking for the different dimensions of the current global shift.

One of the main factors that sold Globalization 3.0 to us was certainly the important role played on the world stage by multinationals from emerging economies. According to a study conducted by the Rotman School of Management in Toronto, companies from developing countries place higher bids, on average, when competing to acquire assets in the Western world.[2] By looking at a sample of

3,806 international bids between 1990 and 2007, they found out that multinationals in developing countries bid 16 per cent higher than their counterparts in the developed world. This behaviour is not only the result of national pride. It is part of elaborate acquisition plans and long-term growth strategies. In other words, these new international players are here to stay. In the past, they might have bought our products, but they will soon be buying our businesses. Working for these new bosses will require exceptional cross-cultural sensibility and world-class communication skills.

We have been focusing on Asia and in particular on China because we believe this country will play a crucial role in triggering demand on a worldwide scale. In the past 14 years, more than 400 million Chinese, one-third of the country's entire population, managed to escape of poverty. And the Chinese middle class is expected to swell to one billion by 2020.[3] However, the rise of China goes far beyond the economic and business sphere. Experts are already talking of a new cultural phenomenon.[4] A global conversation is taking place between the individualist mentality, typical of the Western world, and the collectivist mentality. Where Westerners see individuals, Asians, and in particular Chinese, are more likely to see contexts and relationships.

In our era of digital interconnectedness and cross-border alliances, the ability to develop relationships in new environments has proved priceless. This skill, coupled with a talent for managing ambiguity, is likely to turn China into a major source of communication practices.

The flamboyant ceremonies that accompanied the 2008 Olympic Games in Beijing are a demonstration of how much the country cares about its image on the world stage. It is estimated that China spent over US$40 billion on the games.[5] This hunger for stature represents a unique opportunity for international communicators. China needs our help to realize its global aspirations and build competitive brands.

India is another player to keep on your radar screen. Its population of 1.1 billion is expected to grow by 50 per cent in less than 30 years.[6] According to McKinsey, India's consumer market ranks 12th in the world and is about the size of Brazil's. By 2015, even at a conservative GDP growth rate of 7 per cent, it is expected to be the size of Italy's and will reach the size of Germany's by 2025, which will make it the fifth largest consumer market in the world after the USA, Japan, China and the United Kingdom.[7] India has also been making its mark on the world's creative industry. Bollywood produces more than a thousand films every year. The Western world has woken up to its potential and has been buying major interests in its media and entertainment businesses. NBC Universal bought 26 per cent of New Delhi Television (NDTV), one of Asia's largest television producers, for US$150 million in 2008, while the international financier George Soros bought a 3 per cent stake in the entertainment group AdLabs for US$100 million.[8]

India already has a strong presence in the international business arena with two industrialists, Ratan Tata of the Tata Group and Lakshmi Mittal of ArcelorMittal, who have become icons of the global corporate scene. Tata shocked the world in 2008 with the acquisition of Jaguar and Land Rover, two major status symbols of the global North, for US$2.3 billon. ArcelorMittal led the consolidation of the world steel industry and now ranks as the largest steelmaker worldwide. Indian multinationals' success and their exceptional ability to negotiate international deals are often attributed to the familiarity of Indian business leaders with different cultures.[9] India has 22 official languages and large cultural differences between north and south.

We have also written about the hidden potential of the Arab world in terms not only of news production and media consumption but also of new leadership styles. The progress made by women entrepreneurs in the Middle East has made a strong impression on us. According to the World Bank, 13 per cent of all firms in the Middle East are owned by women. And half of them are managed by their female owners. We are not talking about micro enterprises or small mum-and-pop shops. In countries like Saudi Arabia, Morocco and Egypt, they employ more than 50 people on average.[10] In the United Arab Emirates women make up 20 per cent of the public sector workforce. And 30 per cent of them hold decision-making positions.[11]

Lynda Moore, professor and Fulbright scholar at Zayed University in the United Arab Emirates (UAE), carried out research on Emirati business women and their leadership style. She found that their definition of leadership equals sharing experience, being democratic and accepting ideas from others. Their leadership style is highly inclusive. They tend to treat employees like family and empower them to make their own decisions. They have a strong commitment to social responsibility. Contrary to the general stereotypes, business women in the UAE feel that religion has acted as a support system rather than a barrier to business success. It has given them a sense of identity. Religious values like kindness, simplicity and generosity often inspire their leadership style.

One of the most interesting conclusions of the Arab International Women's Forum's annual conference[12] in 2008 was that Middle Eastern businesses owned by women tend to use online communication and the internet more than those owned by men. Although widely underestimated at present, this development is likely to have a strong influence on the way social media and online marketing will evolve in the region.

In his book *Voices of the New Arab Public: Iraq, Al-Jazeera, and Middle East Politics Today*, Marc Lynch talks about the awakening of new publics in the Arab world. The rise of channels like Al-Jazeera and Al-Arabiya has led to the emergence of a new public sphere more prone to discuss political issues and to challenge the status quo. Talk shows on Al-Jazeera, in particular, have provided an outlet for Arabs to engage in discussions on the future of the region.[13]

Another sign of the new appetite for open dialogue comes from Saudi Arabia, where the talk show of American media mogul Oprah Winfrey has an unprecedented following among young women. It began broadcasting in 2004 through a satellite channel in Dubai and within months became 'the highest-rated English-language program among women 25 and younger'.[14] We are talking about no less than one-third of the country's population. Similarly to the Al-Jazeera talk shows, what makes *The Oprah Winfrey Show* so popular is the fact that issues that are not normally talked about in Saudi society, like self-empowerment and family relationships, are discussed openly on television by women from all walks of life.

The Gulf region, and the UAE in particular, are already serving as a bridge to India and parts of South East Asia. It is the mix of different nationalities that makes the area so attractive for the media sector. News providers from emerging markets are already grabbing the opportunity. NDTV launched NDTV Arabia in 2007 aimed at 100 million homes in the Middle East and North Africa.[15] It provides 'infotainment' for the large number of expatriates, mainly from the Asian subcontinent, living and working in the Gulf. With an office in Dubai, it was the first channel in the Middle East to provide news in English and Indi.

These new international channels are challenging the narrative of the Western world. But they are not the only ones forcing old-school journalism out of the comfort zone. We have written about the lure of citizen journalism and the impact that blogging is having on the way news is produced. Journalists are increasingly looking at bloggers for the 'word on the street' in the way that old-time reporters would work the bars and other gathering places to pick up tomorrow's news. Tim

Gingrich, Weber Shandwick's marketing services executive for Asia Pacific, advises that 'blogs and forums should now be looked to as part of media relations. Treat key bloggers with the same respect that you would a print journalist – and sometimes more. These internet influentials are not doing this as part of their job, but rather out of their interest'.[16]

Social media such as blogs, podcasts and videos are changing the way news is distributed and consumed. For corporate spokespeople, they represent new opportunities to stand out as trusted opinion leaders via peer-to-peer engagement – to become first among equals, if you like. Corporations need to find ways of shifting from the traditional communication model of top-down, one-way pronouncements to incorporate a more personal, authentic engagement with their customers and stakeholders. Engaging with feedback is the new guiding principle. It is the equivalent of coming out of the glass corporate tower and down into the street cafes, rolling up your sleeves and having a good, down-to-earth discussion.

Because social media facilitate online and mobile communication at nil or very low cost, they have become the ideal channel for communications that are immediate or urgent. They enable anyone with a story or a message to bypass the traditional gatekeepers of news distribution such as print and broadcast media.

When asked to explain the transformation currently happening in the world, globalization experts list population growth, shifts in GDP rations and the end of rural society as key elements. Often enough, they forget the internet and the role of social media. We believe online communications to be at the very core of the global shift we are experiencing. In this book, we have been looking at the different aspects of the social media phenomenon. We have treated web 2.0 as a new cultural landscape, similar to the culture of a nation or ethnic group. The only difference is that this new culture shares common interests and passions rather than demographic features and is not geographically contained. Culture is being created by clusters of people coming together in new groupings and tribes. Understanding the way people communicate in an international context today also means understanding the new cyberculture where people use social media as their tool of choice.

In this new environment, a high premium is placed on authenticity and trustworthiness. These values are important in the real world of business and politics too, but on the internet failure to keep to these standards is much more easily identifiable and held up for shaming.

For communicators, corporations and organizations, social media is a cultural and business landscape that cannot be ignored. As we have seen, rising numbers are engaging on blogs, video-, audio- and photo-sharing sites, social networks, web/mobile hybrids to the internet for news, shopping, information and entertainment even if they are not actively seeking out social media spaces. Mobile phones are increasingly bringing that digital landscape to people's pockets so that they are connected 24/7.

We have written about how the new generation, the Millennials, likes to engage with, and have an active approach to, the media of today. In their parents' day, the main media channels encouraged passivity – think of television, radio, LPs, CDs, newspapers and magazines. Their parents are used to sitting back and being sung or played to. Until now, most marketing and communication campaigns have relied on this passivity. The new generation wants to participate actively – to create their own images, videos, text and music and to report on and engage with the news. According to Forrester Research,[17] traditional marketing campaigns predicated on a passive consumer audience do not work on social networking sites. Social network audiences have to be engaged in active participation.

The rise of the Millennials has introduced the need for a new leadership style. We have looked at both the generational and the cultural dimension of leadership. The leader of the postmodern era will have to communicate in environments of unprecedented complexity. In the words of Roger Martin, dean of the Rotman School of Management at the University of Toronto, he or she will have to become an integrator able to aggregate large amounts of information and data. This leader will need a strong communication function able to understand different realities and to broker access to various stakeholders. We are experiencing the dawn of leadership communication. The focus of our profession is shifting from content creation to relationship management and the study of new cultural ecosystems.

At the same time, the communicator 3.0 will be responsible for creating a corporate environment based on knowledge sharing and collaboration. These are the new imperatives of social media. New channels of communication are being opened by blogs, social networks and other tools. They bring people from different parts of a corporation together instantaneously. The communicator of the new era has the double task of introducing these new tools and helping employees to warm up to them.

In this book, we have also tried to take a glimpse at a series of phenomena that are about to change radically the way we do business and communicate about it. These include social entrepreneurship and the multimedia frontier.

We never had doubts about the acceleration taking place around us as a result of technology and the globalized market. What we did not expect, when we set out to write this book, is the formidable shift in gears that came from the near-collapse of the international financial sector in the autumn of 2008. This unprecedented development has added a series of pressure points to the already unstoppable global urge to change. Some experts call it the reversal of the law of greed. Others call it Capitalism 3.0. According to them, the problem with previous versions of capitalism has been its strict focus on wealth creation at the cost of the economic, social and environmental dimensions. It is the corporate model that needs to change. So far it has been stuck in a black-and-white scenario with businesses in charge of creating economic value and non-profit organizations responsible for social value. Globalization 3.0 and the financial crisis have been offering us the opportunity 'to break existing frameworks and create a model of accountability that addresses the realities of the world we're living in'.[18] The new model will need to focus on a new way of creating common value.

This is what social enterprises have been doing. And, according to Victoria Hale, founder of the Institute for One World Health, this approach is spilling over to corporations. In her sector, more and more pharmaceutical giants are realizing that the old way of conducting business is not helping a large part of humanity suffering from terrible diseases. This has forced them to think differently. 'It used to be that whoever had the money had a dominant position', says Hale, 'Not any more. They understand that the old way is not working and are now open to learning from others'.[19]

We have explored the role of the communicator as an agent of change in social business. We believe in the success of social business because it addresses a core need people around the world are feeling.

Humanity is only beginning to understand the impact the internet and social media are having on the way people interact and the effect these interactions are having on the perception of themselves and the rest of the world.

We find it fascinating that corporations have been monitoring online games like World of Warcraft, the multiplayer online role-playing game, to try to understand the influence they are having on the way consumers behave on the internet. Online games, like other internet platforms, are bringing together people who do not have much in common offline. A housewife from New Zealand, a student from Indonesia and a business executive from Rio de Janeiro joining forces to fight the World of Warcraft dragon represent a new reality that we are just beginning to comprehend. These players might not have a common background or outlook on life, but they share a passion for the game.

Online games, like other internet platforms, have been providing people with the means to share their passions on a global scale. And sharing passions leads to bonding. People who meet new internet friends through Facebook or World of Warcraft begin to develop an interest in the countries where they live. All of a sudden they can relate much better to what is happening in other parts of the world. They know what it means to live on a small salary in Bangkok because their internet friends have been talking about it in a chat room. They understand the impact the war in Iraq has been having on the lives of families who took refuge in Jordan, because they have seen the pictures posted by their internet friends on Facebook or Flickr.

This new phenomenon is huge. Never before has technology done so much to change the way human beings bond and share passions at global level. And Web 2.0 is just the tip of the iceberg. Humans have always felt the need to communicate visually. They don't necessarily want to use words on blogs or social platforms. They long for face-to-face connections. This is why we believe that multimedia technology like mobile video and real world interfaces will take global bonding to a higher level. They are the future of communication.

Technology and the interconnectedness of the economies are shrinking the mental and physical distances between people world-wide. New ways of bonding are creating a new awareness and an unprecedented ability to relate to global problems like poverty or environmental devastation. The present epochal shift has many aspects. You can look at it from many angles, but at the core you will always find communication. In the years to come, the communicator will be instrumental in showing corporations and other organizations the direction to take in new environments 3.0 and beyond. We encourage you to become an ambassador for the new role of the communication profession. This is how powerful ideas spread.

Notes

1. F Zakaria, The Rise of the Rest, in *The Post-American World,* p. 3, Penguin Books Ltd, London, 2008.
2. Management Briefing: International Development, timesonline.co.uk, 23 September 2008, http://business.timesonline.co.uk/tol/business/industry_sectors/article4735141.ece.
3. Interconnected We Prosper, iht.com, 23 September 2008, http://www.iht.com/articles/2008/06/25/opinion/edamelio.php?page=1.
4. Brooks: Harmony and the Dream, iht.com, 23 September 2008, http://www.iht.com/articles/2008/08/12/opinion/edbrooks.php.
5. What We Learned, iht.com, 23 September 2008, http://www.iht.com/articles/2008/09/18/opinion/edwang.php.
6. Joe Leahy, Journey into Conflict, *Financial Times,* 15 September 2008, p. 12.
7. Retail in India, ukibc.com, 14 October 2008, http://www.ukibc.com/content.php?contentid=29&sectionid=6.
8. Creative Industries in India, ukibc.com, 14 October 2008, http://www.ukibc.com/content.php?contentid=46&sectionid=6.
9. Peter Marsh, 'We're Not Going to Just Spend Millions', *Financial Times,* 13–14 September 2008, p. 3.
10. Edward Montgomery, Dean of the College of Behavioural and Social Science, University of Maryland, Arab Women's Education, Realising the Potential of Arab Women in the Private and Public Sectors, paper presented at the Arab International Women's Forum Conference, Washington, DC, USA, 24 June 2008.
11. Lynda Moore, Professor and Fulbright Scholar, Zayed University, UAE, Simmons School of Management, USA, Research on Emerati Women Business Leaders: Implications for Leadership Education, Realising the Potential of Arab Women in the Private and Public Sectors, paper presented at the Arab International Women's Forum Conference, Washington, DC, USA, 24 June 2008.
12. Realizing the Potential of Arab Women in the Private and Public Sectors, aiwfonline.com, 14 October 2008, http://www.aiwfonline.com/.
13. Voices of the New Arab Public: An Interview with Author Marc Lynch, motherjones.com, 14 October 2008, http://www.motherjones.com/interview/2006/01/marc_lynch.html.
14. Katherine Zoepf, Oprah Lifts a Saudi veil, *International Herald Tribune,* 20–21 September 2008, p. 1.
15. Leading Asian Media and Broadcast Major NDTV Enters MENA Market, ameinfo.com, 14 October 2008, http://www.ameinfo.com/cgi-bin/cms/page.cgi?page=print;link=136487.
16. Tim Gingrich, Marketing Services Executive, Asia Pacific, Weber Shandwick, in discussion with authors Cambié and Ooi by e-mail, March 2008.

17. Traditional Marketing Failing on Social Networks, vnunet.com, 17 Aug 2007, http://www.vnunet.com/vnunet/news/2196857/traditional-marketing-failing-social-networks.

18. Jed Emerson and Sheila Bonini, Capitalism 3.0: Exploring the Future of Capital Investing and Value Creation, blendedvalue.org, 10 October 2008, http://www.blendedvalue.org/publications/additional.html# capitalism3.

19. Victoria Hale, founder of the Institute for One World Health, in discussion with co-author Cambié, July 2008.

Index